THE MAGIC WORLD OF ORSON WELLES

THE MAGIC WORLD OF ORSON WELLES

James Naremore

SOUTHERN METHODIST UNIVERSITY PRESS   DALLAS

LIBRARY OF CONGRESS CATALOGING-IN-PUBLICATION DATA

Naremore, James.
    The magic world of Orson Welles / James Naremore. — 1st Southern
    Methodist University Press ed.
        p.   cm.
        Bibliography: p.
        Filmography: p.
        Includes index.
        ISBN 0-87074-299-X
        1. Welles, Orson, 1915–   —Criticism and interpretation.
I. Title.
PN1998.3.W45N37   1989
791.43'0233'092—dc20   89-42895
                                                            CIP

Photo credits: RKO, Columbia Pictures, Wisconsin Center for Film and
Theater Research, Universal Pictures.
Cover photograph courtesy of Wisconsin Center for Film and Theater Research.
Book design by Martha Farlow.

10   9   8   7   6   5   4

For my son, Jay, as usual,
and in memory of Rosa Hart, my favorite director

Contents

Acknowledgments

My work on the first edition of this book, published in 1978, was helped by many institutions and individuals. The office of Research and Graduate Development at Indiana University provided me with a summer grant in 1976, and the National Endowment for the Humanities awarded me a summer fellowship the following year. In addition to these agencies, I was assisted by Charles Silver and the staff at the Museum of Modern Art, and by librarians at the New York Public Library, the Library of Congress, and the Wisconsin Center for Theater Research.

Among the individuals, I must first of all thank film director Richard Wilson, an old friend of Welles, who answered my questions, allowed me to glance at the Mercury Theatre files, and gave me a memorable day in Hollywood. Ronald Gottesman, Robert Carringer, and Joseph McBride also helped with their knowledge about Welles. Claudia Gorbman and the late Charles Eckert, my colleagues at Indiana, read early parts of the manuscript and gave important criticisms. Joanne Eustis made a crucially important gift of her extensive library research on Welles, and Bill Kelly, Mark Kemmerle, Robert Ray, and Dennis Turner all read individual chapters and offered comments on the films.

The scope and shape of the book were influenced strongly by my editor at Oxford University Press, James Raimes, who also made a number of important incidental suggestions; for his faith in the project and for his intelligent, sympathetic ear, I owe him gratitude. I want also to thank Ellen Posner for her editorial assistance, and William Stott of the University of Texas, who recommended my work to Oxford at an early stage.

The book would never have been written at all without the enthusiasm of students in Comparative Literature C491 at Indiana, who inspired me and contributed many ideas about Welles's films. And for moral support when the going was roughest, I owe thanks to Ken Gros Louis, Harry and Carolyn Geduld, Lee Chelminiak, and Melinda Giles. Parts of chapter 5, in a different form, appeared in *Literature/Film Quarterly* and *Focus on Orson Welles*, and I am grateful to the editors, Thomas Erskine and Ronald Gottesman, for their encouragement.

I would like to thank Suzanne Comer, Bill May, and the staff of Southern Methodist University Press for making this new edition of my book possible. Special thanks go to Martha Farlow, for her handsome design of this new edition, and to Elli Puffe and Kathy Lewis, who repaired my terrible spelling and helped to correct the multitude of mangled names and printing errors that had found their way into the original version. A few others also deserve mention: Jonathan Rosenbaum generously shared his ideas about Welles and helped me to see some of the late films. William G. Simon and the faculty of the Cinema Studies program at New York University honored me with an invitation to speak on Welles at a symposium they organized in May 1988; my talk on that occasion, subsequently published in *Persistence of Vision*, provided the basis for the concluding chapter of this volume. And Darlene J. Sadlier gave me her advice, support, and love.

Preface to the New Edition

Unfortunately it is now possible for a book about Orson Welles to begin in the same fashion as many of his films, with the death of the protagonist. Welles died in Los Angeles in 1985, at the age of seventy. On the day before his death he taped an appearance on Merv Griffin's television show, where he performed a charming card trick and helped to publicize Barbara Leaming's *Orson Welles: A Biography*. Although he told Griffin that old age resembled a "shipwreck," he had remained quite active. He had recently completed a script entitled *The Big Brass Ring* (posthumously published, with a commentary by Jonathan Rosenbaum), he was at work on an autobiographical screenplay about his and John Houseman's famous WPA production of *The Cradle Will Rock*, and it was rumored that he was about to begin shooting a film with students at UCLA.

Welles had long been "unbankable," but he never ceased to plan and direct movies. For over three decades he had financed his work in the haphazard but heroic manner of *Othello*, the beleaguered Shakespeare adaptation he produced and directed against all odds during the early fifties. (Ironically, the last theatrical picture to be exhibited under his name was *The Filming of Othello*, a François Reichenbach documentary reconstructed as a Wellesian "essay.") Usually he started his projects with insufficient resources to finish them, hoping to raise "end money." Again and again he used his own cash, or he found unorthodox backers whose support was fleeting—a mode of production that sometimes resulted in masterworks like *Chimes at Midnight*, but often had tragicomic or absurdist consequences. For example, one of his last major undertakings, *The Other Side of the Wind* (partly described in chapter 10), was funded by Iranian investors in the days before the revolution; just as it was nearing completion it fell into the hands of the Ayatollah's regime, and is now the object of protracted legal negotiations. Other recent ventures fared no better: in the seventies, unbeknownst to his biographers or critics, Welles actually filmed a complete version of *The Merchant of Venice* with himself in the role of Shylock; but an entire reel of that picture, together with its negative, was allegedly lost by its producers. In the eighties, assisted by Oja Kodar and Gary Graver, he photographed sequences for *The Dreamers*, based on a story by Isak Dinesen; but he could only assemble the footage into a rough cut with an incomplete soundtrack—just as he had done previously, in the case of his ambitious, long-awaited *Don Quixote.*

Some of these films were unknown to me when this book was first published by Oxford University Press in 1978. I have recently seen fragments of all of them, and even in their crudest form—with shots and sounds missing, with optical devices marked in wax pencil—they provide evidence of Welles's undiminished intelligence and artistic skill. The unfinished *Quixote* seems to me especially impressive. Beautifully shot in black and white, using wide-angle perspectives of Spanish landscapes reminiscent of *Mr. Arkadin* and *Chimes at Midnight*, it benefits considerably from the mime of two extraordinary actors, Akim Tamiroff and Francisco Reiguera. Welles has dubbed his own voice in place of theirs, and he also speaks the narration, so that nearly everything remains at the level of *discours* rather than *histoire* (a technique motivated by a framing device in which we were supposed to see Welles telling three episodes from Cervantes to a child). Occasionally the actors address the camera in a fashion similar to the introductory sequences of *The Magnificent Ambersons*, as if they were having a conversation with the narrator, and they often play scenes in contemporary settings; for example, at one point we see Sancho Panza giving Quixote a bath on a rooftop, with a neon sign advertising "Don Quixote Cerveza" visible in the distance. Everywhere we can sense Welles's nostalgia for pre-industrial innocence, and his identification with the aging knight. Clearly he wants us to see this film (and his entire career) in some sense as an impossible, quixotic adventure.

Besides *Don Quixote* and the fragmentary works in progress, a good deal of other information has come to light in the past eleven years. In 1979 Welles's personal papers from the thirties and forties, containing detailed records of all his work in theatre, radio, and film, were purchased by the Lilly Library in Bloomington, Indiana. Partly because of this material, Robert Carringer was able to complete his carefully researched production history of *Citizen Kane* and his forthcoming edition of the script for *The Magnificent Ambersons.* Barbara Leaming and Charles Higham were also able to write biographies of Welles—lengthy books that are often sensationalized and always diametrically opposed in their viewpoints, but nonetheless filled with useful data. (As this edition went to print, a third biography appeared, written by Frank Brady.) More recently, 45,000 feet of *It's All True*—the Latin American "docudrama" Welles shot in 1942—have been discovered in a Paramount vault. Parts of the unedited footage, known as the "Jangadeiros" episode, have been shown at the AFI and in New York. Critics have compared these scenes to Eisenstein's *Que Viva Mexico!*, but in fact they are remnants of a larger, more discursive kind of film—a noble collaborative work about the races and cultures of Mexico and Brazil that has no precedent in world cinema. Richard Wilson is currently attempting to raise the money he needs to transform the Jangadeiros material into a feature; meanwhile the American Film Institute is preserving much of the footage, and one day soon historians in North and South America will publish the whole story of the making (and unmaking) of *It's All True.* Where many other Welles projects are concerned, the manuscripts and production records in the Lilly files have yet to be fully explored, and they will doubtless keep academics busy for years to come.

When I wrote my own book I was working largely from the public record, attempting to exorcise a personal fascination with Welles that dates back to my adolescence. I shared Welles's liberalism and his interest in stage magic and narrative movies, but I also wanted to understand his contradictory place in American culture. If I were beginning the book anew, with the benefit of additional information and the enormous development in film and cultural theory that has taken place over the past decade, it would obviously turn out differently. (At the very least I would change the title, which was Oxford's idea, not mine.) And yet, despite the fact that another "I" wrote most of the following chapters, the "I" of today agrees with most of what they say. The book as it was originally conceived seems to me to remain the most detailed critical discussion of the theatrical films signed by Welles, and it is the only book that tries to link a close analysis of his style with a description of his politics and historical circumstances. I have therefore left the text virtually intact, adding only this preface and a new concluding chapter in which I try to generalize about Welles's career and at the same time comment on unpublished material in the Lilly Library archive. Elsewhere I have inserted several new details, made some corrections of fact, and changed the tenses of a few sentences to indicate that Welles is no longer alive. I have also brought the filmography and bibliographic notes up to date.

In subsequent years, other writers will have more to say about Welles, whose place in the history of American cinema is assured. For the present, I am pleased to have an opportunity to make corrections in my original text, and I hope my additions to the record will be of some use.

Bloomington, Indiana, 1989

THE MAGIC WORLD OF ORSON WELLES

1

The Prodigy

By the age of twenty-six Orson Welles had achieved a success in show business unlikely to be repeated by anyone. He had been the New York Federal Theatre's most dynamic showman; he had co-founded and directed the most critically acclaimed repertory company in America; he had been chiefly responsible for the most sensational radio broadcast in history; he had gone to Hollywood with one of the most generous contracts ever offered by the film factories; he had co-written, produced, directed, and starred in what is still regarded as the most important American movie since the birth of the talkies. A fatalist would say that the gods, or the laws of success, were bound to turn gainst him.

And something ostensibly like that did happen. Welles went on to make an extraordinary series of films after *Citizen Kane*, films that give the lie to the notion that he was "self-destructive" or wasteful of his talent; none of these subsequent projects, however, gave him the same combination of freedom and technical resources, and he was never again to orchestrate such a talented group of people. Even if *Kane* did not exist Welles would still be included in the pantheon of American filmmakers, but having made that picture at an early age, he created expectations for his career that probably no one could have fulfilled.

The spectacular events that led up to Welles's early success have been told many times, most completely in magazine profiles for the *New Yorker* (1938) and the *Saturday Evening Post* (1940), and in two early, now out of print, books, Roy Fowler's *Orson Welles* and Peter Noble's *The Fabulous Orson Welles.* John Houseman and Micheál MacLiammóir, former associates possessed of considerable theatrical and literary talent, have written their own recollections, and Welles himself was interviewed many, many times. I do not propose to go over familiar ground in much detail, but a sketch of the more important episodes, and a description of some early works by Welles which have not been discussed by previous writers, may help place *Kane* and the subsequent films in their proper context.

I

Although Welles was born in Kenosha, Wisconsin, he always reminded his biographers that he was *conceived* in either Paris or Rio, while his parents were on a world tour. From the beginning, therefore, he was a gypsy. He was the second son of prosperous and eccentric midwestern parents, and his upbringing was anything but conventionally bourgeois—in fact it was exactly the sort of childhood that produces a misfit, a prodigy, or both.

Welles's father, Richard Head Welles, was in his forties when the boy was born. He had a good income from several wagon factories and earned still more as an inventor, the money enabling him to be a *bon vivant*—the sort of character his son would grow up trying to emulate. "Dick" Welles had traveled on three continents, maintaining a winter home in Jamaica, making pals with celebrities, and, according to the *New Yorker,* having a restaurant, a cigar, and a racehorse named after him. He married the former Beatrice Ives (stage-named "Trixie"), daughter of a Springfield, Illinois, family which had boasted a friendship with Lincoln. Mrs. Welles, a beautiful, active woman, was a gifted concert pianist; she is known to have written a life of Jesus, and at her death she was preparing to tour the country giving poetry readings to music.

George Orson (named in memory of his distant relative George Ade and Chicago businessman Orson C. Wells) was a sickly child and spent his earliest years in an environment as chaotic as anything he experienced afterward. His parents had a troubled relationship and were divorced when he was six. Beatrice then took the boy to Chicago, where he lived in a musical *salon.* (Even as a baby, he had been in demand as a sort of prop for the Chicago

Opera.) The mother died unexpectedly three years later, and Welles was obviously shaken by the event; he was already an accomplished violinist, but he said that he did nothing with music afterward—althought François Truffaut has called him the most "musical" of directors. After a brief stay with friends, he returned to his father, who by this time had developed an addiction to gin. The two of them made an incredible world trip together, visiting China among other places, and then settled in Illinois at a bizarre hotel that Dick Welles had purchased. Fire destroyed the hotel, the two Welleses moved again, and not long afterward, when Welles was fifteen, the father also died.

During all this time young Orson had been treated as an adult, and was on speaking terms with a number of well-known artistic figures. He was given very little conventional education, partly because of illness and partly because in his earliest years his mother kept him always by her side. Welles claimed to have been learning to read from his mother's copies of Shakespeare at the age of five, and he was smoking his father's cigars at twelve. At various periods in his youth he made a study of Nietzsche, met Harry Houdini, and staged elaborate plays and puppet shows. But if he was like an adult he was also something of a freak, overgrown in body and talent, and he quickly became a subject for child psychologists to examine and reporters to publicize. Such precocity doubtless made him insufferable, yet it did not conceal the essential pathos of his circumstances. Virtually from the time he could walk, he was attracted to playacting, using a makeup kit to fulfill two kinds of pretenses. On the one hand was an aggressive or perhaps defensive disguise: for example, during a brief stay at Washington School in Madison, Wisconsin, he frightened teachers and bullying schoolmates with bloody horror makeup. On the other hand, he liked to change his appearance to make himself as unlike a child as possible: repeatedly he put on whiskers and wrinkles, pretending to be an old man. Interestingly, these two elements—horror and old age—are central to much of his later work.

From 1928 on, Welles was the ward of Dr. Maurice Bernstein, a Chicago physician, family friend, and patron of the opera. Dr. Bernstein had divorced his wife and married a soprano, but the resemblance to Charles Foster Kane stops there; purportedly an expert with gifted children, Bernstein had the wisdom to enroll Welles at the progressive Todd School in Woodstock, Illinois, a town the boy later described as "a Victorian posy under a bell of glass." It was the happiest time of Welles's youth, largely because of his friend Roger Hill, the peaceful surroundings, and the free rein he was given with his imagination. Among Welles's accomplishments were a huge mural for the school and several dramatic productions that were virtually one-man shows; for example, he was Brutus *and* Cassius, Androcles *and* the lion in productions he also directed and designed.

Despite Welles's obvious dramatic talent, first his father and then Dr. Bernstein tried to focus his attention on art. The father tried to make him a cartoonist, introducing him to Bud Fischer (the elder Welles's acquaintances included not only creators of comic strips but William Randolph Hearst himself), and Dr. Bernstein subsequently encouraged him to study at the Chicago Art Institute. Finally, using part of the inheritance Dick Welles had left, Bernstein sent the young man on a painting tour of Ireland; the Irish climate, for some unexplained reason, was supposed to be good for Welles's chronic hay fever, and the landscape would give him a subject for his art. But the experiment did not work. Welles found his way to Dublin and the Gate Theatre, where he auditioned for Hilton Edwards and Micheál MacLiammóir, claiming to be a veteran of the New York Theatre Guild. (He did not try the Abbey, which was better known in America, because there he would have to be an Irish citizen with at least a marginal proficiency in Gaelic.) No one really believed Welles's lie about the Theatre Guild, but he was such a curious and demonic overactor that he was immediately given roles to play, and from his first performance as the villainous Duke in *Jew Süss* he was a small sensation. After his triumphant stay at the Gate, however, he found it difficult to get a work permit for the more famous theatres in England; more travel and some writing followed, and he finally returned, somewhat disillusioned, to the Midwest, where he occupied himself with a variety of activities. With William Vance he directed his first film, a silent expressionist farce called *Hearts of Age*, which Joseph McBride has described in detail. It is actually a short but elaborate home movie, with Welles and the other players nearly unrecognizable under layers of makeup. Welles appears in the role of Death, garbed as a stage Irishman, dancing about and leering around corners or through windows. The movie is virtually plotless, and is filled with the camera trickery and heavy-handed symbolism of the avant-garde, all of it presented in the form of a crude parody.

At about this same time, when he was eighteen, Welles collaborated with Roger Hill on the editing of *Everybody's Shakespeare* and the writing of a play about John Brown, entitled *Marching Song*. He also wrote another play on his own, which he called *Bright Lucifer*. No one seems to have shown interest in either project, although as late as 1938 Welles spoke fondly of *Bright Lucifer* to an interviewer from the *New Yorker* and talked of having it produced. It happens that the manuscript of this play survives in the Arnold Weissberger Collection at the University of Wisconsin's Center for Theater Research, and while it is hardly the product of genius, it is valuable for its revelation of the young Welles's personality—in fact, the title seems to me an apt description of his whole career in America. Like many of Welles's best-known films, *Bright Lucifer* is a curious blend of philosophic argument and Gothic fantasy, loaded with playful and sometimes troubling autobiographical references; it indirectly summarizes Welles's childhood and adolescence, and it foreshadows much of his later work.

The three-act play is bound in a folder that looks almost like a child's copybook. It is covered with handwritten revisions, and on the opening page is an impressive sketch by Welles of the only setting—the main room of a sportsman's cabin, sparsely furnished but darkened with atmospheric shadow. Three characters have gathered here on an island for a few days of fishing: a middle-aged newspaperman named Bill Flynn, editor of a Sunday feature which is described at one point as an "inquirer"; Bill's younger brother Jack, a burned-out actor of Hollywood horror films; and Bill's ward, Eldred Brand, a demonic adolescent who is the "bright Lucifer" of the title. Eldred is a precocious, sexually ambiguous, and quite insane child whom Jack calls a "busy little bitch boy." In many respects he resembles the young Welles: he is an orphan, a victim of hay fever, a cigar smoker, and a devotee of Nietzsche; he also has more than a little in common with Shakespeare's Edmund, the chief villain in one of Welles's favorite dramas. Indeed the play is so filled with situations drawn from the author's experience that one cannot help wondering what Dr. Bernstein would have thought of the following exchange between Eldred and his foster father, Bill:

ELDRED: You never miss a chance, do you, to remind me that I'm an orphan—an adopted orphan?

BILL: Please, Eldred—

ELDRED: If it had just happened that you were my father instead of the man that beat you to it—

BILL: Please, Eldred—(pause) I've never denied that I loved your mother, but I loved your father, too.—And Sonny, I love you, but you're getting past the age—

ELDRED: You've tried to be just like a father to me, haven't you? All those years tucking me into bed. I have my mother's eyes, haven't I? I used to wear bangs and we went on little walks together and you taught me the alphabet. Yes, and Christ knows you've taught me that litany! *All these years!* . . . my adored old stepmother . . .

BILL: Listen, Sonny, your mother and I—

ELDRED: My mother? You mean *Martha, that* woman?

BILL: *Eldred!*

ELDRED: She hates me! She hates me, Bill! It's true! She's jealous of our love for each other. So's [Jack]!

BILL: Eldred, my God!

ELDRED: I tell you I've seen it in his eyes all day, jealousy and hatred and craziness—

Naturally it is Eldred who is crazy, and one should hesitate before imputing a purely autobiographical motive to these lines. Even at eighteen, Welles had a highly developed sense of the Eldred-like roles his voice and body had destined him to play. He was too sophisticated a writer not to disguise his private life, and his emphasis on Oedipal rivalry may be less a considered analysis than an attempt to be *au courant*. The passage does, however, prefigure a tendency in his later work, where he constructs fantasies loosely based on his own life, often projecting himself into the role of a possessed, pathologically troubled character whose behavior is the result of misplaced libidinal energy. The demonic, self-destructive urge for power in this character grows out of a Freudian conflict, and the fictional world Welles constructs belongs in a tradition somewhere between old-fashioned Gothic melodrama and psychological "realism."

Despite the setting, the play is dominated by themes of savagery and devil worship, symbols of Eldred's troubled consciousness, and the staging suggests Welles's later experiments in the Voodoo *Macbeth*. A group of Indians—probably based on the Menominee of northern Wisconsin—are encamped near the island, engaged in a burial ceremony for a squaw; the sound of their drums keeps entering from offstage, providing eerie background for the contest between Jack's sanity and Eldred's affection for the "dark gods." Ultimately, the monster actor is no match for the real thing. While Bill is momentarily away, Eldred takes advantage of a conversation about practical jokes in order to convince Jack that a trick can be played on the Indians: Jack will dress up in his Hollywood costume (which happens to have been brought along on the fishing trip) and appear at the ceremony outside. Jack agrees to this adolescent scheme, but he is carried away by his own performance; he kidnaps the squaw from the frightened Indians, and spends most of the night running through the forest carrying a dead body. Eldred has somehow anticipated all this and is trying to engineer Jack's madness. When the actor returns to the cabin, shaken and guilty, Eldred helps him conceal the facts from Bill, and proposes that he put on the monster costume once more, in order to give Bill a good laugh. Again—somewhat implausibly—Jack capitulates; and when Bill sees a horribly realistic "ghoul" standing in the cabin, he dies of a heart seizure. Eldred and Jack are left confronting one another in the lonely cabin, Eldred raving madly about the triumph of evil and offering to become Jack's "manager" for any hauntings in the future. Jack seizes a revolver and shoots Eldred dead, but as he stands over the body an apparition appears—a ghoul, looking exactly like Jack himself in the monster costume. Jack rushes out into the night, screaming Eldred's name. The devil drums begin sounding outside, and Welles's stage directions remark that "Something old and dark has got its way."

This contrived story provides some basis for psychological speculation about Welles, who has put so much of his public self into the character of Eldred. As we shall see, a great deal of Welles's work can be explained in terms of the conflicting demands of his humanism, personified in this case by Jack, and his romantic rebelliousness, represented by Eldred. It is as if characters like Eldred give him the opportunity to express an anger that the more rational side of his personality then corrects and criticizes. But clearly his imagination and passion were fired by the notion of the tragic outlaw; usually he makes such characters the victims of some kind of determinism, and in so doing he gives a certain humanity to their rebellion. They remain villains, but they also function as critics of bourgeois society and as scapegoats; after all, there is a little of Eldred in Jack, and by extension in everyone. In one sense, therefore, the Eldreds of the world have nearly the same perverse appeal for Welles as Milton's Satan had for writers of the nineteenth century; they become symbols of the desire to reject one's hated circumstances and gain control over destiny.

On a less speculative level, *Bright Lucifer* is interesting for the way it embodies Welles's major themes. The mixture of midwestern pastoral, grotesque terror, and "family drama" vaguely suggests both *Kane* and *Ambersons,* and when the white man/red man conflict is added, we find ourselves at the veritable center of American literature. The spiritual tension of the play—the contest between a somewhat flawed humanist and a power-hungry maniac who models himself on the devil—will appear again and again in Welles's later work, most obviously in stage productions of *Faust, Julius Caesar,* and *Danton's Death,* and in films like *Kane* and *Touch of Evil.* On one side of this battle are liberal reason and good feeling; on the other are the demons of psychoanalysis and the supernatural. Whenever Welles depicts such a contest he comes to the same potentially radical conclusions that are implicit in most Gothic fiction: he shows that evil characters have both power and consistency, whereas liberals are either complacent, badly flawed, or swept up into the tyrant's own madness. In his more obviously political dramas and films, he will present the conflict in terms of a social dilemma, his moral being somewhat pessimistic: evil always wins, the one consolation being that the tyrant's hubris leads to his downfall.

For all its interest, however, *Bright Lucifer* is only child's play. At one point in the text, in a line Welles has lightly crossed out, the frustrated actor Jack remarks of his career, "I wanted to scare people on a big scale. . . . Not lousy movies. No, I mean artistically—a huge practical joke." Relatively soon afterward Orson Welles would be able to fulfill this ambition; fascinated with trickery and hoaxes, he inadvertently pulled the biggest Halloween prank of them all.

II

Had Welles been able to get work in the English theatre after his experience at the Gate, he might have remained an expatriate; luckily, he found his way back to America during one of the most interesting periods in the nation's theatrical history. He soon landed a job with a road company headed by Katharine Cornell, met John Houseman, and began the association which led to the New York Federal Theatre and the Mercury group.

Welles entered the New York theatre just at the high point of what Gerald Rabkin has called "committed" drama—the period 1934-36, when Theatre Union and New Theatre League had produced Odets's *Waiting for Lefty* and Irwin Shaw's *Bury the Dead*. His major work, however, occurs in a period of relative quiet, when the New Deal had become the chief subsidizer of social plays and even the Communists had become moderate. By the middle of the decade the Popular Front had been established, creating an alliance between Marxists and anti-fascist writers such as Hemingway and Archibald MacLeish. (Welles's first important American role was as a doomed capitalist, a sort of ur-Kane, in MacLeish's political drama *Panic*.) Throughout this time Welles was in sympathy with the left, and like most intellectuals he regarded Roosevelt as a hero; he belonged to what might be called the Henry Wallace wing of the Democratic party, and was to remain an outspoken, active supporter of Soviet-American friendship, an antagonist of racism and fascism, until late in the forties. (In the McCarthy era he became a sort of expatriate after all, though not out of any direct political pressure.) His political consciousness was shaped by the Popular Front. At various times he called himself a Socialist, remaining strongly anti-fascist yet somehow within the "pragmatic" ethos of New Deal reformers. In fact the remarkable sense of inner tension and contradiction which can be seen in a film like *Kane* is in some ways a reflection of the subtle complexities and contradictions in Welles's own political situation.

Welles had also come to prominence during a period of collective consciousness, when the major theatrical achievements were the result of group activity. Even the clearly non-Marxist dramatists like Sherwood Anderson, S. N. Behrman, Sidney Howard, and Robert Sherwood had formed a loose alliance in the Playwrights' Company, and New York was bustling with small theatre collectives. (It was toward the end of this period that Welles and Houseman dissolved their partnership; according to Houseman, their egos had begun to conflict—a foreshadowing of the loss of collective spirit in the arts generally.) Of all the groups in those days easily the largest was the Federal Theatre, which brought employment to actors and drama to people on a scale that has never been duplicated; in New York alone there were four major Federal Theatre companies, so that Welles and Houseman accounted for only a small part of the total. Quite naturally, the project was attacked by the conservatives, particularly by the Hearst press, which called it "an adjunct of the New York Leftist literary junta." Although only about 10 percent of the productions had an overt political content, the very existence of such theatre was troubling to Republicans. At first Hallie Flanagan, the executive in charge, resisted censorship of the plays, but political pressure from the right mounted steadily. This no doubt contributed to the trouble Welles and Houseman encountered when they tried to stage Marc Blitzstein's "labor opera," *The Cradle Will Rock*, their only venture into truly proletarian theatre, which was summarily closed by government agents and forced into a stunning improvised performance down the street in the aisles of the Venice Theatre. Welles immediately resigned his job with the New Deal, and Houseman was fired.

But if they had departed the government officially, Welles and Houseman retained their New Deal approach to theatre. They formed a repertory company with an investment of ten thousand five hundred dollars, lifting the name "Mercury" from a copy of *Mercury* magazine lying in a corner of an empty fireplace at Welles's home. The company eventually had thirty-four members, and took over the old Comedy Theatre on Forty-first and Broadway, announcing four productions for its first year of operation. With the blessing of Brooks Atkinson, the Mercury's foundation was headlined in the Sunday drama section of the *Times*, where Welles and Houseman alluded to their previous Federal Theatre projects as a way of explaining what the new undertaking would be like. (Welles had already declared himself an enemy of government-controlled theatre, but his opinions in this matter tended to vacillate; a short while later he appeared in Washington to testify on behalf of the Pepper-Coffee bill, hoping to establish a Federal Bureau of Fine Arts.)

Although the Mercury was to be dominated by Welles's personality and by publicity about him, it presented itself as a group project trying to entertain and inform a mass public. The Mercury Manifesto, written by Houseman, declared that the group would play to the same audience that saw the WPA productions of *Dr. Faustus* and *Macbeth*: "this was not the regular Broadway crowd taking in the hits of the moment. . . . here were people on a voyage of discovery in the theatre." The Mercury also promised plays that would have an "emotional or factual bearing on contemporary life," observing that social consciousness would not substitute for "good drama," but that a "socially unconscious theatre would be intolerable." Welles even spoke of establishing a Mercury Laboratory for

Sunday nights, in which young playwrights could experiment—an idea that the WPA itself had once tried unsuccessfully on a small scale. True to most of their words, the Mercury kept their idealistic plan going for a remarkable length of time, maintaining a repertory schedule, pausing in the midst of financially successful productions like *Julius Caesar* in order to make way for different plays and other actors, all the while keeping the *Caesar* actors on the payroll.

But even though the Mercury was fostered and nurtured by the political ethos of the thirties, in many other respects Welles was out of step with the times. Partly because he had been steeped in classical theatre since childhood, partly because he had developed his style and temperament in the "provincial" Midwest and in Dublin repertory, his productions often drew from the spirit of the twenties as much as from the thirties. The "new" theatre was didactic in tone and Brechtian in style, whereas most of Welles's work harked back to a decade-old tradition of expressionism; the Gate had once been a center of such activity, and during the same period America saw Theatre Guild productions of Kaiser and Čapek, Lawson's *Roger Bloomer*, and Rice's *Adding Machine*—to say nothing of German expressionist cinema and O'Neill's *The Hairy Ape*. Welles's work, which was inspired by this older style, consisted mainly of revivals or adaptations of classics, plays mounted in starkly dramatic fashion with visual effects that prefigure the look of his later films. Here, for example, is Houseman's description of the set Welles designed for the modern-dress *Caesar*:

> First came the main downstage playing area—fourteen feet deep including the apron—which rose to a gentle rake to meet a set of shallow steps running the full width of the stage. These led to an eight-foot plateau, the mid-stage playing area, then rose again to a final narrow crest, six and a half feet above stage level, before falling back down in a steep, fanning ramp that ended close to the rear wall of the theatre. This gave the stage an appearance of enormous depth and a great variety of playing areas. Steps and platforms were honeycombed with traps out of which powerful projectors were angled upward and forward to form a double light curtain (the "Nuremberg lights") through whose beams all actors . . . were suddenly and dramatically illuminated before descending to the playing areas below.

This production, like so much of Welles's theatrical work, was a heady mixture of twenties aestheticism, anti-fascist political drama, and New Deal *esprit de corps*. It was not, however, nearly so didactic or leftist as *The Cradle Will Rock*. The confrontation between Brutus and Antony—an out-of-depth idealist and a cynical politician—was not unlike the confrontation we have already seen between Jack and Eldred in *Bright Lucifer*, and it resembles the pairings of characters we find in Welles's film projects—Marlow and Kurtz, Leland and Kane, O'Hara and the Bannisters, Vargas and Quinlan. Here, as later, Welles was so honest in his criticism of liberalism that a few people took the play as an attack on democracy. Welles felt he had to explain his theme to a *New York Times* reporter, who wrote as follows:

> Brutus, as Mr. Welles understands him, was the prototype of the bewildered liberal in a confused world, a great man with all the faults and virtues of liberalism. So was Caesar a great man. Why present him otherwise just because the play is anti-Caesar? That is . . . the error of left-wing melodrama, wherein the villains are cardboard Simon Legrees.

Welles's defense was accepted by most, even though doubts lingered. Brooks Atkinson, for example, remarked that the play has "the somewhat ambiguous effect of implying that there is no use rebelling against the fascist state—which may be true, although a great many people hate to think so."

In any case *Julius Caesar* was a great success; like most of Welles's productions it was a triumph of "director's theatre," and became one of the most celebrated American presentations of Shakespeare in this century. "Bard Boffola," said the headline in *Variety*, reporting on the avalanche of critical praise. Reviewers were awed by the brutal simplicity of the staging (a "simplicity" which, as Houseman has noted, was achieved at considerable expense, using batteries of complex lights and a series of tricky ramps), by the inventiveness of Welles's editing of the play (for one of the most impressive moments, the execution of the poet Cinna by a violent mob, he had borrrowed lines from *Coriolanus*), and most of all by the frightening modern-dress parallels with contemporary fascism. When *Caesar* was followed by equally successful productions of *The Shoemaker's Holiday* and *Heartbreak House*, Welles became a sort of hero of the American theatre. *Time* magazine, for example, described him as the "brightest moon that has risen over Broadway in years. Welles should feel at home in the sky, for the sky is the only limit his ambitions recognize."

It was this sort of publicity that helped the Mercury company obtain a contract with CBS radio. Here Welles continued his policy of adapting classic literature in a Gothic style, and although the politics of the Mercury radio shows were seldom overt, there remained a sort of New Deal, populist urge behind the broadcasts. "Radio," Wells said to the press, "is a popular, democratic machine for disseminating information and entertainment. . . . The Highbrows are still sniffing at it. But when television comes—and I understand it is not far off—they will be the first, in all probability, to hail [radio] as a new art form."

Of course Welles was not new to the popular arts; he was well known as "The Shadow," and he would become even better known as the man who caused the Mars panic. His more important contributions, however, had to do with the form of radio dramatics. This moribund art is usually regarded as an extension of playwriting, but Welles always thought of radio (and later television) as a narrative medium rather than a purely dramatic one. "There is nothing that seems more unsuited to the technique of the microphone," he said, "than to tune in on a play and hear the announcer say, 'The curtain is now rising on a presentation of—' . . . this method of introducing the characters and setting the locale seems hopelessly inadequate and clumsy." Welles wanted to eliminate the "impersonal" quality of such programs, which treated the listener like an eavesdropper. The radio, he recognized, was an intimate piece of living-room furniture, and as a result the "invisible audience should never be considered collectively, but individually." (This, incidentally, was an idea FDR had understood better than any other politician of the era.)

Welles's solution to the problem was simple and effective. With his magnificent voice, he could become the perfect storyteller. Explaining the technique, he compared radio to oral narrative: "When a fellow leans back in his chair and begins: 'Now, this is how it happened'—the listener feels that the narrator is taking him into his confidence; he begins to take a personal interest in the outcome." The Mercury program would therefore be called *First Person Singular* (a more egocentric title one could not imagine), and all its broadcasts, from *A Tale of Two Cities* to *Hamlet*, would be done in first-person narrative, together with related devices such as stream of consciousness, diaries, and letters. Most programs were dominated by Welles's voice reading great swatches of prose from well-known novels, and by Bernard Herrmann's music;

indeed few contemporary composers have understood so well the function of music as a narrative device. The Mercury players and the sound effects technicians also got into the act, but passages of pure dramatic dialogue were introduced selectively. As a result novels adapted for the program came out in something very close to their original form, moving effortlessly between pure narration and dialogue, jumping across time and space with the speed of cinema. The *New York Times* review of *Treasure Island* commented that Welles's voice was "more personal" than that of the standard radio announcer; "this . . . abetted by just enough sound effects of surf and shouts, screams and scheming, 'paints' the picture."

The technique of Welles's earliest broadcasts can be heard in the second half of the well-known *War of the Worlds* recording, where a Princeton professor, having survived apocalypse, takes over in his own voice and brings the story to its conclusion. Of course nobody then or now has paid much attention to the second half; by all accounts, even the opening of *War of the Worlds* was not one of Welles's most aesthetically satisfying productions, and contrary to popular opinion it got one of his lower ratings. Like his other shows, however, it was calculated to utilize properties inherent in the medium, and it did so better than anyone anticipated, catapulting Welles to international fame and linking his name forever to the greatest hoax (however unintentional it may have been) in the history of broadcasting.

Presumably it was Welles's idea to have writer Howard Koch update H. G. Wells's science fiction novel by casting the first part of the program in the form of fake news bulletins, with Herrmann imitating everything from "Ramon Raquello and his orchestra" to a solitary piano playing Chopin. At first an announcer breaks into a music program to say that "disturbances" have been sighted on the planet Mars, and then gradually the whole show is taken over with reports of disaster. At the midway point, a reporter (Ray Collins) is heard from atop "Broadcasting Building" on Times Square, describing the destruction of New York and ultimately falling dead at the mike. A ham radio breaks the silence, asking, "Isn't there anyone on the air?" and then, after ten seconds of absolute quiet, a CBS announcer gives a station break.

Everyone concerned has recalled that they had little respect for the script, which they thought was silly, and at the last moment Welles almost withdrew the project in favor of an adaptation of *Lorna Doone.* But when the broadcast finally aired on Halloween eve 1938, it was acted with customary intensity, and at 8:30, halfway through the program, the cast was surprised to learn that some listeners had been taking the whole thing seriously. For several hours afterward, groups of people from coast to coast were thrown into panic, believing that monsters from Mars, flying invulnerable spaceships and armed with poison gas, were destroying the earth. Luckily nobody committed suicide or died of heart failure, although people of widely different social classes and educational backgrounds behaved irrationally. They prayed, took flight in cars, or ran out to warn their neighbors that the world was ending; church services were interrupted by hysterics, traffic was jammed, and communications systems were clogged. At Princeton, two distinguished geologists rushed out to search for the Martian "meteor" which was reported to have landed nearby, and scores of citizens were medically treated for shock.

Four times during the show listeners were told that they were hearing a dramatization, and at the end Welles jovially announced that it had all been a friendly joke: "That grinning, glowing, globular invader of your living room is an inhabitant of the pumpkin patch, and if your doorbell rings and nobody's there, that was no Martian . . . it's Hallowe'en." Nevertheless for many of those who tuned in late to the first half of the program, the news seemed quite real. Welles and Koch had used actual settings like Grovers Mills, New Jersey, for the rocket landings, and had taken full advantage of public familiarity with "on the spot" news coverage, such as the classic broadcast in which a reporter is heard breaking down at the sight of the Hindenburg explosion. Although a fictional network called "Intercontinental Radio" was invented for the news announcements, and although the entire destruction of the world took only thirty minutes of air time, the early sections of the program were quite good at creating the illusion of real events. Most of the names used on the show were slightly garbled versions of live persons—even "Professor Richard Pierson of Princeton" sounded rather like Newton L. Pierce, an assistant in astronomy at the university, and an announcement of a nationwide emergency was made by the "Secretary of the Interior" in a voice exactly like FDR's. What was particularly effective was the way Welles as director had manipulated the audience's sense of time, keeping to real duration at the beginning of the show and then dramatically collapsing the action once the basic illusion was established. At several points, notably in the beginning, he allowed dead silence on the air, and he dragged out "Ramon Raquello's" rendition of "La Comparsita" for an excruciatingly long period; all this, of course, made the later, more speeded-up and implausible occurrences seem real.

Listened to today, the program seems quite naïve, and despite Welles's and Koch's occasional cleverness one finds it difficult to believe that so many people were deceived. Several explanations have been offered for the phenomenon: the show aired just after the Munich crisis, a war scare which is alluded to at the very beginning of the broadcast, and which may have influenced some to think that the reported invasion wasn't extraterrestrial at all. Sociologist Hadley Cantril, who made a book-length study of audience response, believed that people were fooled because of an anxiety "latent in the general population," caused by years of economic depression and in some cases by educational deprivation. The world was clearly ripe for radio demagogues, he noted, and the problem lay less in radio than in "the discrepancy between the whole superstructure of economic, social, and political practices and beliefs, and the basic and derived needs of individuals."

The program ultimately became important as a case study of mass hysteria, but in the immediate aftermath of the broadcast it was not clear whether Welles would be remembered as a hero or as a monster. The morning papers described public reaction as a "tidal wave of panic," and the chairman of the FCC issued a statement calling the program "regrettable." An angry H. G. Wells threatened to sue because of what he claimed was a misuse of his novel, and for a while there were rumors of government retaliation against CBS. When Orson Welles stepped forward to interview reporters on the day after the show, he was taking not only the credit for the broadcast, but also the possible blame. He had unwittingly become the world's newest and perhaps most dangerous manipulator of the public.

In retrospect, however, it is easy to see how Welles's fascination with the media had tended to comment indirectly on the demagoguery latent in the times. By choosing to imitate news announcements, tinny hotel orchestras, silences, breakdowns, and various forms of wireless communication, he and Koch achieved an ironic distance between themselves and their sign-system, as if they were trying not only to grip the listener but to joke about the power of radio itself. In much the same way, Welles's films would tend to comment on movies or photographic images, and in his late work, such as *The Immortal Story* and *F for Fake,* he would become preoccupied with the relationship between fictional versions of an event and the shifting, evasive "reality" underlying the fictions. He remained, in other words, both enamored of his abilities as a showman and slightly guilty about those abilities. Like Jack, the actor in *Bright Lucifer,* he seemed to feel a Faustian temptation behind his talent, a danger of becoming the role he played.

However it foreshadows Welles's later work, and whatever its virtues as drama, *War of the Worlds* at least ensured that Welles would come to Hollywood on a wave of publicity. Even before the Mars panic he had been on the cover of *Time* and had signed a radio contract with Campbell's Soup; but *War of the Worlds* made him the first true creation of what Robert Brustein has called "news theatre." Soon his need of money to keep the Mercury stage productions afloat, plus his fame (now almost equivalent to Hitler's), would conspire to bring him to RKO. Not that he was the reluctant intellectual or the filmmaking *naïf* some writers have made him seem. He had made one complete movie and his stage work showed his interest in films as clearly as Eisenstein's had done in the twenties. Welles had, in fact, read both Eisenstein and Pudovkin, and for the Mercury Theatre production of *Too Much Johnson* he had shot a fifty-minute film (now lost) which was integrated with the play. He had projected snippets of movies in his other productions, and his massive stage show, *Five Kings,* had deliberately tried to create "cinematic" montages, fades, and dissolves on stage. In June 1938 he remarked during a lecture to a convention of English teachers in New York that the entertainment value of legitimate theatre had become "vastly inferior to the movies." Clearly, he wanted to try Hollywood (although he had rejected an offer from MGM that would have required him to serve an apprenticeship under King Vidor), and it is not surprising, given his new reputation, that his early projects on the West Coast tended to be about demagogues who manipulate the masses.

III

MGM was known for quality, Warner Brothers for "social realism," and Paramount for sophistication. RKO, on the other hand, was chiefly a designer's studio. It never had a stable of important actors, writers, or directors, but quite by accident it was rich in artists and special-effects technicians. As a result its most distinctive pictures contained a strong element of fantasy—not so much the fantasy of horror, which during the thirties was the province of Universal, but the fantasy of the marvelous and adventurous. At RKO Willis O'Brien and his team had created *King Kong;* the Disney group had released the first animated feature, *Snow White and the Seven Dwarfs;* and talents like Perry Ferguson, Van Nest Polglase, and Vernon Walker produced fascinating, otherworldly sets and artwork. Given such a tradition, it is difficult to imagine Xanadu being conceived anywhere else.

Unfortunately, the studio never quite made it to the major leagues, though it tried nearly everything, from modestly budgeted spectaculars like *Kong* to low-budget horrors like Wheeler and Wolsey's *Cracked Nuts.* One problem was that RKO was owned by a succession of people with interests outside the movies, and it was notorious for going through reorganizations: from 1926, when it was called FBO Pictures, until 1933, it had six different production chiefs, and by the mid-forties it had gone through six more. When Welles arrived, it was under the control of two kinds of money— southwestern and eastern—representing two philosophies of management. On the one hand was economy-minded Texas industrialist Floyd Odlum, who was interested mainly in quickie program features; on the other was an RCA–Rockefeller Center group, headed by David Sarnoff and Nelson Rockefeller, who wanted a "quality" image. ("Quality" did not necessarily mean big budgets; one reason for all those special-effects people was that the studio put a premium on ingenuity.) In 1937 the eastern group had prevailed, hiring George Schaefer to take charge of production. Schaefer, formerly a Goldwyn assistant, tried to be a prestige producer in the mold of the Thalbergs, Selznicks, and Scharys, but he was to prove much less successful. Through him Welles was put under contract (a choice that reflected the studio's old-time policy of bringing radio stars to the movies), and he remained a supporter of the Mercury organization until he was forced out in 1942, the year of the *Ambersons* tragedy.

As long as Schaefer was in, things went relatively smoothly, but it would be a mistake to assume that Welles ever had *total* freedom. He had been hired as a jack-of-all-trades who would produce a picture a year, and though he seemed to have half the classic literature of the Western world on his list of proposed films, his stay at RKO was littered with rejected or abandoned scripts. The most important of these, *Heart of Darkness,* has been excerpted in *Film*

Comment, with an excellent commentary by Jonathan Rosen-baum. *Smiler with a Knife*, based on the Nicholas Blake thriller, is a script I have been able to examine briefly through the courtesy of Richard Wilson, and a third project, which was proposed in advance of *Kane* and then developed as Welles's second feature for the studio, can be found in the Weissberger Collection at the University of Wisconsin. This last item, an untitled manuscript very loosely based on the Calder-Marshall political novel *The Way to Santiago*, was described by the production staff as a "Mexican Melodrama." Gregg Toland was to photograph the film, partly on location, and Welles would star; Welles also wrote the screenplay and was scheduled to direct, although he later announced that Norman Foster, his collaborator on *Journey into Fear*, would take over the job. Even had Foster directed, however, it seems likely that Welles would have supervised much of the work.

Two things about the *Smiler with a Knife* project are worth noting. First of all, although it was based on a spy novel it was to be an essentially comic film (at one point Welles wanted Lucille Ball to star, and the whole idea was later abandoned when Carole Lombard rejected it). Welles's own notes to himself when preparing drafts of the script indicate that he was most pleased by the antic moments, and wanted to revise the sections where he thought the satire was weakest. Second, and most interesting, the script contains an important foreshadowing of *Kane*. Midway through the movie, Welles planned to insert a *March of Time* sequence, at the conclusion of which the camera would track away from a movie screen and discover two of the important characters seated in a theatre audience—all this a year in advance of Welles's collaboration with Herman Mankiewicz, whom Pauline Kael believes to have been the principal author of the *Kane* script and the man responsible for its movie satire and "thirties comedy."

The scripts for *Heart of Darkness* and the "Mexican Melodrama" are worth a longer comparison, because they not only illustrate Welles's early preoccupations but imply interesting things about his working conditions. Throughout his stay in Hollywood, Welles had to do at least one or two thrillers of the "Mexican Melodrama" variety for every *Ambersons* or *Macbeth*. (It is said that he offered to do *Smiler with a Knife* for free if RKO would let him proceed with the expensive Conrad film.) He once said that he preferred stories that affected the "heart" rather than the "spine," but like any good Hollywood director he had to adapt his thematic interests to a genre, often making his films interesting through the sheer force of style. This is not to say that Welles regarded the thriller as an inherently bad form; he had been doing thrillers on radio for years, and for a New York actor he was refreshingly free of snobbery. There was, however, a certain tension between his ambitions and the demands of Hollywood. *Heart of Darkness* and the proposed Mexican film show this tension fairly clearly, chiefly because they have so much in common. Both are concerned with demagoguery and manipulations; both involve a perilous journey into the heart of a jungle; and both use a doppelganger theme, in which a liberal protagonist is set off against a fascist lookalike. (Welles was to play a dual role in *Heart of Darkness*, and he might ultimately have done the same for the Mexican film.) In fact the two projects are so similar that the "Mexican Melodrama" could be described as an attempt at redoing Conrad in a more popular, less experimental form.

Certain aspects of the Conrad script ought to be re-emphasized because they make an interesting comparison with the later undertaking. An important theme in both projects (somewhat concealed by the melodramatic form of the second film) is the irrational drive to evil that can be detected in the most humane of men. The Conrad novella (which Welles and Koch had done on radio soon after the Mars broadcast) develops this theme against the background of nineteenth-century Belgian imperialism in the Congo. Welles's script updates the story to make it apply to the rise of fascist dictatorships, but in most respects he is faithful to the original. Welles himself would play Kurtz, a man who, according to Lionel Trilling, embodies all the extremes of his civilization. Like Welles, Kurtz is a latter-day Renaissance man—a painter, a writer, a musician, and a public speaker with a powerfully hypnotic voice; but we gradually learn that he is also the most hugely successful agent in the exploitation of the Congo. He has gained ascendancy over the Africans by persuading them that he has magical powers, and he has exercised his rule with extreme cruelty, giving himself over to acts of lust and violence that Conrad cannot even name.

The powerful effect of this character study derives largely from the fact that it is told impressionistically, through the eyes of the semi-autobiographical narrator, Marlow. Marlow's gradual discovery of Kurtz's secret, first by secondhand reports and then by a voyage up the Congo, is like a glimpse into the abyss, transforming him from a complacent European romantic (resembling Conrad's readers) into a wiser but more troubled character. What troubles Marlow most of all is that he recognizes a subtle affinity between himself and Kurtz, a potential for evil that he believes is at the heart of civilization itself—as if all our ego-ideals could barely protect us from monsters of the id. Hence the story has a double edge: it is an attack both on European imperialism and on Rousseau's view of humanity.

Welles understood these themes—indeed he had been concerned with them since adolescence—and he recognized that the effect of the novella depended upon its limited, first-person viewpoint. On the stage this technique would be nearly impossible to achieve, but in the movies, which can fuse theatrical spectacle with the narrative potential of the novel, it offered interesting possibilities. Welles's idea was to substitute the eye of the camera for the "I" of Conrad's narrator; the camera would become Marlow, whose voice, that of Welles himself, would be heard offscreen. He even wrote a brief prologue to the film, hoping to "instruct and acquaint the audience as amusingly as possible with the technique." After the regular RKO trademark title, followed by the Mercury title, it begins this way:

FADE OUT

DARK SCREEN

WELLES'S VOICE: Ladies and Gentlemen, this is Orson Welles. Don't worry. There's just nothing to look at for a while. You can close your eyes if you want to, but—please open them when I tell you to. . . . First of all, I am going to divide this audience into two parts—you and everybody else in the theatre. Now then, open your eyes.

IRIS INTO

INTERIOR BIRD CAGE—

1. *Shooting from inside the bird cage, as it would appear to a bird inside the cage, looking out. The cage fills the entire screen. Beyond the bars can be seen the chin and mouth of Welles, tremendously magnified.*

WELLES'S VOICE: The big hole in the middle there is my mouth. You play the part of a canary. I'm asking you to sing and you refuse. That's the plot. I offer you an olive.

A couple of Gargantuan fingers appear from below cage and thrust an enormous olive towards CAMERA, *through bars of cage.*

WELLES'S VOICE (*cont'd*): You don't want an olive. This enrages me.

Welles's chin moves down and his nose and eyes are revealed. He is scowling fiercely.

WELLES'S VOICE (*cont'd*): Here is a bird's-eye view of me being enraged. I threaten you with a gun. *Now the muzzle of a pistol is stuck between the bars of the cage. It looks like a Big Bertha.*

WELLES'S VOICE (*cont'd*): That's the way a gun looks to a canary. I give you to the count of three to sing.

Nothing could have made a more dramatic transition from radio to cinema, and nothing could have announced more clearly the director's potential authority over the audience. In fact the whole prologue seems designed to establish the illusion of Welles's omnipotence. One imagines his amused, slightly hypnotic voice filling the theatre, giving the impression that the ultimate magic trick is about to be performed. "You aren't going to see this picture," he says at one point, "this picture is going to happen to you." And the "you" here is of course singular, because in the movie theatre everyone sees the same thing, the camera becoming the collective eye of the audience, which is manipulated by Welles's unseen hand.

It is worth noting that in contrast to the typical Hollywood production of the period, which tried to conceal its mechanics, Welles's movie would never let the audience forget that the whole thing was being cleverly managed. Thus after leading the audience through a series of unpleasant situations, including a scene where "you" become a condemned man about to die, Welles concludes the prologue with a couple of visual jokes meant to underline his point:

WELLES (*cont'd, looking straight into lens*): Now, if you're doing this right, this is what you ought to look like to me.

DISSOLVE

INTERIOR MOTION PICTURE THEATRE (painting)

5. SHOT *of inside of theatre as it would appear from the stage* **or rather from the center of the moving picture screen!** *Beginning on the projection booth,* CAMERA PANS DOWN *taking in the orchestra floor of the theatre, dimly lit by the reflected light from the screen.* **The audience is entirely made up of motion picture cameras.** *When this has registered:*

WELLES'S VOICE: I hope you get the idea.

FADE OUT

FADE IN

BLACK SCREEN
6. *A human eye appears on the left side of screen. Then an "equal"
sign appears next to it. The capital "I." Finally the eye winks and
we* DISSOLVE.

I hasten to add that all this hardly amounts to an "alienation effect." Welles was aware, after all, that a good magician can be
appreciated if you know something about the skill involved in
creating his tricks. Nevertheless, in a period when most technique
was supposed to be invisible, concealing the labor behind the product, Welles's approach was anomalous. It cut against the grain of
the impersonal factory style, serving both as an entertaining device
and as a commentary upon the illusory, potentially authoritarian
nature of the medium. Indeed his prologue to *Heart of Darkness*
underlined the theme of manipulation and demagogic deception
which was central to the story; on another level, it helped establish
the sense of pervasive evil, the subtle link between the audience
and Kurtz which Conrad himself had implied. As Jonathan Rosenbaum has observed, "the multiple equations proposed by the introduction, whereby I = eye = camera = screen = spectator, are extended still further in the script proper, so that spectator = Marlow
= Kurtz = Welles = dictator."

The subsequent "Mexican Melodrama" touches upon many of
these same issues, but it transposes them into a Hitchcock-style,
"wrong man" thriller. It also abandons the camera eye technique,
opting for a more conventional, perhaps more workable subjectivity. On the untitled cover of the script Welles wrote a brief explana-
tory note: "My part in this story has no name. The character will
therefore be referred to in the first person." The importance of this
device becomes apparent from the opening shot, which plunges us
immediately into a bewildering, Kafkaesque situation, revealing
Welles's grand egotism as strongly as the opening of *Heart of Darkness*:

MY FACE FILLS THE FRAME.
ME: I don't know who I am.
THE CAMERA PULLS BACK TO REVEAL *me seated in the middle of a big,
bare white-washed room, dressed only in a sheet. I am surrounded
by a lot of men, representatives of nearly every race. With a
sudden rush of sound, they begin firing questions at me.*
"Where did you come from?"
"When did you arrive?"

"Who attacked you?"

"How did you get into the country?"

These and more questions in as many languages as there are men to speak them: —Spanish, German, French, Italian, English and Japanese. I don't know any of the answers.

ME: I don't know who I am. I don't know my name. I don't know where I come from.

Here the subjectivity is achieved by a method precisely opposite from *Heart of Darkness.* The camera aims *at* the central consciousness, and the objective world enters from offscreen. From this point on, Welles conveys emotions through simple reaction shots, the audience staying with the protagonist until late in the film, finding their bearings and learning the meaning of events only as he does. The technique is similar to the way Hitchcock treats Roger Thornhill in *North by Northwest,* but with one difference: in this case the protagonist suffers from amnesia. We soon discover that he has been struck on the head by political enemies, stripped, and brought to a police station; but we have no more idea of his identity or what country he is in than he does. At least Thornhill knows he is not Kaplan, but when the protagonist of this film is told his name is Kellar, he believes it. As he tells us later in the film, he has been born full grown (the opening image of Welles clad in a sheet contributes to the metaphor) and must find his way like a child.

The result of this narrative strategy is to make the audience's identification with the protagonist at once intense and uneasy—a situation rather different from the typical film. At first we are not sure whether we are in the mind of hero or villain, and even the settings add to the discomfort. We gradually learn that we are in Mexico, but the protagonist speaks no more Spanish than the majority of the American movie audience, so that it becomes difficult to make sense of events. The early scenes add to the confusion because they are filled with a mélange of national types and languages. When one of the men in the police station, an American reporter named Johnson, treats Welles with amused contempt, offering to buy him a dress suit and dinner if he will come to a party, we move to some sort of official function in the Presidential Palace, where "every race in the world, every color, is represented . . . Diplomats, big businessmen, correspondents, politicians, labor leaders, American, English, Germans, Russians, Spaniards, a predominance of Indians."

In the palace Welles is treated as a sensation—people stand around muttering and whispering about him, sometimes hissing. Johnson leads him through the crowd and introduces him to a beautiful Mexican named Elena (to be played by Dolores del Rio) and to a certain General Torres, who is described as weighing over four hundred pounds with a face like a "pockmarked bullfrog." Welles is greeted as "Mr. Kellar," and is treated civilly but with some uneasiness, as if everyone were surprised at his presence. It becomes clear that Johnson has brought him to the party as a malicious joke on General Torres. Elena whispers an aside: "The General's presence here is in itself an embarrassment to the President. As we wished it to be. But *you!*—Mr. Kellar—isn't this a mistake?" She quickly arranges for a meeting at midnight, in a nightclub called "El Chango," and then melts back into the party.

The paranoid atmosphere is sustained throughout the first twenty-five pages of the script, with Welles always at the center of an unfamiliar crowd and the threat of violence always near. From the Presidential Palace we go to a plaza, where "thousands of Mexicans (credit Verne Walker) are waiting, their eyes turned towards the balcony of the Palace." It is the Mexican day of independence, and as Johnson leads Welles through the milling people, fireworks begin to explode; suddenly Johnson gasps and falls, the victim of a bullet which, we subsequently learn, was intended for Welles. After more confusion, Welles sneaks past a throng of people and hides aboard a sightseeing tour bus filled with "lady schoolteachers from Woodstock, Illinois," and a group of Shriners from Wisconsin who are drunkenly singing "If You Want to Be a Badger." Several people on the bus are talking excitedly, in an overlapping style, about the murder outside, and at last Welles learns exactly who he is. He overhears gossip about an infamous radio personality named "Mr. England," a fascist propagandist who has turned up in Mexico and been attacked by "radicals." Glancing down at a discarded newspaper on the bus, he is shocked to see his own face on the front page, under a caption reading "LINSAY KELLAR—MR. ENGLAND." (There is no Kellar in the novel upon which the script is based, nor is there an amnesia victim. Even the choice of the broadcaster's name is part of Welles's signature—from Kurtz to Kane to Kellar, he was enamoured of Kafka's initial K.)

Kellar, or "Mr. England," is a character who suggests the real-life "Lord Haw-Haw," an English radio commentator hired by the Nazis during the war. As the film develops, we learn that "Mr. England" has been sent to Mexico to broadcast to the United States from a secret radio station at Santiago, an obscure island off the coast of central Mexico. The fascists plan to start a Mexican version of the Spanish Civil War, and they hope to keep the U.S. neutral with the help of Kellar's propaganda. The twist in the plot is that the amnesia victim played by Welles is not Mr. England at all, only a look-alike who never learns his real identity. For a long time, Welles believes that he is Kellar; he is instinctively anti-fascist, but he fears that this is only an effect of the amnesia. He refuses to sleep because a doctor has told him that his memory might return after a rest, and when he is sent on a torturous journey to Santiago, he hopes somehow to foil the enemy.

Much of the script involves a wonderfully atmospheric journey through the jungle toward the radio station. The Mexican generals soon grow wary of Welles and hire a guide, an altogether repulsive but somehow charming killer, to see to it that he never reaches his destination. The plot fails, however, and when Welles reaches the island of Santiago he discovers that the real man has been hiding there all along, trying to keep his presence a secret from the world. Welles is taken captive by "Mr. England," an urbane gentleman who, it turns out, actually comes from Minnesota; he is also tortured, but to no avail. After a complicated series of events the film reaches its climax. While a group of Germans and Mexicans are meeting in Santiago to plan a *coup d'état*, Welles manages to escape and force his way into the radio station, where he goes on the air with a broadcast aimed at North America. For the first time in the film, we find ourselves taking a point of view different from the protagonist's:

. . . *everybody shuts up to listen to the radio. (It is important to note that from here to the finish of this entire sequence, my speech is continuous.)*

MY VOICE: —very important! You haven't any reason to believe me. But this time you've got to. I'm telling the truth . . .

MR. ENGLAND: There's the station. —He must be speaking from there.

Mr. England starts away, but my next words on the radio stop him.

MY VOICE: Listen! Listen to this. *(Effect)* Hear that sound? The sound of ticking? *(Pause—Effect very clear)* That's a time bomb. I don't know just when it's going to explode. But I think that before it does there'll be just enough time for me to tell you about October first.—

ITURBIDE: The date! That's the date!

ONE OF THE LATINS: Now everyone knows it! . . .

MY VOICE: I want you to know all about October first before I die. You see, I'm going to die any minute now because I'm holding the time bomb in my hand.

A moment's pause filled with the sound of ticking. Then Mr. England starts away. . . . As he leaves, CAMERA *starts slowly closing in on the* RADIO.

MY VOICE *(during the above):* I'm broadcasting from a munitions dump. This microphone is located over a warehouse containing over a thousand tons of high explosives . . .

THE FACES OF THE CONSPIRATORS . . .

MY VOICE: Maybe if you got here in time, and you'd have to come quick, you'd see a big steam yacht making out to sea. It might be interesting for you to know who's on board.

DISSOLVE TO:

A BIG CHART—*the Island of Santiago, almost filling the screen. A pencil in someone's hand checks the location.*

CAMERA PULLS BACK TO REVEAL: INT. A GOVERNMENT OFFICE IN MEXICO CITY. *My voice continues from a small radio in the office. Several officials are listening. . . .*

MY VOICE: I think you'd find big men in the Americas. The wrong kind . . .

OFFICIAL *(on the telephone):* Larga distancia—Washington.

DISSOLVE

INT. LOWER MIDDLE CLASS AMERICAN HOME

MY VOICE *(on this):* These, the ones that don't belong—

FATHER *(at phone):* Hello—is this the Inquirer?

MY VOICE: They're the real power in this revolution—

FATHER *(at phone):* Say—there's a fellow on the radio—

DISSOLVE

A BIG LOUDSPEAKER. CAMERA PULLS BACK TO SHOW: THE FACADE OF A MUSIC STORE IN A LARGE MEXICAN TOWN, *a crowd of Mexicans of various classes gathered before the loudspeaker. . . . A Mexican is translating my words to the crowd. . . .*

DISSOLVE: THE PRESIDENT'S PALACE—MEXICO CITY. . . .

MY VOICE: On the sixteenth of September the people of Mexico celebrate their Independence Day. The president rings a bell and cries out in the square—"Viva Mexico! Viva La Republica!" Years ago, a priest named Hidalgo rang that bell and gave that cry for the first time in that country. They call it the Grito. —Well, here's another Grito. I hope it'll be heard. —I hope—

SUDDEN SILENCE. *The sound of ticking has stopped, too. Complete silence. . . .*

AN EXPENSIVE-LOOKING BAR IN RIO DE JANEIRO. *Men, and women too,*
who have gotten up from their tables and are gathered by the
radio at the bar . . .
THE LOUDSPEAKER: IN FRONT OF THE MUSIC STORE. *The Mexicans*
listening.
THE GOVERNMENT OFFICE—MEXICO CITY. *The officials listening.*
The one at the phone lowers the receiver.
A GOVERNMENT OFFICE IN WASHINGTON—*American officials. . . .*
THE AMERICAN HOME. *The family listening.*
THE FATHER: That must have been an awful explosion.
DISSOLVE: INT. THE WAREHOUSE. *I am standing by the microphone. In*
one hand, I hold an alarm clock!

For a time Welles has chosen to keep the movie audience deceived along with everyone else; happily, however, the radio broadcast is a reverse of *War of the Worlds*, a hoax that saves people
instead of putting them in danger. The trick takes on added interest in the perspective of Welles's whole career, because he was
always preoccupied with the notion of art as a medium for lies; in
this case the big lie of the fascists is exposed by another lie—"I'm
telling the truth," the Welles character insists at the beginning of
his broadcast, and in a sense he is, but even in this relatively
ordinary Wellesian effort, truth and deception are inextricably
linked, the difference between demagoguery and benign illusionism growing very vague indeed.

Despite such ironies, Welles's Mexican film was fairly direct
propaganda for the war, its more pessimistic qualities suggested
only in the bizarre, *film noir* treatment of some scenes. It was a
likely project, partly because it would have made an exciting melodrama and partly because it was well suited to the politics of RKO.
Throughout the thirties and early forties, that studio had under-
taken a kind of "good neighbor" policy, staging everything from
Fred Astaire musicals to Disney cartoons in a Latin American setting. One of the underlying motives for these films was Rockefeller
oil holdings in Latin America, and the concern to keep those holdings within the orbit of the United States. (Welles's script actually
refers to an oil industry in Mexico which is being threatened by
the Germans; it does not, however, suggest that the Americans
themselves might have been guilty of economic imperialism—a far
cry from the way American oil would be depicted in *Touch of Evil*.)
As it happened, however, the script encountered objections from

the Mexican government itself, and because RKO was sensitive to the Latin American market, the project was shelved.

Thus both *Heart of Darkness* and the "Mexican Melodrama" remain sketches for possible films. Perhaps it is just as well that they were not produced—Welles was able to employ their themes and style in other works (in place of a Kurtz discovered at the heart of darkness he gave us a Kane discovered in the center of a labyrinth), and by any standard his first two films represent a more impressive debut.

But in advance of any direct discussion of these films, it will be helpful to pause and consider the typical qualities of Welles's staging of a story for the camera—his work as a director rather than as a script writer.

2

The Magician

According to John Houseman, Welles was "at heart a magician whose particular talent lies not so much in his creative imagination (which is considerable) as in his proven ability to stretch the familiar elements of theatrical effect far beyond their normal point of tension." Left-handed as the compliment may seem, Welles was in fact a magician, and watching his movies is sometimes like attending a performance by Blackstone or Sorcar. In *Citizen Kane*, for example, there is a famous shot where the camera moves in to a closeup of a group photograph of the *Chronicle* staff while Kane talks about what good men they are; suddenly Kane walks right into the photo, and as the camera pulls back from the assembled journalists we find ourselves at an *Inquirer* party six years later. Near the beginning of *The Magnificent Ambersons* Welles reads Booth Tarkington offscreen while the house across the street from the Amberson mansion is shown in long shot; slowly the sky darkens, a moon appears, and the house is festooned with lanterns—as if by magic, a winter day is transformed into a summer night. Moments like these are not merely functional; they also draw upon a cinema of illusionism as old as Méliès. Even if we were to disregard such obvious showpieces of movie trickery, Welles's films would still seem flamboyant, filled with magic and "theatrical effect."

Most people are attracted to Welles's work because of this spectacular quality, despite the fact that he liked to think of himself as a man of ideas. Before considering any of his films as narratives or philosophic statements, therefore, let us look at their surfaces— not so much the elaborate special effects as the typical dramatic scenes within a given film. For at this level Welles's handling of the medium constitutes an idiolect, a personal style with as many historical, cultural, and psychological implications as his more public ideas or themes.

The obvious place to begin is with *Kane*, and within that film a logical starting point is the wide-angle, deep-focus photography that became one of the most distinctive features of Welles's style. As we shall see in later chapters, his methods were to change some- what, growing more fluid, various, and in some ways more daring as he gained experience and encountered other cameramen after Toland; in fact he seldom returned to a really elaborate depth of field—as in those grotesque shots where a giant head only a few inches from the screen is in equally sharp focus with a figure that seems to be standing a mile away. Nevertheless, the principle of exaggerated perspective was suited to his temperament, and re- mained an essential quality of his work. Like much of the acting in his films, it creates a slightly hallucinatory effect, marking him from the beginning of his career as anything but a purely represen- tational or conventional artist. Indeed in every feature of his early work—from the photography, to the sound, to the acting—Welles's style is mildly unorthodox, implicitly rebellious against the norm. These points will become clearer, however, after we have exam- ined a few scenes.

I

One of the best-known and most written about moments in Welles's first movie is the boardinghouse segment, where we meet Kane in his youth. The camera pans slowly across a handwritten line of Thatcher's memoirs—"I first met Charles Foster Kane in 1871"—and then, accompanied by Bernard Herrmann's lilting "Rosebud" theme, the image dissolves from the white margin of the page into an unreal land of snow where Charlie frolics with his sled. At first the black dot against pure white echoes the manu- script we have been looking at, but it swoops across the screen counter to the direction the camera has been moving, in conflict with the stiff, prissy banker's handwriting, suggesting the conflict

between Kane and Thatcher that runs through the early parts of the movie. The camera moves in closer, and an insert establishes the setting when one of the boy's snowballs strikes the sign over Mrs. Kane's boardinghouse. Following this shot is a single, characteristically Wellesian, long take. The camera retreats from the boy, and moves through the window where his mother stands admonishing him not to catch cold; she turns, accompanied first by Thatcher and then her husband, walking the full length of the parlor, the camera tracking with her until it frames the whole room. She and Thatcher sit at a table in the foreground, and the camera holds relatively stationary for the rest of the scene. By this means Welles deliberately avoids conventional editing techniques and lets each element—the actors and the decor of the home—reveal itself successively, until everything is placed in a highly symbolic composition.

Toland's photography is of course much sharper than this reproduction of a frame can indicate. The deep focus enables us to see everything at once, and the wide-angle lens slightly enlarges the foreground, giving it dramatic impact. As is typical in *Kane*, the camera views the action in terms of three planes of interest: in the foreground at the lower right, Mrs. Kane and the banker sit negotiating the child's future; in the middle distance, Mr. Kane makes agitated pacing movements back and forth, whining and complaining to his wife; far away, framed in the square of the window as if in the light at the end of a tunnel, Charlie plays in the snow. While the parents and banker converse inside, the sound of the boy's play can be heard through the window, which Mrs. Kane has insisted must be left open. According to the RKO cutting continuity, the boy's shouts are "indistinct," but if you listen closely you will hear some of his lines. As his mother prepares to sign him over to a guardian and thus dissolve her family, the boy shouts, "The Union forever! The Union forever!"

Undoubtedly Welles's theatrical experience led him to conceive movie images in this way; the *Julius Caesar* sets, as we have seen, had been designed to allow for just this sort of in-depth composition. Actually, however, Welles's long takes are in some way less conventionally theatrical than the typical dialogue scene in a Hollywood feature, which does nothing more than establish a setting and cut back and forth between closeups of the actors. Hollywood cinema was basically a "star" medium, designed to highlight faces and words, whereas Welles tried to introduce a sense of visual conflict and directorial presence, even in the absence of cutting. In the scene at hand, the three planes of interest have been as carefully "reconstructed" as any montage, and they function in a roughly similar way. One important difference is that the spectator has an immediate impression of the whole, of several conflicting elements presented not in sequential fashion, but simultaneously. The movies, after all, are not an exclusively linear medium; if the director wishes to preserve the temporal continuity, he has a second dimension—depth—along which the fragments of an idea can co-exist. Thus while the story of *Kane* moves briskly forward on the reel, we occasionally have the sense of slicing through a cross section of a moment, looking down a corridor of images and overlapping events.

Welles designs the boardinghouse scene in such a way that we cannot help looking down Mrs. Kane's parlor to the window that neatly frames and encloses the boy's play, seeming to trap him at the very moment when he feels most free. At virtually the same time we are aware of Mrs. Kane seated with the banker in the foreground, her face the image of stern puritanical sacrifice; Thatcher hovers over officiously, while in the middle distance, caught between son and mother, the weak, irresponsible Mr. Kane keeps saying he doesn't like turning the boy over to a "gardeen." The faces, clothing, and postures of the actors contrast with one another, just as the slightly blurred, limitless world of snow outside the window contrasts with the sharply focused, gray interior. Clearly, the shot was meticulously organized in order to stress these conflicts; in fact it took Welles and Toland four days to complete the sequence, because everything had to be timed with clockwork precision. As a result *Kane* has a somewhat authoritarian effect; Welles may not be so Pavlovian a director as Eisenstein, but neither is he quite willing to let the spectator choose what he will see. He keeps the actors and the audience under fairly rigid control, just as the characters in this scene seem under the control of Fate.

Abetted by Toland's extreme-depth photography, Welles uses

the long takes in *Citizen Kane* in highly expressive ways. As in the shot described above, the actors often take unnatural positions, their figures arrayed in a slanting line that runs out in front of the camera, so that characters in the extreme foreground or in the distance become subjects for the director's visual commentary. Actors seldom confront one another face to face, as they do in the shot/reverse shot editing of the ordinary film. The communications scientists would say that the positions of figures on the screen are "sociofugal," or not conducive to direct human interaction, and this slight physical suggestion of an inability to communicate is fully appropriate to the theme of social alienation which is implicit in the film.

Space in the conventional Hollywood film—especially in action genres like the gangster movie or the western, which used a sharp, relatively "deep" photography—had been freer, more mobile, and certainly less symbolic than this. Oddly, however, Welles's long takes have frequently been praised for their heightened "realism." For example, in the course of his fine early essay on *Kane,* David Bordwell has written that the boardinghouse scene demonstrates the self-effacing quality of Welles's direction: "despite the complexity of the set-ups, we gain a sense of a reality—actual, unmanipulated, all of a piece." Elsewhere he remarks that key features of Welles's technique are designed to create the illusion of a "real world." "The spatial and temporal unity of the deep-focus, the simultaneous dialogue, the reflections and chiaroscuro, the detached use of the moving camera, the intrusion of sounds from outside the frame—all increase the objectively realistic effect."

Bordwell's notions about technique seem to derive, with some modification, from André Bazin, whose famous essay "The Evolution of Film Language" has been a major influence on Welles's critics. Indeed Bazin's commentary on *Kane* raises so many interesting questions that no study of Welles's deep-focus compositions can afford not to give it a brief review. Summarized, his argument runs as follows: between 1920 and 1940, there had been two kinds of filmmakers—"those who put their faith in the image and those who put their faith in reality." By the "image" Bazin meant "very broadly speaking, everything that the representation on the screen adds to the object there represented"; by "reality" he was referring to an unmanipulated phenomenal world spread out in front of the camera, a world which he believed could leave its essential imprint on the film emulsion. According to Bazin, a director had two ways of adding to the object represented and thereby diluting the "reality." He could manipulate the "plastics" of the medium—the lighting, the sets, the makeup, the framing of a shot, etc.—or he could employ montage, which would create "a meaning not proper to the images themselves but derived exclusively from their juxtaposition." Around 1940, according to Bazin, the principle of "adding" to the reality was challenged by directors like Jean Renoir, William Wyler, and Orson Welles. Thanks to the depth of field in *Kane,* Bazin wrote, "whole scenes are covered in one take. . . . Dramatic effects for which we had formerly relied on montage were created out of the movements of the actors within a fixed framework." In Welles and in his predecessor Renoir, Bazin saw "a respect for the continuity of dramatic space and, of course, its duration." Indeed, he said, the alternation of expressive montage and long takes in *Kane* was like a shifting back and forth between two tenses, or between two modes of telling a story.

Because the many deep-focus shots in *Kane* eliminated the need for excessive cutting within a scene, because they theoretically acted as a window upon what Bazin regarded as the ambiguous phenomenal world, he praised the film as a step forward in movie "realism." Furthermore, he argued that the deep-focus style was appropriate to ideas expressed in the script. "Montage by its very nature rules out ambiguity of expression," he wrote, and therefore *"Citizen Kane* is unthinkable shot in any other way but in depth. The uncertainty in which we find ourselves as to the spiritual key or the interpretation we should put on the film is built into the very design of the image."

Bazin was certainly correct in describing *Kane* as an ambiguous film, and as a departure from Hollywood convention; nevertheless in his arguments about "realism" he underemphasized several important facts. For example, if in some scenes Welles avoided using montage to "add to the object represented," this left him all the more free to add in another way—through what Bazin had called "plastics." Interestingly, some of the deep-focus shots in the film were made not by simple photography, but by a literal montage, an overlaying of images in a complicated optical printing process which created the impression of a single shot. *Kane* is one of the most obviously stylized movies ever made; the RKO art department's contribution is so great, Welles's design of every image so constricting, that at times the picture looks like an animated cartoon. Indeed this very artificiality is part of the meaning—especially in sequences like the election rally and the surreal picnic in the Xanadu swamplands. Technically speaking, Welles has made the ultimate studio film; there is hardly a sequence that does not make us aware of the cleverness of various workmen—makeup artists, set designers, lighting crews, and perhaps most of all Orson Welles. Critics as diverse at Otis Ferguson, Paul Rotha, and Charles Higham have complained that *Kane* calls attention to its style, making the audience aware that they are watching a movie. Even François Truffaut and Joseph McBride, who are strongly influenced by Bazin's aesthetics, seem to prefer Welles's less obtrusive films— *Ambersons*, say, or *Falstaff.* "When a director matures," McBride says, "his work becomes more lucid, more direct, allowing room for deeper audience response; as Truffaut has put it, what is in front of the camera is more important." Behind this axiom one can feel the whole weight of Bazin's theories, although to McBride's credit he acknowledges a flaw in the argument. When he met Welles, he asked about the relative simplicity of the later European films: "I asked him why, in recent years, his movies have had less and less of the razzle-dazzle of his youth. Could it be a kind of growing serenity? 'No, the explanation is simple,' he said. 'All the great technicians are dead or dying.' "

Yet the statements of both Welles and Toland, in other contexts, seem to foreshadow or confirm Bazin's notions about realism. Toland has claimed that Welles's idea was to shoot the picture in such a way that "the technique of filming should never be evident to the audience," and in his well-known *American Cinematographer* article, we repeatedly encounter comments such as the following: "The attainment of approximate human-eye focus was one of our fundamental aims"; "The *Citizen Kane* sets have ceilings because we wanted reality, and we felt it would be easier to believe a room was a room if its ceiling could be seen . . . "; "In my opinion, the day of highly stylized cinematography is passing, and being superseded by a candid, realistic technique." The last statement finds an echo in Bazin's notion that *Kane* is part of a general movement, a "vast stirring in the geological bed of cinema," which will restore to the screen the "*continuum* of reality" and the "ambiguity of reality." The same general argument can be heard in Welles's own remarks. In an interview with Peter Bogdanovich, he was asked why he used so much deep focus. "Well," he replied, "in life you see everything at the same time, so why not in the movies?"

One should remember that the term "realism" (often used in

opposition to "tradition") nearly always contains a hidden ideological appeal, and that the word has been appropriated to justify nearly every variety of revolution in the arts. But if "realism" is intended simply to mean "verisimilitude," then Welles, Toland, and Bazin are at best half right. It is true that deep focus can preserve what Bazin called the "continuum" of reality, and that three-dimensional effects on the screen (which owe considerably to Welles's blocking and Toland's skillful lighting) can give the spectator the impression of looking into a "real" space. Nevertheless Welles and Toland are inaccurate when they imply that the human eye sees everything in focus, and Bazin is wrong to suggest that either reality or human perception is somehow "ambiguous." On the contrary, human vision is exactly the opposite of depth photography, because humans are incapable of keeping both the extreme foreground and the extreme distance in focus at the same time. The crucial difference between a camera and the human eye is that the camera is nonselective; even when we are watching the deep-focus composition in *Kane* we do not see everything in the frame at once. We are aware of an overall composition which exists simultaneously, but, as Bazin has noted, the spectator is required to make certain choices, scanning the various objects in the picture selectively. Welles seems instinctively aware of this fact, because he has designed his images quite rigidly, sometimes blacking out whole sections of the composition or guiding our attention with movement and frames within the frame. Welles's movies make relatively greater intellectual demands upon the audience, giving them *more* to look at, but the information which is crowded on the screen has been as carefully manipulated and controlled as in any montage.

Still another and perhaps more important factor needs to be taken into account in any discussion of the phenomenal "realism" of Welles's technique. Toland claimed that he was approximating the human eye when he stopped down his camera to increase the depth of field, but what he and most other commentators on the technique do not emphasize is that he also used a wide-angle lens to distort perspective. *Kane* was photographed chiefly with a 25mm lens, which means that figures in the extreme foreground are elongated or slightly ballooned out, while in the distance the lines formed by the edge of a room converge sharply toward the horizon. Thus if Toland gave the spectator more to see, he also gave the world a highly unnatural appearance. In fact Welles's unusual images fundamentally alter the relationship between time and space, calling into question some aspects of Bazin's arguments about duration. Here, for example, is an extract from an interview with the British cameraman/director C. M. Pennington-Richards:

Of course using wide angle lenses the time-space factor is different. If you've got a wide angle lens, for instance a 1" lens or an 18mm, you can walk from three-quarter length to a close-up in say four paces. If you put a 6" lens on [i.e., a telephoto], to walk from three-quarter length to close-up would take you twenty paces. This is the difference: During a scene if someone walks away and then comes back for drama, they come back fast, they become big fast. There is no substitute for this—you only can do it with the perspective of a wide-angle lens. It's the same with painting; if you want to dramatize anything, you force the perspective, and using wide angle lenses is in fact forcing it.

These comments signal the direction that any discussion of photography in *Kane* should take. But while there has been a great deal of theoretical discussion about depth of field in the film, rather little has been said about forced depth of perspective, which is the *sine qua non* of Welles's style, and which accounts for a great deal of the speed and energy of his work. And the technique is effective precisely because it lacks verisimilitude. Most directors operate on the principle that the motion picture image should approximate some kind of human perception; the virtue of Welles's films, however, is that they work in a different direction, creating what the Russian formalist critic Victor Shklovsky would call a poetic "defamiliarization."

There were, of course, several purely practical advantages to Toland's use of this special lens. It increased the playing area, not only in depth but in width, allowing the director to integrate characters and decor. Although it made panning movements somewhat ugly by Hollywood standards (there are relatively few in *Kane*), it greatly enhanced the dramatic power of tracking shots, giving impact to any movement forward or backward, whether by the camera or the players. Indeed the values of this technique were so many that a 35mm lens, once considered extreme, is now standard, and much shorter lenses are used regularly in horror films. (On television these lenses are used frequently, partly because they compensate for the small screen. One problem, however, is that TV directors use dual purpose lenses; to save time and money, they zoom in on details instead of tracking, thereby losing the dramatic shearing away of space that is produced by wide-angle camera movement.)

In retrospect, what was really innovative about Toland and Welles was not their sharp focus but their in-the-camera treatment of perspective. Depth of field was less unusual than Toland and later historians have made it seem; like the photographing of ceilings, it was at least as old as Griffith and Bitzer—indeed there are beautiful examples of it in Chaplin's *The Gold Rush.* A certain "normality" of spatial relationships, however, had been adhered to throughout the studio years, with only an occasional photographer or director behaving differently; filmmakers used a variety of lenses, but they usually sought to conceal optical distortions by means of set design, camera placement, or compensatory blocking of actors. When Welles and Toland deliberately manipulated perspective, they foreshadowed the jazzy quirks of movement and space that were to become almost commonplace during the sixties and seventies.

Not that wide-angle perspectives were new when *Kane* was made. Welles's favorite director, John Ford, had used them extensively in *Young Mr. Lincoln* and *Stagecoach,* and Toland had made some interesting experiments with them in *The Long Voyage Home,* sharing a title card with Ford. In 1941, the same year as *Kane,* Arthur Edeson photographed *The Maltese Falcon* at Warner Brothers using a 21mm lens, which, at least theoretically, distorted space even more than in Welles's film. It is instructive, however, to contrast the effect of *Falcon* with that of *Kane.* The space in the John Huston film, far from seeming exaggerated, seems cramped; nearly the whole action is played out in a series of little rooms with the actors gathered in tight, three-figured compositions. Huston, like most other Hollywood directors, stayed within limits of studio conventions, underplaying Edeson's offbeat photography. Welles, on the other hand, used the lens distortion openly, as an adjunct to the meaning of the story; in fact the peculiar exaggeration of perspective in *Kane* is equivalent to effects one sees everywhere in German expressionist cinema, where sets are usually built in tunnel-like designs. Toland's wide-angle photography is therefore made to contribute to the "horror movie" feeling of the film, and is the perfect visual equivalent to Welles's earlier theatrical productions. In *Kane,* space becomes demonic, oppressive; ceilings are unnaturally low, as if they were about to squash the

characters; or, conversely, at Xanadu rooms become so large that people shrink, comically yet terrifyingly dwarfed by their possessions. (This effect is enhanced by the set design. At one point Kane walks over to a huge fireplace and seems to become a doll, warming himself before logs as big as whole trees: "Our home is here, Susan," he says, absurdly playing the roll of paterfamilias.)

Again and again Welles uses deep focus not as a "realistic" mode of perception, but as a way of suggesting a conflict between the characters' instinctual needs and the social or material world that determines their fate. He continued this practice, fantastically exaggerating space in his later films (*Touch of Evil* was shot largely with an 18.5mm lens), making exaggeration a key feature of his style. The short focal-length of the lens enabled him to express the psychology of his characters, to comment upon the relation between character and environment, and also to create a sense of barely contained, almost manic energy, as if the camera, like one of his heroes, were overreaching.

This highly charged, nervous dynamism of imagery and action can be found everywhere in *Kane*, and is produced by other techniques besides photography. Fairly often Welles will stage important moments of his story against some counterpointing piece of business, as if he were trying to energize the plot by throwing as much material as possible onto the screen. One of the most obvious examples is the party sequence in the *Inquirer* offices, where Leland and Bernstein debate about Kane's character. Here again the shot establishes three planes which are set in conflict with one another (see above). To the left is Leland, a young, handsome, fastidious WASP a little like the "New England schoolmarm" Kane will later call him. To the right and slightly nearer is Bernstein—slight, ugly, Jewish, and as loyal as a puppy. Leland is bareheaded, but Bernstein wears a Rough-Rider's hat as a sign of his allegiance to Kane's war in Cuba. The contrast is further emphasized by the dialogue: throughout the scene Leland refers to Kane as "Charlie," implicitly recognizing that they belong to the same class, whereas Bernstein always refers to his boss as "Mr. Kane." (Incidentally, we have just heard a song about Kane. Charles Bennett, the entertainer at the head of the chorus line, asks, "What is his name?" The chorus girls sing, "It's Mr. Kane!" The whole crowd joins in, singing, "He doesn't like that Mister/He likes good old Charlie Kane!")

The brief conversation in this scene is important, because it underlines Leland's growing disillusionment and Kane's increasing ambitions. In the original Mankiewicz-Welles script, the dialogue was played at an interlude in the party, while various members of the newspaper staff danced with the chorus girls. By the time of the actual filming, however, Welles had decided to stage the conversation simultaneously with Kane's dance. Leland and Bernstein literally have to shout to be heard over the raucous sounds of the orchestra and chorus, and our eyes are continually pulled away from them toward the antics in the background. Even when Welles cuts to a reverse angle, we can still see Kane and one of the girls reflected in the glass of a window.

This shot contains an echo of the composition in the boardinghouse; once again Kane is supposed to be at play, and once again a window frame seems to mock his apparent freedom. The violent overlappings and baroque contrasts of space are used here not only on the visual level, but also on the soundtrack. Welles did not invent overlapping dialogue any more than he and Toland invented deep focus, but the complex, hurried speech in *Kane* and the various levels of sound within a scene are especially effective corollaries of the complex photographic style. To complement what Toland had publicized as "pan focus," Welles devised a sort of "pan sound," drawing on his years in radio, where he had gained a reputation as an experimenter. Indeed this reputation is alluded to in a biographical profile for the *Saturday Evening Post*, written before the idea of *Kane* was conceived, when Alva Johnson and Fred Smith comment on the powers of Welles's "auditory nerve":

Recently he was in a restaurant with some people who became interested in the dialogue at the table on the left; they eavesdropped eagerly, but without catching more than an occasional word. Welles then gave a full account of the discussion at the table on the left and threw in for good measure the substance of the discussion at the table on the right. . . . Welles insisted that the triple-eavesdropping faculty could be acquired by anyone who practiced earnestly.

Welles probably believed that a complex soundtrack like the one at the *Inquirer* party is more "real," more true to the welter of conversations in life; we know from testimony of people like John Houseman that Welles's radio dramas had gone to extraordinary lengths to achieve documentary-like speech or sound effects. Here again, however, the technique is in fact an expressive device. Despite Welles's demonstration in the restaurant, the listening ear doesn't make sense of overlapping speech or the chaos of sounds in the environment. Like the eye, it is highly selective, and needs to screen out unwanted noises. The microphone, on the other hand, is as non-selective as the camera—that is why the sounds in *Kane*, like the images, have been carefully orchestrated to blot out unwanted distractions and to serve symbolic functions, even while they overheat the spectacle and make the spectator work to decipher it.

Critics have often pointed to the "radio" sound in *Citizen Kane*. (In fact, the first words that Welles speaks in the film, after the whispered "Rosebud," are a reference to his Mars broadcast: "Don't believe everything you hear on the radio," he chuckles.) As evidence of Welles's expertise with sound, commentators always mention the "lightning mixes"—scenes in which one character's speech will be cut off abruptly, only to be completed by another character in another time and place. These charming tricks, however, are a logical extension of the Vorkapitch montages Hollywood used so often in the thirties, and there is nothing especially original about them; one finds similar transitions in *Trouble in Paradise* and *Gold Diggers of 1935*. What is more interesting and perhaps more "radio-like" is the degree to which music and sound in Welles's films become natural adjuncts to the "layered" principles of deep focus. The best example of the technique, it seems to me, is not in *Kane* but in the snow scene in *The Magnificent Ambersons*, where jingling sleigh music is first alternated and then intertwined with the dissonant squeaking of an automobile handcrank. These sounds are subtly combined with the excited chatter of six characters (all of them, as in the earlier ballroom sequence in the same film, post-synchronized by RKO technicians), creating a true montage of conflicts and reinforcing a major theme. Similar effects are at work in a modest way in the boardinghouse episode and the *Inquirer* party in *Kane*, where the sound in the background is meant to contrast with the sound in the foreground. In the climactic moments of *Touch of Evil*, the technique can be seen in its most radically expressive form, as if Welles's work were evolving toward greater, not less, stylization.

There are, of course, other moments in Welles's movies when the dialogue and incidental sound have been made deliberately and "realistically" chaotic, because the director has been willing to sacrifice clarity for pure speed. By the middle thirties, a fast-talking, breezy manner had become virtually the norm for American movies, and Hiram Sherman, one of the stars of the 1938 Mercury stage production of *Shoemaker's Holiday*, recalls that Welles was particularly fond of the technique:

He loved you to bite the cue. Everything had to mesh, go together. You didn't finish a speech that someone else wasn't on top of you. All the time. This kind of repartee was very effective in *Shoemaker*. It was going lickety-split all the time. We didn't even have an intermission. We tried it for one preview, but Orson decided to cut that out and plow right on.

Sherman's emphasis on how "everything had to mesh, go together," is an important key to the overall style of a movie like *Kane*, where so much depends on superimposition and simultaneity, one scene dissolving into the next, one account of Kane's life slightly overlapping the succeeding account, one actor biting the other's cue. In its first half, the film is as rapidly paced as a Howard Hawks comedy, but not so much for the sake of realism as for the sheer thrill of the zesty atmosphere.

Furthermore, this sense of pace and energy depends more on cutting than is usually noted. Even Bazin, who was interested chiefly in the long take, recognized that "superimpositions" were characteristic of Welles's work. What Bazin did not emphasize, as Brian Henderson has pointed out, is that "the long take rarely appears in its pure state." In fact, Henderson notes, "the cut which ends a long take—how it ends and where—determines or affects the nature of the shot itself." For example, toward the end of the scene in Mrs. Kane's boardinghouse, Agnes Moorehead rises and walks back toward the window, the camera slowly following her. She pauses, and Welles cuts to a reverse angle, looking past her face toward the opposite side of the room. The scene as a whole is

not a long take but a shot/ reverse shot combination which is fundamental to narrative movies. There are, however, some interesting differences between this particular editing style and standard Hollywood practice: for one thing, the rhythm of the cutting is not keyed to the rhythm of the dialogue—instead it imposes a structure on the narrative, holding off the crucial closeup until the most effective moment. Equally important, the editing of shots such as this one, photographed with a wide-angle lens, creates a slightly more violent effect than the editing of normal perspectives, and makes the audience more aware of the cutting process. The exaggeration of space gives the reverse angle an unusual force, as if we had been jerked into a radically different viewpoint. Thus Mrs. Kane's face looms up in the foreground, and the impact of this image is reinforced by having her call loudly out the window to Charles. The cut emphasizes the mother's pain and her pivotal role; behind her, we can see the figures of the father and the banker standing awkwardly in the distance, dwarfed by the size of her head.

Because of the many wide-angle views in *Kane*, shot/reverse shot editing takes on new dramatic possibilities. Consider, for example, the scenes of Kane and Susan separated by the vast halls of Xanadu, where a simple over-the-shoulder editing style becomes a powerful and witty statement about alienation and loneliness. Earlier, in the newspaper office, a reverse angle is used to convey Kane's anger at Leland: Leland emerges from a drunken stupor and stands at the door of his office, looking out toward where Kane is composing a review of Susan's opera debut; we cut to a reverse shot composed in extreme depth (so deep, in fact, that it was created by the optical printing I have mentioned), showing Kane's massive head at the left of the screen and Leland stepping out of the door in the far distance. Simultaneous with this violent change of perspective, Kane pushes back the typewriter carriage with a loud slam; the sound of the typewriter, which was tiny in the previous shot, suddenly becomes close up and frightening.

Elsewhere in the film, Welles avoids reverse views altogether, playing out whole scenes in one take and "editing" by revealing successive playing areas. In some of his more elaborate montages he will throw a brief wide-angle shot on the screen with stunning effect, as in the *Inquirer* party, where a distorted closeup of a smiling black man coincides with a blast of music. In many other scenes, however, he uses an ordinary shot/reverse shot style and even an ordinary lens—consider the argument between the young Kane and Carter in the newspaper office, or the meeting between Kane and Susan in her apartment. Ultimately, therefore, it might be said that the chief difference between *Kane* and the standard film has less to do with an unusual editing style than with the size and relative perspective of the shots Welles puts on the screen, plus his tendency to animate the space around the actors. Generally he keeps the camera at a distance, using the wide-angle lens to increase the playing area, so that he can draw out the individual shots and fill them with detail. Although there are far more close-ups in *Kane* than Welles himself remembered, we seldom see an actor's face isolated on the screen. Welles wanted the audience to "read" a complex imagery, wanted them to appreciate his skill at rapid manipulation of the magic-show qualities of the medium. In other words, his work ran somewhat against the grain of classic studio movies, which encouraged the audience to forget technique and identify with the players.

The acting in Welles's early films is determined by similar principles, being slightly overwrought and at times self-consciously inflated. George Coulouris, who played Thatcher in *Kane*, has remarked on this quality:

> I made many films after *Kane* and one thing I've noticed is its intensity and power—more than would be tolerable in many films. The scene in which we argue back and forth in the newspaper office is not conventional movie acting. With other actors or another director, it would have been "brought down" a lot and lost a good deal.

In fact the argument between Kane and Thatcher—and virtually the entire Thatcher section of the film—is a foreshadowing of a technique which would become increasingly evident in Welles's later work; the players "project" their lines to a greater degree than in the ordinary movie, as if they were oblivious to the idea that acting for a camera ought to be low-key and naturalistic. The Thatcher section is a subtle, deliberate echo of Victorian melodramatics, but even the later episodes are particularly high-pitched, creating a sort of repressed hysteria. Agnes Moorehead, Ray Collins, and Dorothy Comingore are a bit more wide-eyed and loud than they need to be; Collins, for example, underplays the villainy of Jim Gettys, but he stays in one's mind as a vivid portrait largely because he handles the quieter lines of dialogue almost like a stage actor, preserving the illusion of calm while he speaks at a high volume. Later, in the scene where Susan attacks Kane for allowing Leland to write a negative review of her singing, the sound technicians seem to have added an extra decibel to her already piercing voice: "What's that?" she shouts as Kane opens a letter from Leland. "A declaration of principles," he says, almost to himself. "*What?*" she screams, the sound cutting at the audience's ears and making Kane flinch as if from a whiplash.

Welles's own remarkable performance in the central role is in keeping with this stylized quality. The resonant, declamatory voice speaks its lines very rapidly, almost throwing away whole phrases but then pausing to linger over a word, like a pastiche of ordinary excited speech. A masterful stealer of scenes, Welles also knows that if he glances away from the person to whom he is speaking he will capture the audience's attention. His slightly distracted look, plus the gauzy photography he prefers for his own closeups, gives his acting what François Truffaut calls a "softly hallucinated" tone, something of a counterpoint to the more nightmarish mood of the rest of the movie. (At this point, however, one should note that Welles's screen persona and some of his directorial mannerisms may have developed less out of taste or theory than out of necessity, because he always disliked his own body. A massive, fascinating presence, he was nevertheless somewhat flat-footed and graceless in movement, and his best performances were in the roles of very old men. As the young Kane he is usually photographed sitting down; when he does move—as in the dance at the *Inquirer* party or in the scene where he destroys Susan Alexander's room—his stilted, robot-like behavior is acceptable because it is in keeping with the highly deterministic quality of the script and the visuals.)

Keenly aware of his acting range, Welles has designed every shot in *Kane* to accommodate his physical limitations; partly as a result of this habit, he has also been very fussy about the choreography of the other actors, who, as we have seen, are locked into rigidly structured patterns. Unlike Hawks, Ford, or any of the "action" directors of the time, he gives us very few moments when the camera sits passively by and allows an actor's body its own natural freedom. Yet in Welles's first two films there are individual scenes which go beyond artifice and bring an extraordinarily truthful, unmannered quality to the acting. In both cases—Kane's rage in Susan's bedroom and Aunt Fanny's hysterical outburst near the end of *Ambersons*—the emotions seem to rise out of a sexual frustration that has been building throughout the plot, and in both cases the actors are no longer quite pretending. (After the bedroom scenes Welles is rumored to have remarked, "I really felt it." Aunt Fanny's collapse, on the other hand, was reshot dozens of times, until Agnes Moorehead was literally shedding tears of exhaustion.) On the screen, these moments feel so authentic that they almost break through the fictional context, but in their own way they are as unconventional as the otherwise slightly exaggerated, artful playacting. By the early forties American movies had developed a slick, understated acting style that avoided behavioral extremes; when characters cried, their tears seemed real but never really disturbing. Among the chief performers of the decade, only James Stewart was able to convey psychic breakdowns with an intensity comparable to the ones in *Kane* and *Ambersons*, but his anguish was usually softened by Frank Capra's sentimental, optimistic stories. Welles's films were slightly different; they made the audience conscious of psychological pain—and also of the art of acting—in a way that was more common to the theatre. Hence a movie like *Citizen Kane* may have been a dreamworld, a wondershow, but it was also capable of touching upon important emotional realities.

II

Welles was slightly unorthodox and special, but of course he had been assisted by the RKO staff and learned most of what he knew from watching the films of his Hollywood predecessors, including Ford, Lubitsch, Sternberg, and Murnau. In fact Murnau's *Sunrise* contains nearly all the essential ingredients of Welles's visuals, down to a sharply focused shot which modestly prefigures the famous attempted suicide in *Kane:* in the foreground is a glass containing a spoon; in the middle distance a woman reclines on a bed; in the far distance we can see activity outside a window. In turn, Welles's own work was to influence American cinema throughout the forties: stylish melodramas such as Ulmer's *Ruthless* and Farrow's *The Big Clock*, to cite only two examples, are filled with flashbacks, elaborate tracking shots, long takes, compositions in depth, and even set designs which are vaguely reminiscent of *Kane*.

Nevertheless, if the "classic" studio cinema ever existed (and by "classic" I mean movies that used chronological narrative, invisible editing, minimal acting, and a muted photographic expressionism—everything designed to immerse the audience in "content" and make them forget the manipulations of style), then Welles's individualism was a challenge to the system. Furthermore, whatever the derivation or influence of Welles's techniques, the peculiarities of his cinema seem to me to consist of different elements from the ones emphasized by Bazin. *Citizen Kane* has a crisp, three-dimensional photography, an accurate sense of period manners and decor, and a depiction of social caste almost as vivid as Eisenstein's. To these ostensibly "realistic" qualities it adds an almost shrill acting style and a *mise-en-scène* distinguished not so much by its ambiguity as by its density and multiplicity. Thus Welles's movies contrast with others of the period because they contain such a fine frenzy of performance and information; the overriding quality of his work is not its phenomenal realism but its distortion and excess. And the progress of his American films was to be a fairly steady movement away from the conventions of cinematic reality toward the bizarre and surreal.

Most of his later pictures, made under severe contractual restraints and without the Mercury company, are characterized by a sort of dazzling aesthetic unrestraint, and are contemptuous of naturalism, reason, and decorum. The images he projects on the screen are ostentatious distortions of the natural world, lacking the orderly planes of classical expression, as if he were trying to break down a visual frontier by dramatically emphasizing any movement forward or backward along the tunnel of space in front of the camera. In this regard he becomes the exact opposite of an equally ostentatious but popular director like Hitchcock, whose films have several parallels with his own, but whose imagery is always lucid and orderly. (Interestingly, Hitchcock once told students at the American Film Institute that he disliked deep-focus compositions as a rule, and that he thought the wide-angle lens caused too much exaggeration.) Like Hitchcock, Welles inherited certain mannerisms from the Germans: an authoritarian blocking of actors; heavy, dramatic lighting; and a fondness for shooting from radical angles. But when these attributes are added to the forced perspective of his imagery and the unusually crowded, intense effect of his action and dialogue, the result is an impression of a romantic temperament gone completely unchecked. In fact the very density and bravado of this style may have helped RKO executives to fuel the myth of extravagance that still surrounds Welles's life and work. Welles never went drastically over budget and was never responsible for a true financial disaster; nonetheless the idea persisted that he was a waster of studio money. This, together with his satiric vision of America and his lack of box office success, severely limited his ability to work in Hollywood.

Welles's artistic flamboyance and unrestrained power also had a somewhat paradoxical effect on the films themselves, because from the beginning of his career his leading themes were the dangers of radical individualism and unlimited power. As we shall see, most of his films are about tyrannical egotists, men who try to imitate God. His major characters usually try to live above the law, in contempt of ordinary human restraint, and as a result they cut themselves off from their community, becoming prisoners of guilt, self-delusion, and old age. Nevertheless, Welles's own public philosophy was consistently humanistic and liberal, and nearly all his Hollywood films were grounded in social commentary. The question naturally arises, then, whether there was not a tension or contradiction between Welles's philosophic stance and the personality which is implicit in his style.

Clearly there was such a tension, and it is echoed in other aspects of Welles's work, especially in the nest of conflicts and oppositions in *Citizen Kane*, which will be discussed in the next chapter. For example, Welles's typical way of dealing with a film story was to begin at the level of social satire and then to become preoccupied with "tragic" issues, so that he seemed to be responding to two distinct urges. His preference for the Gothic or "expressionist" mode is a further sign of an emotional dualism: Gothic writers have typically been political rebels of a sort, trying to depict the corruption and degeneracy of an entrenched order; even so, as Leslie Fiedler has noted, there is a contradiction between the "liberal uses and demonic implications, the enlightened principles and reactionary nostalgia of the tale of terror." Thus the tyrants at the center of Welles's films are usually more fascinating and sympathetic than the naïve, commonplace figures around them—this in spite of the fact that Welles puts many of his own political sentiments into the mouths of "starry-eyed idealists" like Jed Leland, Michael O'Hara, and Mike Vargas. Actually, the demonic, obsessive drives of the tyrant begin to take on a sort of moral purity, as if egomania and self-delusion were partly a reaction against a sickness in the society at large.

Welles never attributed the sickness to any clear systemic causes: in fact he was more given to explaining his sympathetic tyrants in terms of neurotic sexual obsessions, or to contrasting the madness of America with momentary glimpses of pre-industrial "innocence." But the stylistic quality I have been describing above—the density and manic extremism of Welles's typical scenes—is perfectly expressive of the displaced libidinal urges that cause his protagonists to launch their frustrated drives for power. And even though Welles was critical of these Faustian types, they had something deeply in common with the personality of the director himself, as it is suggested in the gorgeous excess of his style. According to his friend Maurice Bessy, Welles lamented the fact that he was "made to follow in the footsteps of the Byronic adventurer, even though I detest this sort of man and everything he stands for." Such a remark suggests an extraordinary division in Welles's own character, and may help explain why he often portrayed the romantic egotist as a driven and deeply interesting person; certainly his ironic treatment of Kane or the Ambersons did not conceal his sympathy, his fascination with their absurd grandeur. His overreachers tend to be tyrants in spite of themselves, pathetically trying to determine their own fate even while they are doomed by their childhood and victimized by a society beyond their control. As Bessy has pointed out, the Wellesian tyrant, for all his destructiveness, is a wielder of sham power: Kane tries to construct his own world at Xanadu; George Minafer thinks he can become a "yachtsman"; Macbeth believes he is a king; Mr. Arkadin imagines he can eradicate his past; Mr. Clay attempts to gain immortality. The ambitions of these men are at once awesome and laughable, much like the young Welles himself. None of them is really in control, and most of them are naïvely, ludicrously out of touch with reality, motivated by sexual urges they never fully understand. Therefore the Faustian proto-fascist in a Welles movie usually turns into a sort of perverse Don Quixote, a man in tragicomic rebellion against a world that conspires to inhibit his dream of autonomy and control.

When Welles's films are viewed in this way, the connection between his heated, sometimes outrageous style and his rather philosophic subject matter becomes more apparent. In one sense Welles was critical of romantic egotism—that is why he often combined German expressionism with the sort of absurdist comedy that has always been at the heart of the American Gothic. At the same time, however, the Orson Welles who tried to master Hollywood was himself a victim of his childhood and his romantic character. While intellectually Welles may have been a liberal, emotionally he was something of a radical; as we shall see, his fascination with passing time and human mortality, his preoccupation with characters who are slightly out of step, his interest in a past when everything was somehow better than it is now—all these things indicate that at one level he was both a rebel and, in one sense, a reactionary. Thus John Houseman was right to say that Welles pushed "theatrical effect" far beyond its "normal point of tension." In this way, Welles's films suggest how much he had in common with his characters, to say nothing of what he had in common with the romantic agony that runs throughout American literature. It is precisely this quality of his style that made his career in American movies so difficult, and that made his own life seem to imitate that of one of the protagonists of his stories.

3

Citizen Kane

Citizen Kane is the product of an individual artist (and a company of his associates) working at a particular movie studio at a particular historical moment. This fact ought to be self-evident, but one needs to state it because the question of the "authorship" of *Kane* has become the oldest, worst-tempered, and most confused argument in movie history. The debate has been revived in recent years by Pauline Kael, whose long essay for *The Citizen Kane Book* forced numerous angry replies from movie historians eager to defend Welles's contribution to the script. For those readers interested in a more complete, authoritative account of exactly who wrote what and when on *Citizen Kane*, I recommend Robert Carringer's study of the production history of the film. Carringer, who researched the RKO archives, examined all seven revisions of the script, and spoke to most of the people concerned, found documentary proof that Welles was one of the principal authors of the screenplay. In other words, the credits as they appear on the screen are fairly accurate: *Kane* was produced by Welles's company, co-authored by Herman Mankiewicz and Welles (John Houseman was offered screen credit, but declined), and directed by Welles, who also played the leading character.

Notice, however, that there are *two* sets of credits for the movie: at the beginning we are told that *Kane* is a Mercury production "by Orson Welles," and at the end, after the coat-grabbing finale, we are given a complete list of contributors, in which

Welles's name plays a subsidiary role. Interestingly, both of these views of the film's authorship are correct—the first does not cancel out the second, and the truth of the film's origins can be understood only by keeping both in mind simultaneously.

Actually, the entire film works according to an identical principle, so that everything evokes its opposite and all statements about the protagonist are true in some sense. There are, to choose one minor example of the method, two snow-sleds. The first, as everyone knows, is named "Rosebud"; the second is given to Kane as a Christmas present by Thatcher, and is seen only briefly—so briefly that audiences are unaware that it, too, has a name. If you study the film through a movieola or an analyzing projector, you will discover that for a few frames sled number two is presented fully to the camera, its legend clearly visible. It is named "Crusader," and where the original has a flower, this one is embossed with the helmet of a knight.

Welles was probably unconcerned when his symbolism did not show on the screen. "Crusader" was a tiny joke he could throw away in a film that bristles with clever asides. I mention it not only because I am foolishly proud of knowing such esoterica, but also because it is a convenient way to point up the split in Kane's character and in the very conception of the film. In many ways it is appropriate that Thatcher should try to win the boy over with a sled named "Crusader." Kane will repay this gift by growing up to be a crusading, trust-busting newspaperman, out to slay the dragon Wall Street. (Hearst, his counterpart, had been known for the way he embarked on crusades, and in his earlier days, when it suited him, had been the enemy of the traction trust.) On another level, the two sleds can be interpreted as emblems of a sentimental tragedy: Kane has lost the innocence suggested by "Rosebud" and has been transformed into a phony champion of the people, an overreacher who dies like a medieval knight amid the empty Gothic splendor of Xanadu.

The essence of the film, in other words, is its structure of alternating attitudes. It is an impure mixture of ideas, forms, and feelings—part magic show, part tragedy; part satire, part sentiment—as divided as Kane himself. In fact the contrast between "Crusader" and "Rosebud" is only the most superficial instance of the way the film deliberately sets images, characters, and ideas against one another, as if it were trying to illustrate Coleridge's notion that good art always reconciles discordant elements. Thus the Freudian aspects of the screenplay create an ironic, almost playful effect, whereas the imagery of "Rosebud" tries to pull the audience's emotions back in the direction of mystery, demonic energy, and pathos. Nearly everything in the story is based on this sort of duality or ambiguity, so that we are constantly made aware of the two sides to Kane. He has not only two snow-sleds but two wives and two friends. The camera makes two visits to Susan Alexander and two journeys to Xanadu; it even shows two closeups of "Rosebud," once as it is being obliterated by the snows of Colorado at Mrs. Kane's boardinghouse, and then again as it is incinerated in the basement of Kane's Florida estate. Finally, in the most vivid clash of all, we are given two endings: first the reporter Thompson quietly tells his colleagues that a single word can't sum up a man's life, and the camera moves away from him, lingering over the jigsaw pieces of Xanadu's artwork; after Thompson's exit, however, the same camera begins tracking toward a furnace, where it reveals the meaning of "Rosebud" after all. The film has shifted from a darkened, intellectual irony to a spectacular dramatic irony, from apparent wisdom to apparent revelation.

Such perfect contrasts keep our feelings qualified, in suspension, leaving most audiences unsure whether to regard *Kane* as high seriousness or as some kind of brilliant conjuring trick. At every level the movie is a paradox: Kane himself is both a villain and a romantic, Faustian rebel, as much like Welles as he is like Hearst. The style of the film—and under this rubric may be included the various contributions of script, acting, and camera—is both derivative of earlier Hollywood models and self-consciously critical of them. The leftist political implications of the project adversely affected Welles's entire career, and yet in many ways *Kane* evades the concrete issues; it does, of course, mount a powerful attack on Hearst, but the attack is somewhat oblique—actually, *Kane* is almost as deeply concerned with the movies themselves, and with the potentially deceptive, myth-making qualities of the media, which are linked by extension to the deceptions of the Hearst press. Hence it produces a certain ambivalence not only toward its subject but toward the very methods which are used to disclose the subject.

Some of these tensions and internal divisions may be seen in the following close descriptive analysis. Taken together, they help make *Kane* not only a rich psychological portrait but a subtle commentary on its own text—a film that reveals all the paradoxes and contradictions of the Welles myth in general.

I

The movie opens with an act of violation. The dark screen slowly lightens to show a "No Trespassing" sign which the camera promptly ignores. To the strains of Bernard Herrmann's haunting, funereal "power" music, we rise up a chain link fence toward a misty, bleak, studio-manufactured sky. The camera movement is accompanied by a series of dissolves which takes us first to a new pattern of barbed-wire, elongated chain links and then to an arrangement of iron oak leaves, presumably adorning a gate. I say "presumably" because the opening montage is meant to captivate and confuse the audience, leaving them slightly unsure of where they are at any given moment. The point here is not to reveal Kane's private world but to provide fascinating glimpses, frustrating the viewer with a baffling subjectivity. Thus, as we are taken beyond the gigantic "K" atop the fence and progressively nearer to a lighted window in a castle, we encounter a surreal combination of images: monkeys in a cage, gondolas in a stream, a golf course. Only the window provides continuity; in fact it seems to defy the logic of space by remaining at exactly the same point on the screen in each shot, growing portentously larger with every dissolve.

Kane's castle looks a bit like the home of a sorcerer, chiefly because of the stereoptic, *Snow White*-like effect of the RKO art work. Welles has to be credited for the way he allowed the talents of Perry Ferguson, Van Nest Polglase, Vernon Walker, and the Disney animators to come into play throughout the film. He had the wisdom to turn the rough cut of "News on the March" over to the newsreel department for editing, since they could best duplicate the style, and here he is able to use the art department with equal intelligence. Who else but Hollywood designers could have created such a spooky, compelling, vulgar design, a brilliant mixture of kitsch and idealism, satire and mystery? Except for the crepuscular lighting, their vision of Xanadu compares with the architecture of a Hearst-like estate which had recently been described by Aldous Huxley in *After Many a Summer Dies the Swan* (1939):

On the summit of a bluff and as though growing out of it in a kind of stony efflorescence, stood a castle. But what a castle! The donjon was like a skyscraper, the bastions plunged headlong with effortless swoop of concrete dams. The thing was Gothic, mediaeval, baronial—doubly baronial, Gothic with a Gothicity raised, so to speak, to a higher power, more mediaeval than any building of the thirteenth century. . . . It was mediaeval, not out of vulgar historical necessity, like Coucy, say, or Alnwick, but out of pure fun and wantonness, platonically, one might say. It was mediaeval as only a witty and irresponsible modern architect would wish to be mediaeval, as only the most competent modern engineers are technically equipped to be.

Our approach to this bizarre domain is as voyeuristic as anything in Hitchcock. The camera is drawn like a moth to the lighted window, where its journey is frustrated; the light immediately clicks out. Notice that the same forward movement of the camera, usually accompanied by dissolves, will be used throughout the film, until it becomes a stylistic motif. One thinks, for example, of the way the camera twice crawls up the walls of the El Rancho nightclub and moves toward a broken skylight; a dissolve takes us through the broken glass, enabling us to peer at Susan Alexander. There are a number of less obvious instances of the same technique, and some of them are worth listing here:

1) When Thompson (William Alland) enters the vaults of the Thatcher Memorial Library, the camera starts moving forward toward him, only to have a great iron door close in its face; a dissolve takes us beyond the door, the camera peering over Thompson's shoulder at the pages of Thatcher's diary.

2) When the flustered editor Carter (Erskine Sandford) leaves the offices of the *Inquirer*, sent by Kane to drum up sensational news, the camera stands looking at an artist's rendering of the building; a slow forward movement begins, a dissolve taking us closer to a window where Kane is writing his declaration of principles; another dissolve takes us through the window and inside the room.

3) When Kane first meets Susan and goes up to her apartment, the camera stand quietly in the hallway looking through an open door; Kane shuts the door and the camera rushes forward impetuously, almost anxiously, stopping only when Susan opens it again.

4) Near the end of the film, Kane walks out of Susan's bedroom at Xanadu, going past a mirrored hallway that casts reflections of his aging body off into infinity; after he passes, the camera zooms slightly forward toward the darkness of the empty glass.

5) In the climactic moments, the camera glides forward over

Kane's possessions, a collection that looks like an aerial view of a metropolis. A dissolve takes us closer, the camera moving past the flotsam of Kane's life: a symbolic toy-box, a set of old newspapers bound in twine, a photo of Kane circa his first marriage, an iron bedstead from an earlier scene, another photo of Kane as a boy with his mother, and finally the snow-sled. Just as the camera draws near this final object, and before we can read the inscription, a workman enters and carries the sled away; another dissolve takes us to the furnaces, where the camera continues moving forward directly into the flames, at last coming to rest on the burning "Rosebud."

The constant forward movement of the camera through windows and doors and into dark corners is of course perfectly in keeping with the film's attempt to probe Kane's sexual unconscious, and it creates an appropriately eerie effect. Moreover, the ultimate revelation of the burning sled produces a vivid feeling of entropy— as if the camera had pushed as far as possible and the source of Kane's mystery were being consumed at the very moment when it is being discovered. There is still another sense, however, in which the technique of the opening segment becomes a part of the film's structure and meaning. It establishes the camera as a restless, ghostly observer, more silent and discreet than the journalists who poke about among Kane's belongings, but linked to them in certain ways. Like Kane's own newspapers, the camera has become an "inquirer," its search implicating the audience in a desire to find Kane's private rather than his public meaning.

The periodic frustrations the camera encounters—a door closing, a light clicking out—are like affronts to the audience's curiosity. They also create a sense of mystery and subtle anxiety which is enhanced by other elements in the opening of the film; consider, for example, the fascinating but confusing imagery we encounter inside Xanadu. When the camera reaches Kane's window only to have the light turned out, we dissolve to an equivalent reverse angle inside the bedroom. All we see, however, is a deeply shadowed figure lying as if in state. Throughout this sequence Kane will be photographed in expressionist shadow, or else the camera will be placed so near his figure that we can barely read the image. A gigantic closeup of the dying man's lips is the largest single shot, but until the lips move and whisper the crucial word, we have no idea what we are looking at. Even when they do move, they create a slightly ludicrous impression: a big mustachioed mouth seen from so close it looks like the mountains of a strange planet.

Nearly everything in Kane's bedroom is presented in this dreamlike, subjective, slightly confusing way. The inexplicable closeup of a cottage (a still photo superimposed with moving snow) turns out to be a paperweight, and when the camera pulls back to reveal this fact some confusion lingers, because everything—Kane's hand, the paperweight, and the background—is covered with snowflakes. From this shot we cut to another view of the hand, this time shown on the opposite side of the screen—a deliberately chaotic and "bad" editing style that does not allow the audience to orient itself inside the room. When the paperweight rolls down the steps and crashes (another piece of trickery created by several images spliced together) we cut to the most confusing shot of all: a reflection in a convex piece of broken glass, creating an elaborate fish-eye effect which is virtually a parody of the lens Toland will use to photograph the movie. We can barely make out a nurse opening a strange ornamental doorway and entering; another cut, to a low angle near the head of Kane's bed, shows the nurse placing a sheet over a body.

These fragmentary glimpses of Kane's world have been so fantastic, so enshrouded with darkness and mystery, that they hide more than they reveal. They tantalize the audience, only to cap the effect suddenly, without warning, by introducing the "News on the March" title card. The newsreel, once it gets under way, allows viewers to settle momentarily into a new, more logical narrative mode, grounded in presumably objective, documentary facts. It illustrates the dramatic curve of Kane's public life, explaining the origins of the strange castle we have just seen, and providing a general map for the various local instances which will be developed later in the film. Thus, as David Bordwell has pointed out, the two opening segments are like *hommages* to the fountainheads of cinematic "perception"—the fantasy of Méliès and the documentary realism of Lumière. Nevertheless these two modes do not achieve a synthesis. The newsreel, as much as the opening scenes, tends to remind the audience of the voyeurism inherent in the medium, and leaves Kane as much an enigma as ever. If the private Kane was seen too subjectively, too close up, the public Kane is seen too objectively and usually from too far away.

"News on the March" is a wonderfully funny parody of the

hyped-up journalism that Hearst and Luce had helped to create; in fact Welles and about a fourth of the Mercury players had previously worked in the radio version of "The March of Time," and had borrowed freely some of its famous catch-phrases, such as "this week, as it must to all men, death came to . . ." But for all its self-important tone, the newsreel offers mainly a compilation of Kane's public appearances, usually filled with scratches and photographed from awkward vantage points. Repeatedly Kane is shown alongside politicians, allying himself first with the progressives and then with the fascists; in his early career he is shown waving and smiling at the public in awkward gaiety, but in the later pictures he becomes somber and camera-shy. We are told that "few private lives were more public," but actually we have only disturbing glimpses into Kane's domestic habits: a doctored photo of one of his Xanadu parties; a shot of him sitting beside an empty swimming pool, swathed in towels and going over a manuscript; a peep through a latticed gate, as a hand-held camera with a telephoto lens tries to show the old man being pushed in a wheelchair. The newsreel gives the impression that Kane was always being interviewed, investigated, or eavesdropped upon, but it leaves little sense of what the man was like and only a superficial notion of his influence on public affairs. Even "1941's biggest, strangest funeral" is shown only as a brief shot outside a pseudo-Gothic pile; the image is grainy (Toland's imitation of newsreel stock is always perfectly accurate) and the sky is a giant diffuser of light, so that we can see only a few rich mourners from a distance, over the massed heads of reporters.

Throughout this "documentary" there is a comic disparity between the awesomeness of Kane's possessions and the stilted old codger we actually see, as if the newsreel were trying to establish him both as a mythical character like Noah or Kubla Khan and as something of a joke. Kane consistently supports the wrong politicians; he marries a president's daughter and then gets caught in a sex scandal with Susan Alexander; he drops wet concrete over his Edwardian coat at a public ceremony; he vouches for the peaceful intentions of Hitler. He is so bumbling and foolish that little remains of him but his wealth, and even that is treated as a believe-it-or-not curiosity. But if we are awed at Kane's money and contemptuous of his behavior, we also begin to dislike the reporters who poke microphones in his face. This feeling is reinforced when Welles detaches us from the newsreel, suddenly breaking the illusion by cutting to a side view of the screen and the projection lights, then making an aural joke: the projector clicks off and the pompous musical fanfare groans to a stop, as if somebody were giving "News on the March" a raspberry.

The ensuing conversation among reporters is derived from a colorful presentation of a scene inside a movie theatre in the 1937 Theatre Guild production of Sidney Kingsley's *Ten Million Ghosts*; it is also one of the most self-reflexive moments in the film—shot in an actual RKO screening room which has been made to look more like a region of the underworld. The air is smoky and the reporters are sinister shadows; indeed they remain shadows throughout, even in the closing scenes, when a group of them tour the bric-a-brac of Kane's estate. The corners of forties-style suits are outlined against a blank white movie screen, and the editor (Philip Van Zandt) is shown from a radically low angle, gesturing against a "Nuremberg" light beaming down from the projection booth. Rawlston and his yes-men correctly perceive the emptiness and inconclusiveness of the newsreel, but their solution is to find an "angle." "It isn't enough to tell us what a man did," Rawlston says, "you've got to tell us who he was." The solution to this problem is the dying word "Rosebud," a gimmick worthy of Hearst himself, a device that will unify the story and give the newsreel viewers a sentimental insight into Kane's character.

Rawlston gives Thompson a tap on the shoulder and a shark's smile, ordering him to go out and get "Rosebud" "dead or alive." Notice, however, that the audience is not allowed to feel comfortably superior to this scene. We have already been made curious about "Rosebud," which, after all, has exactly the same function for Welles and Mankiewicz as it does for Rawlston. Indeed, Welles indirectly admitted this fact in one of his interviews with Peter Bogdanovich, where he talked about his discomfort with the sled idea: "Rosebud remained, because it was the only way we could get off, as they say in vaudeville." In other words, without "Rosebud" the movie would lack a neatly rounded plot and a nicely punctuated ending, in much the same way as Rawlston's newsreel lacks the proper impact until some oversimplified "key" has been concocted to explain Kane's life.

The projection room segment therefore serves to criticize the script and the whole process of filling a blank movie screen; it becomes ironically appropriate to have Herman Mankiewicz, Joseph Cotten, and Erskine Sandford barely visible in the shadows of the room, playing the roles of reporters who scoff at Kane's dying words. Everybody, the audience included, has been involved in a dubious pursuit; Welles has stimulated our curiosity only to make us feel cautious. The three opening sections of the film have helped initiate the search for "Rosebud," but they are filled with so  many ironies and opacities that they threaten to undermine the search before it has started.

The story now becomes a series of reminiscences by the witnesses to Kane's life, who create a "rounded" picture of the man. And here it is important to note that the script is fundamentally different from a movie like *Rashomon:* it does not becloud events by presenting separate versions of an unknowable reality, but instead gives different facets of a single personality—a method similar to the one Herman Mankiewicz's brother Joseph was later to use successfully in such pictures as *All About Eve* and *The Barefoot Contessa.* Kane's life is depicted more or less chronologically, through the memories of five characters who knew him at progressively later stages in his life. We never have the feeling that these characters are distorting the truth (even though Leland recounts domestic events he could not possibly have seen), and if we discount the opening and closing moments of the film, and the details of Thompson's search, the private life of Kane is shown in nearly as straightforward a fashion as the public facts of the newsreel. For all its juggling of time, therefore, *Kane* has a logical, rational structure; it is a film about complexity, not about relativity.

Thompson's quest is initiated with a thunderclap and a Gothic rainstorm, in a scary but comic contrast to Rawlston's last words ("It'll probably turn out to be a very simple thing."). We see a garish, dripping poster of a blonde woman, and the camera moves upward, sliding over the roof of the El Rancho and down through the skylight. (The name of the club is significant: El Rancho was the name Hearst gave his California ranch in the days before he built San Simeon.) Here again we are made to feel that the search for "Rosebud" is tawdry and sensational, notably so in a deep-focus shot that concludes Thompson's abortive interview with Susan. Thompson steps into a phone booth and his hat brim is silhouetted at the right corner of the screen; he closes the door and the headwaiter (Gus Schilling) moves just a fraction to the left so that he is framed by one of the rectangular glass panels; in the distance, her head bowed drunkenly over a table, is Susan. We are made aware of her sordid life, and we see a chain of predators arrayed in front of her. The waiter is trying to spy on Thompson, who has been trying to learn about Kane; Thompson, in turn, has to convey information to his boss at the other end of the line. "Hello, Mr. Rawlston," he says. "She won't talk." The composition of the shot is all the more troubling because the extreme depth of perspective makes the chain of predators seem to extend out into the audience, bringing the viewers by implication into the film's corrupt world.

The El Rancho scene ends with still another kind of self-conscious flourish, a blackout joke. Thompson tries bribing John, the headwaiter, who comments innocently, "Thank you . . . thanks. As a matter of fact, just the other day, when the papers were full of it, I asked her. She never heard of Rosebud." Fade out, with an ironic, playful chord of Herrmann's music. Nearly all the fragments of the narrative have been structured this way, with a mild shock or a witty image at the beginning and a joke or an ironic twist at the end. It is exactly this quality which made Pauline Kael describe *Kane* as the epitome of "thirties comedy," a genre which she points out was fathered on Broadway by George S. Kaufman in the twenties; Kael is particularly good at describing the "fullness and completeness" with which the film manipulates this tradition, becoming, at least in its opening parts, a collection of sketches "arranged to comment on each other." The striking thing about *Kane*, however, is that the cynical, wisecracking style of the Kaufmans and Hechts has been put to the service of something more difficult, the movie achieving a rare commingling of brittle artifice, tough social realism, and romantic tragedy. The "thirties comedy" is there, of course, especially in the early scenes, but the ultimate feeling is different, affected by Welles's and Toland's Germanic staging, by the unsentimental acting of players like Dorothy Comingore (whose voice bears a prophetic resemblance to Marilyn Monroe's), and by the indirect influence of impressionist novelists like Conrad and Fitzgerald. To call *Kane* essentially a comedy or a "newspaper" yarn is therefore to place the main emphasis on certain features in the first third of the story, and to oversimplify its scope and tone.

Just how complex this tone is may be seen in the next sequence—Thompson's visit to the Thatcher Library—which begins with another joke. Herrmann plays his "power" motif with a flat, stale brass; the camera tilts down from the model of a huge, ugly statue of Thatcher and locates Thompson speaking with a prototypi-

cal lady librarian, who reminds him of the rules pertaining to all manuscripts. Obviously the library has been designed to emphasize Thatcher's vanity and coldness: the inner vault seems as long as a football field, and at the far end is a small safe from which an armed guard extracts a volume of a diary, bringing it forward as if he were bearing the Eucharist. The whole ridiculous edifice appears to have been constructed to house Thatcher's tiny memoirs, but the effect of the imagery is more than simple invective.

The mannish librarian stands at military attention while the guard, caught in the beam of a "Nuremberg" light, brings forth a glowing book. Thompson is closer to the foreground, so that he looks a bit like Kafka's Joseph K. come before the Courts of Law. The Gothic lighting is meant partly to create a comic irony, yet at the same time it produces an awesome scene, an effect of wonder coexisting with the satire. Lawrence Goldstein and Jay Kauffman, in their book *Into Film*, have described the vault as a "way station between heaven and hell ... the guard becomes a divine messenger bringing the fiercely glowing documents out of the darkness [like] the tablets offered Moses; and the hard mahogany table that will receive the documents burns with the glint of a sacred altar." Throughout *Kane*, this aura of sacredness is mixed with elements of hokum and profanity, so that we are aware of banal material goods being mystified into a spiritual netherworld. The lighting style, like nearly everything in the movie, resists being described either as pure satire, as seriousness, or as old-fashioned "movie magic"; instead it is carefully designed to underscore one of the film's leading themes—the transformation of money into myth.

The principle of contrast which guides the film is repeated when, from one of the darkest moments, we move to one of the lightest. The "Thatcher" portion of the film, which grows out of Thompson's reading of the diary, is at first somewhat Dickensian in mood, as befits Thatcher's generation. Thatcher himself is a coldhearted moneybag, and his story tells how a poor child rises suddenly to great expectations. Within a few moments we see Charles Foster Kane being lifted from a snowy playground in front of his mother's boardinghouse and set down at a richly Victorian Christmas celebration, although in both places the atmosphere is chilly, the boy surrounded by menacing adult figures. George Coulouris (made up to look rather like John D. Rockefeller) plays Thatcher in broad caricature, delivering his lines at top speed; in a charmingly exuberant and altogether anti-realistic montage which foreshadows the opening of *The Magnificent Ambersons*, he constantly turns to face the camera, muttering in disgust as the young Kane grows up, founds a newspaper, and then attacks Wall Street. But Kane rises only to have an ignominious fall; the narrative as a whole covers the period between the winter of 1871 and the winter of 1929, when Kane, ironically forced to turn part of the control of his newspapers over to his former guardian, broods on his failure, telling Thatcher that he would like to have been "everything you hate." By the end, we are made to feel that Capital has always been in charge of Kane's life, and that the market crash has done little more than solidify the power of America's major bankers by placing the *Inquirer* in Thatcher's hands. At the same time a nostalgic evocation of the nineteenth century has given way to a somber present; indeed the deep-focus shot of the room where Kane signs part of his rights away bears a vague resemblance to the tomb-like Thatcher Library.

The portrait of Kane which emerges from these memoirs contains as many ironies and ambiguities as the plot. In the boardinghouse scene, where for once we might expect to see Kane as the innocent victim of social determinism, he is depicted as something of a brat; in fact, the closeup of Mrs. Kane hovering protectively over her child is almost comic because he looks like such a mean kid. By contrast, he is at his most charming and sympathetic during the early scene in the newspaper office, where his potential danger is underlined, but where he is shown as a darkly handsome, confident young man, loyal to his friends and passionate about his work. This is, in fact, the point of Welles's full-scale entry into the film, and it is predictably stunning: Thatcher, who has been reading a succession of *Inquirer* headlines, lowers a paper ("Galleons of

Spain off Jersey Coast") to reveal Kane sitting at his editorial desk. Here at last, greeted by a triumphal note of Herrmann's music, is the young Welles of Mars panic fame, propped easily in a swivel chair, clad in shirtsleeves, sipping coffee. He has been made up to look casually rich and beautiful, and he glances at Thatcher with a bemused, Machiavellian glint in his eye. In the same shot Leland and Bernstein enter the frame, Leland calmly taking a cigar from the desk (he is an addict, as we see later), and Bernstein scurrying past on official business. Throughout the scene, Welles makes himself a calm figure at the center of a storm, blithely dictating a telegram which echoes one of Hearst's most famous comments to a reporter ("Dear Wheeler, you provide the prose poems and I'll provide the war"), and, in a large, climactic closeup, thumbing his nose at Thatcher's warnings ("You know, Mr. Thatcher, at the rate of a million dollars a year I'll have to close this place—in sixty years").

In this scene, as in other episodes from the same period in his life, Kane seems generous with money and disrespectful toward stuffy Victorian authority; perhaps most importantly, he says he is committed to the "people" as opposed to the "trusts." Thatcher and the elderly editor Carter—a harrumphing old banker and a genteel incompetent—are perfect foils to his rebelliousness. They behave like outraged schoolmasters, making Kane's yellow journalism and his attempt to start a war in Cuba seem like a combination of boyish pranksterism and creative energy. But Kane's bullying attitude and what he actually says tend to suggest a totally different sort of character. He himself offers an explanation for our mixed emotions: "The trouble is," he tells Thatcher, "you don't realize you're talking to two people." On the one hand is the Kane we see, the pretty young man who claims to represent the interests of the public; on the other hand is the Kane who has investments in Wall Street and who knows down to the penny the amount of his holdings ("eighty-two thousand, three hundred and sixty-four shares of Public Transit Preferred"). "If I don't look after the interests of the underprivileged," he remarks, in one of the places where contradictions are reconciled, "maybe somebody will—maybe somebody without money or property."

When Thompson closes the diary and exits the library ("Thanks for the use of the hall"), he goes to interview Bernstein, who maintains the spell of Kane's charm. Bernstein talks mainly about the period between the founding of the newspaper and Kane's marriage to Emily Norton, a woman who "was no Rosebud."

The only real apologist for Kane in the film, Bernstein is basically a likeable character, and evokes sympathy. Except for the reporters, he is the only person who has remembered Susan after Kane's death ("I called her myself the day he died. I thought maybe somebody ought to"). He is also completely free of self-importance and moral superiority, and even his reactionary comment on the Panama Canal arises more from a defense of his dead friend than from any self-serving motive. He is realistic about old age and death (old age is the "only disease you don't look forward to being cured of"), as well as about his position in life ("Me? I'm chairman of the board. I got nothing but time"); nevertheless he seems spry and at peace with himself. Even the setting for his interview is conducive of a melancholy serenity: shadows fill the room, but rain falls outside the high windows and a fire burns in the hearth. Bernstein sits in a big leather chair, his face reflected in the polished surface of his desk as if in a quiet pool. Here, photographed in a long take which contains some of the most discreet camera movements in the film, he tells the little story about seeing a girl in a white dress on the Jersey Ferry (Welles's favorite moment, beautifully acted by Everett Sloane, whose voice and manner come dangerously close to suggesting an old crone) and he reminds us that he is the only character who has been with Kane until "after the end."

And yet the kindness and the cozy atmosphere do not conceal the fact that Bernstein's friendship has been compromised. We soon learn that he has been more like a devoted child, and his devotion has had sinister consequences. All his judgments rise logically out of his character as an over-faithful associate, from a different social class than Kane, who has become a kind of stooge. The furthest removed from the patrician Leland, he is described, in a scene that was dropped from the completed film, as having once been in the "wholesale jewelry business"; his talents, Kane says wryly, "seemed to be what I was looking for." Thus even though Kane will tell Emily in no uncertain terms that Bernstein may pay a visit to the family nursery, there remains a discreet distance between the two men; we see Leland and Kane arrive together at the *Inquirer* offices in a hansom cab, dressed in the height of New York fashion, while Bernstein tags along atop a delivery wagon, fulfilling his purpose as the guardian of Kane's possessions. Later, at the political rally and at Susan's concert, Bernstein will be photographed in the company of Kane's goons; as Kane's financial agent and unquestioning companion, he has been responsible for whatever dirty work needed doing, and it is clear that he has always placed loyalty above principle. Hence there is a deep irony in the comfortable serenity of his old age, a luxury which has come to him like a "tip" from his employer.

Bernstein's reminiscences are chiefly about adventure and male camaraderie; even so, further ironies are obvious. Kane sweeps into the *Inquirer* and turns it overnight into a twentieth-century paper, flamboyantly promising to be a knight-errant for the people, "a fighting and tireless champion of their rights as citizens." Only a few moments before, however, he has cynically concocted a lurid news item about sex and murder, during which he tells Carter, "if the headline is big enough, it makes the news big enough." Bernstein himself acknowledges these warts on Kane's character, but interprets them as ingredients of a tragic flaw. "I guess Mr. Leland was right about the Spanish-American War," he says, but he defends Kane anyway, describing him as a man connected with the destiny of the country.

During Bernstein's flashback, the sense of manifest destiny and the exhilaration of seeking Kane in action give the film most of its feel as a "newspaper" picture, although it is a picture of such ambition and intelligence that it makes others of the type seem shallow. It manages to show all the contradictions in liberal democracy through a single editorial desk, the newsroom literally becoming a focal point of social history, where we see the country moving through various stages of democratization—each attempt at progress generating new conflicts and new evils. Here, as later in *The Magnificent Ambersons*, Welles found a way to combine the chronology of individual characters with the chronology of the nation at large; America moves from the age of the Tycoon, through the period of populist muckraking, and into the era of "mass communications," with turn-of-the-century types like Kane being destroyed by the very process they have set in motion. Perhaps in this respect Bernstein's defense of Kane has a historical validity. Kane is in fact the quintessential "American" that Mankiewicz's original title for the film (*American*) had called him—a man designed to embody all the strengths and failings of capitalist democracy.

As I have already suggested, the film's ambiguity and ironic detachment about Kane, its acute sense of the relation between character and history, spills over into the portraits of the minor players. Bernstein and Leland, for example, are marvelously paired, the tensions and contrasts between them becoming indistinguishable from the separate aspects of Kane's own personality. Leland, whom Thompson now visits in a geriatric ward, is often regarded as the spokesman for the "moral" of the film, but while it is true that he serves as a sort of conscience for Kane, he is as flawed and human as the doggedly loyal Bernstein. Like everyone else, he has been placed in a social and psychological context: the last member, the ultimate refinement, of a fading and effete New England aristocracy ("one of those old families where the father is worth ten million bucks and then one day he shoots himself and it turns out there's nothing but debts"), he is an aesthete who despises the capitalists but who seems out of place among the workers. Clearly he lacks Kane's vitality, and is fascinated with Kane for that very reason. A dandy and a puritan, he is very much the "New England schoolmarm" Kane has named him; in fact, the film may be hinting that his involvement with Kane is partly a displacement for sexual feelings. Mankiewicz and Welles were prohibited from showing a scene in a bordello where Kane unsuccessfully tries to interest Leland in a woman, but even without this scene Leland seems to have no active sex life. As a young man in the Bernstein section he barely conceals his admiration for Kane, who has been his benefactor and who apparently shares his idealism. When he grows disillusioned, there is inevitably a "loose" woman involved: at the big *Inquirer* party, his frowns of disapproval and complaints about the war with Spain are intercut with images of Kane making time with one of the chorus girls, and when the "love nest" with Susan Alexander brings an end to Kane's political career it is Leland, not Emily Kane, who behaves like a jilted lover.

In his old age, Leland suggests an idealist who has degenerated into a cynic. (Joseph Cotten's makeup here has always seemed to me a bit overdone, but he has been perfectly cast in the role, his voice suggesting a "weak" version of the slightly genteel, upper-class Southern lilt one hears in Welles's own speech.) He has grown a bit smug, but his mock senility and his bitter jokes do not completely hold off despair. He tells Thompson that "a lot of us check out with no special conviction about death. But we do know what we're leaving . . . we believe in something." These words, which can be taken as a valid criticism of Kane, are relatively small comfort. Leland himself is so lacerated with age and disillusionment that he now has only cigars to sustain him. He is charming of course, but his wit has a hollow, grotesque quality, resembling nothing so much as a dried-out Hollywood script writer. The setting itself emphasizes sterility and death—a purgatorial hospital sunroof where a few ghostly figures in wheelchairs are attended by ugly nurses, and where even the sunlight seems cold.

The atmosphere of Leland's interview is particularly ironic in view of the story he tells. Although Bernstein has suggested that "Rosebud" might be a woman, it is Leland who talks about Kane's love life; a more intimate friend than Bernstein, he recounts the period between Kane's first marriage and his attempt to turn Susan Alexander into an opera star. From a sociopolitical study of Kane, the script now begins to shift toward straightforward, though rather simplified, psychoanalysis.

At this point in his history, Kane is a greater public figure than ever, his politics constantly being played off against the crisis of his personal life. The two women he meets are as much physical and social opposites as Leland and Bernstein have been, yet in their own way both are connected to his desire to assert mastery, his need to find what Leland calls "love." The celebrated breakfast-table montage showing the disintegration of Kane's marriage to Emily (Ruth Warrick, whom Leland describes aptly as "like all the girls I knew in dancing school") is followed by the comic toothache scene in Susan Alexander's apartment, the allegro pace dissolving into a sweet, intimate rendezvous. Aided by what is surely the least ostentatious, most persuasive makeup job in the film, Welles turns rapidly from an ardent husband wooing a president's niece into a tired businessman courting a salesgirl.

Susan's toothache is a typical Hollywood "meet-cute" device, and as if he were acknowledging his own cleverness Welles casts shadow pictures on the wall to amuse her: "Gee," she says, "you know an awful lot of tricks. You're not a professional magician are you?" Kane, however, is as much the victim of illusions as their creator. He sentimentally imagines that Susan has a mother like his own, and the scene where he presides quietly over her "recital" is followed immediately by the opening of his campaign for governor—the sexual conquest linked to a hubristic attempt to dominate the populace. In fact, the closing line of Susan's song concerns the theme of power: it comes from *The Barber of Seville*, and roughly translates "I have sworn it, I will conquer."

The ensuing political rally is almost pure expressionism, and is a good example of how the film creates large-scale effects with a modest budget and the optical printer. In place of a crowd of Hollywood extras, the figures in the audience are obviously painted and abstracted, revealing both Kane's delusions of grandeur and the crowd's lack of individuality. Everything is dominated by Kane's ego, from the initial "K" he wears as a stickpin, to the huge blowup of his jowly face on a poster, to the incessant "I" in his public speech; now and then, however, we cut away to the back of the hall, the oratory becoming slightly distant, Kane suddenly looking like a fanatical puppet gesticulating on a toy stage. He talks about "the workingman and the slum child," and meanwhile the frock-coated men behind him are arranged to resemble the bloated rich of a Thomas Nast cartoon, one of them leaning on a polished walking stick while his silk top hat lies casually on the floor. The atmosphere is somehow both Germanic and purely American, Kane's stem-winding campaign speech taking place in a setting that subtly evokes newsreel shots of Hitler's harangues to his political hacks.

Throughout the rally Kane's supporters—Leland, Bernstein, Emily, and his young son—have been isolated in ironic, individual closeups, but his political rival, Boss Jim Gettys (Ray Collins), stands high above the action, the stage viewed over his shoulder, so that he dominates the frame like a sinister power. It is Gettys who is truly in control of this campaign, and the showdown he subsequently arranges between himself, Kane, Emily, and Susan—a private conversation in perfect contrast to the rally—is one of the most emotionally effective scenes in the film. There are over a dozen shots in the sequence, one of them a rather long take, but no closeups; the characters are dynamically blocked, with Kane, Susan, and Gettys alternately stepping into complete shadow as the tide of the conversation changes. On the whole, however, the scene is as much a triumph of ensemble acting as of direction. The evil Gettys, who is surely as much a monster as Kane, is underplayed by Collins, who suggests a nice family man with just a touch of crudeness; knowing his power, he behaves courteously to Emily, even though he tells Kane that he is "not a gentleman." "You see, my idea of a gentleman . . . Well, Mr. Kane, if I owned a newspaper and didn't like the way somebody was doing things . . . I wouldn't show him in a convict suit with stripes, so his children could see him in the paper, or his mother."

One mamma's boy has taken revenge on the other, and as a result Kane explodes. "I can fight this all alone," he shouts, and then screams, "Don't worry about me. I'm Charles Foster Kane! I'm no cheap, crooked politician trying to save himself from the conse-

quences of his crimes. Gettys! I'm going to send you to Sing Sing!"
What makes the scene even more powerful are the voices of the
two women, who provide a virtually musical counterpart to the
male contest. Emily's voice is quiet, determined, and formal: "There
seems to be only one choice for you to make, Charles. I'd say that
it's been made for you." Meanwhile Susan, who is completely ignored by everyone, pipes shrilly, "What about me? Charlie, he said
my name'd be dragged through the mud."

Here, at the same moment as the political issues are about to be
brought forward, the film has shifted almost completely into its
examination of Kane's sexual life. In fact the only concrete evidence we are given of Kane's tyranny, the only person we will
actually see being damaged by his actions, is Susan Alexander. The
issue seems to warrant a brief digression, because in this respect
Kane contrasts vividly with the usual muckraking accounts of
William Randolph Hearst's career. Although Mankiewicz and
Welles alluded to many of the deceptions described by writers like
Ferdinand Lundberg, they underplayed the violence associated
with the real Hearst empire, suggesting it only through occasional
asides and the imagery of the political rally. Thus Hecht and Mac-
Arthur's *The Front Page*, for all its amoral, rover-boys comedy,
actually does a good deal more to convey the seamy side of Hearst's
endeavors. For example, during the newspaper wars of early twentieth-century Chicago, Hearst had employed gangsters to rout his
competitors; gunmen like Dion O'Bannion had beaten up rival
newsboys and even shot innocent civilians, while Hearst's editors
blamed the trouble on "labor agitators." Through most of the century Hearst was a vigorous opponent of unions and child labor
legislation, and his mining interests in Peru were more or less
forced labor camps. Lundberg had charged that Hearst's employees
were not merely the victims of sweat shops: "they have, in many
instances, been literally enslaved, indentured for long periods, and
kept in employment against their will, under the muzzles of guns."
Citizen Kane's only apparent reference to such crimes is to show
Bernstein in the company of hired toughs, and to have Leland
berate Kane for his paternalistic attitude toward workers. Just
when Leland meets the politically broken Kane in the abandoned
newsroom and accuses him of swindling the public, the film veers
off into the most intimate details of Kane's love affair with Susan.

Such a phenomenon is all the more interesting if we look back
at some of the previous Hollywood movies about capitalists—*The*

Power and the Glory (Fox, 1933), for example, or *I Loved a Woman* (Warner Brothers, 1933)—where, as in *Kane*, the treatment of the tycoon's public life gives way to a preoccupation with his private affairs. Several critics have already stressed the similarity between *The Power and the Glory* and *Kane*; the earlier film is not especially liberal in tone—in fact it contains a vicious and even racist scene in which the protagonist, Spencer Tracy, heroically puts down a mob by insulting a thickly accented labor organizer. Nevertheless, screenwriter Preston Sturges's flashback technique and certain of his characterizations were undoubtedly known to Mankiewicz and Welles. Spencer Tracy's floozy mistress, for example, slightly resembles Susan Alexander, and the scene in a child's nursery where the love affair is brought to an end is reminiscent of the climactic moments in Susan's bedroom at Xanadu. Equally influential, it seems to me, is *I Loved a Woman*, which not only suggests certain features of Kane's character, but also foreshadows the whole Emily-Susan side of the plot. *I Loved a Woman* concerns John Hayden (Edward G. Robinson), a Chicago meat packer's son who begins life as an aesthete and becomes a monopolist and profiteer. "I'm a human puzzle," he says at one point, referring to his penchant for art collecting. Hayden marries a cold, ambitious socialite, a scheming woman who gradually changes him from a fop into a ruthless meat baron. Miserable in this loveless marriage, he is attracted to a young opera singer (Kay Francis), who needs his financial backing. Midway through the film she invites him up to her apartment; there, in a scene remarkable for its parallels with *Kane*, the aspiring singer plays "Home on the Range" on an old piano, while the tycoon sits back in a cozy chair and remarks that the song reminds him of his mother.

Although *I Loved a Woman* contains some veiled references to the career of Samuel Insull, it, like *The Power and the Glory*, is a mediocre and sentimental film, interesting chiefly for its possible relationship to *Kane*. And what both of these earlier works show is that Mankiewicz and Welles were using one of the oldest and most effective ploys of Hollywood melodrama: they were disguising, condensing, and displacing the social issues—using a love story to illustrate the character flaws that would presumably make the tycoon a danger to the public. The only difference at this level between *Kane* and previous films is the degree to which its politics are tilted to the left.

But even though the shift into sexual themes results in a kind of evasion, the basic issues are not entirely subverted. Susan Alexander is only roughly similar to Marion Davies, but that is obviously not because Welles and Mankiewicz feared Davies's wrath or wanted to protect her. Susan serves as a reminder to the audience of Hearst's domineering patronage of his mistress, and more importantly she becomes a symbol for his treatment of the society at large. As Leland tells us, she represents for Kane a "cross-section of the American public." She has had a middle-class mother who gave her music lessons, and when Kane meets her she is also a working girl, undereducated and relatively innocent. (Like most of the characters in the film, Susan has mixed motives; she is not the addle-brained gold digger some critics have made her seem.) She comes from a social level similar to that of Kane's own parents, and his relationship with her is comparable to his relationship with the masses who read his papers. It is true that Kane showers her with wealth, but this merely confirms Leland's remark in the desolated, post-election newspaper office: "You just want to persuade people that you love them so much that they ought to love you back." In fact, all of Leland's accusations and prophecies about Kane's relationship to his readers are fulfilled in Susan's part of the film. "You talk about the people as though you owned them," Leland says. Kane's treatment of Susan is a confirmation of this charge, and it also reminds us of the violence he is willing to use to have his way; thus in the last reels, which show Kane retreating more and more from public life, Susan is reduced from a pleasant, attractive girl to a harpy, and then to a near-suicide.

The film emphasizes the fact that Susan sings unwillingly, at the command of her master. During the election campaign, Kane establishes his "love nest" and the relationship is summarized in a single shot: in the foreground Susan is poised awkwardly at a grand piano; farther back in the room, Kane is enthroned in a wicker chair, applauding slowly and grinning in satisfaction; still farther back in the frame, visible through the archway to another room, is a sumptuous double bed. After his marriage to Susan, Kane tells the reporters, "We're going to become an opera star," and he hires Matisi to begin the arduous, comically inappropriate series of music lessons. The backgrounds in this part of the film grow more and more opulent, while Susan becomes increasingly driven and humiliated. Her singing becomes not only a painful form of work but a kind of involuntary servitude. As a result, her resemblance to Marion Davies fades. She looks more like those Peruvians toiling at gunpoint in Hearst's copper mines, even though she is certainly getting better pay.

The choice of opera rather than movies for Susan's career is also significant. It not only brings references to Welles's boyhood, to Insull, McCormack, and Sybil Sanderson into the film, but it also highlights the difference in social class between Susan and the patrons for whom she works. We see her kneeling on satin pillows, pitifully frightened and garishly made up, singing "Ah! Cruel" to a dozing, tuxedoed audience, while up in the rafters a laborer holds his nose and shakes his head sadly. "I'm not high-class like you," Susan tells Kane in an even shriller voice when she kneels again on the floor and reads the Leland-Kane review, "and I never went to any swell schools." She attempts to quit the opera, reminding Kane that "I never wanted to do it in the first place." Kane, however, orders her to continue because "I don't propose to have myself made ridiculous." In a scene remarkable for the way it shows the pain of both people, his shadow falls over her face—just as he will later tower over her in the "party" scene, when a woman's scream is heard on the soundtrack.

Leland has warned that the workingman will not always tolerate Kane's patronage: "you're not going to like that one little bit when you find out it means your workingman expects something as his right and not your gift." This, of course, is one reason why Susan leaves Kane. Naturally we sympathize with Kane when he recalls "Rosebud" and when the camera reveals his secret in the closing moments; in some ways the Susan Alexander plot has clouded the issues, replacing political with personal concerns, but in other ways it shows how the public and sexual concerns are interrelated. Rather like the symbols in a dream, Susan helps to censor the content even while she preserves its underlying significance.

But if concrete political issues are somehow present in the film, Kane himself continues to be depicted as a mystery to be unraveled. The wide-angle, deep-focus photography in the later sections enhances the mystery by frustrating Welles's inquisitive camera, setting up a feeling of space that can never be crossed no matter how many "No Trespassing" signs are disregarded. Throughout, Kane has been presented with a mixture of awe, satiric invective, and sympathy. He has provoked widely different responses from the people around him: in the newsreel he has been attacked for different reasons by both capital and labor; at his death, the *Inquirer* has shown a distinguished-looking photo with the banner headline, "CHARLES FOSTER KANE DIES AFTER A LIFETIME OF SERVICE," while the rival *Chronicle* has pictured him glowering under a dark hat brim, with the headline reading "C. F. KANE DIES AT XANADU ESTATE." To Thatcher, Kane was a spoiled do-gooder who was a menace to business; to Bernstein, he was a hero who helped build the country; to Leland, he was an egomaniac who wanted everybody to love him but who left only "a tip in return." Ultimately the audience has been made to feel that no single response is adequate, and near the end, the disparate judgments take the form of a single, complex emotion. Thompson, functioning as the audience's surrogate, remarks to Susan Alexander, "You know, all the same I feel sorry for Mr. Kane." Susan, the only character we've actually seen Kane victimize, the only person who could condemn the man outright, gives Thompson a harsh look and a terse reply: "Don't you think I do?"

Susan's comment crystallizes the film's divided attitude. In the later sequences where Kane nearly destroys Susan, the images of his massive form towering over the submissive woman are more than simple evocations of tyranny: we fear along with Susan, but we also feel sympathy for Kane, who is pained by age and thwarted desire. This feeling of pity is especially strong toward the end, where the most powerful and intense moments, the enraged breaking up of Susan's room and the discovery of the paperweight, are played off against the predatory Raymond (Paul Stewart) and the vast, chilly labyrinth of Xanadu. As the inquiry has deepened, the tone of the film has shifted subtly; the comic blackout sketches that characterize the Thatcher and Bernstein sections have been replaced by a darker, more grotesque mingling of comedy and tragedy that belongs to Leland and Susan—the scenes near the big Xanadu fireplace, for example, with Susan's voice echoing, "A person could go crazy in this dump"; or the gaudy picnic, with a stream of black cars driving morosely down a beach toward a swampy encampment, where a jazz band plays "This Can't Be Love" against a matted background of sinister RKO bats. Each phase of the movie becomes more painful than the one before, until we arrive at the most cynical of the witnesses, Raymond, who is ironically responsible for the most intimate part of the story: Susan leaves, her image receding down a corridor into infinity (another brilliant use of optical printing), and Kane blindly destroys her room, the crisis bringing back memories of childhood loss and rejection.

As Kane has grown increasingly isolated, the camera has

stressed the space between him and other people; Thompson never emerges from the shadows, but by the end of Raymond's story he has become less like a reporter and more like a sympathetic, slightly troubled onlooker. (It seems to me a mistake to speak of him as a fully developed character, as some commentators do. Even the acting of the role is clumsy—William Alland being in fact an amateur who suggests a man wandering into the fiction from outside.) Finally he gives up his search, knowing too much to expect a simple answer. We, of course, are in a more privileged position, and are given, if not a rational explanation, a vision of "Rosebud," an image which both transcends and unifies the various witnesses to Kane's life.

Of course Welles was uneasy about the whole snow-sled idea. He dismissed "Rosebud" in a famous remark, calling it "dollarbook Freud" and emphasizing that Herman Mankiewicz thought it up. Pauline Kael has said that it is "such a primitive kind of Freudianism that it . . . hardly seems Freudian at all." It should be noted, however, that some of the psychoanalytic ideas in *Kane* might indeed have come straight from a textbook. According to Freudian terminology, Kane can be typed as a regressive, anal-sadistic personality. His lumpen-bourgeois family is composed of a weak, untrustworthy father and a loving, albeit puritanical mother; he is taken away from this family at a pre-pubescent stage and reared by a bank; as an adult he "returns" to what Freud describes as a pregenital form of sexuality in which "not the genital component-instincts, but the *sadistic* and *anal* are most prominent" (*General Introduction to Psychoanalysis*, 1917). Thus, throughout his adult life Kane is partly a sadist who wants to obtain power over others, and partly an anal type, who obsessively collects zoo animals and museum pieces. His childhood, as Joseph McBride has pointed out, seems far from idyllic; nevertheless, it is a childhood toward which he has been compulsively drawn.

The burning sled, whether it is classically Freudian or not, contributes to a coherent and, it seems to me, a psychologically valid characterization. The closing scenes also provide a fascinating commentary on the limits of human power; more specifically, they are a statement about the disparity between the world as it is and the world as imagination would have it be. Throughout the film, Mankiewicz and Welles have underlined the fact that Kane is essentially child-like, a man who, for all his power, can never be completely in control of his life; just as he is not a "self-made" tycoon, so he is not the creator of his private destiny. All of his energies are spent in trying to create his own world, or in rebelling against anyone who asserts authority over his will. He despises Thatcher of course, and when he can no longer "look after" the little people he begins to hate them. He tries to maintain a dangerous but awe-inspiring daydream, of which Xanadu is only the most obvious manifestation. Whenever the dream world is threatened, he responds with a child's rage. For example, when Thatcher interrupts Kane's play in the snow, the boy defends himself by striking out with his sled; when Jim Gettys interrupts the political game, Kane breaks into a terrifying but pathetic fury, his enraged voice cut off as Gettys exits and calmly closes a door; when Leland and Susan assert their independence, Kane retaliates with all the force of his pent-up anger. When we last see him he throws a literal tantrum, regressing to the state of a child destroying a nursery.

Whatever his influence in other spheres, Kane cannot control his own fate. (In 1941, with the New Deal in ascendance and the United States entering a war against fascism, it must have seemed to Welles that Hearst was in a similar position.) He is forever imprisoned by his childhood egotism, living out power fantasies and converting everything into toys. The film is full of these toys: first there is the sled, then the newspaper, then the Spanish-American War. (Notice, in fact, how the war has been depicted as a child's game, with the *Inquirer* reporters sporting little wooden rifles and funny hats.) Toward the end there is Susan, with her marionette-style opera makeup and her dollhouse room in a fantasy castle. The final toy, the paperweight Kane discovers after his tantrum, is probably the most satisfactory image of them all; it represents not so much a lost innocence as a striving after an imaginary, "adult" autonomy. It symbolizes an ideal—a self-enclosed realm, immune from change, where Kane can feel he has control over his life. The sled burning at the heart of the furnace therefore becomes less a purely Freudian explanation than the logical conclusion to Kane's tortured romantic idealism. It is one of those images, known to passion and the imagination, that Yeats called "self-born mockers of Man's enterprise."

After our discovery of this sled, *Citizen Kane* concludes with still another reminder of the camera's inquisitiveness, a near complete reversal of the process with which it began. The camera retreats from the magic castle, staring at the awesome smoke of corruption in the sky, settling at last on the "No Trespassing" sign outside the gate. Even the title has been a contradiction in terms.

II

As an aesthetic object and as a psychological portrait, *Kane* becomes a highly satisfying film, representing what is probably the limit to which a story could move toward self-conscious "art" and "significance" while still remaining within the codes of the studio system. As a portrait of an archetypal tycoon, it is so effective that it has become part of American folklore. And its central images keep returning in contemporary life—Nixon secluding himself in San Clemente, or Howard Hughes, before his death, owning a retreat in the Bahamas which he called the "Hotel Xanadu." For all its evasiveness about Hearst's crimes, *Kane* is also a deliberately political film, growing directly out of the ethos of the Popular Front. As we have seen, it continually reminds the viewer of things outside itself—either the movies, or Hearst, or the "Welles phenomenon." Before leaving it, therefore, one needs at least briefly to shift discussion away from formalist analysis and closer to the *auteur* and the audience. In this way, one can see that *Kane*'s biographical, autobiographical, and political complexities are logical extensions of the aesthetic and psychological tensions I have been describing.

We may begin by noting that *Kane*'s splendidly artful ambivalence toward its central character is not shared by the major biographies of Hearst written during the thirties: in fact these books are as much in conflict as Thatcher and the labor spokesman in the *Kane* newsreel. The authorized portrait, Mrs. Freemont Older's *William Randolph Hearst, American* (1936), makes Hearst a paragon of civic virtue, a sort of philosopher-king. Ferdinand Lundberg's *Imperial Hearst* (1937), which I have already mentioned and which was cited in an absurd plagiarism case against Mankiewicz and Welles, is a muckraking journalist's account of Hearst's crimes. Interestingly, W. A. Swanberg's "definitive" *Citizen Hearst*, which appeared in 1961, takes a middle-of-the-road view; although Swanberg does not acknowledge it, his title and the structure of his narrative clearly were influenced by the movie.

All this data about Hearst is valuable to students of *Kane*, not only for its own sake, but because it shows how the film delights in making references to its primary source. Even the *New York Inquirer* is significant. In real life a paper with that title, which was published by the Griffin brothers, was owned by Hearst. "From the legal standpoint," Irving Hoffman wrote, "they might as well have referred to the paper in the picture as the *Journal-American*."

Nevertheless, it is important to remember that Kane and Hearst are not identical. Welles was at least technically correct when he said that Kane was a fictional character partly based on several turn-of-the-century tycoons. In translating the yellow journalist into a creature of fiction, he and Mankiewicz had borrowed freely from other lives. They had departed from biographical fact in a number of crucial ways, each of them important to the dramatic and perhaps also the ideological effect of the film.

Unlike the biographers, Welles and Mankiewicz chose to concentrate on a private life rather than the public structuring of an empire. They also gave Kane a humble birth, which was not true of any of his possible models; it was certainly not true of Hearst (the whole point of Dos Passos's famous sketch had been that W. R., born into Phoebe Hearst's "richly feathered nest," could never understand his public), and it was not true of McCormack or Insull or Welles or Mankiewicz. Last, and in some ways most significant because more than anything else it aroused the ire of the Hearst press, they made Susan Alexander into a tormented, unhappy creature who walks out on her supposed benefactor—this in contrast to the Hearst-Davies relationship, which was generally happy. Indeed when death finally came to Hearst, it was very different from Kane's death in the film. Hearst did not spend his last days alone in the caverns of his estate; several years earlier he had moved to the less resplendent Beverly Hills mansion of his mistress, and he died with her close at hand. His last words were unrecorded.

These changes imply that Welles and Mankiewicz were trying to create sympathy for Kane by playing down his menace. As a tycoon in the grip of a psychological compulsion, as a poor boy suddenly given wealth, he becomes less, not more, representative of his class. To some viewers he has looked like a great man doomed by his own good fortune, an embodiment of the same "American Dream" myth that is often applied to Welles. When the script is summarized, Welles's and Mankiewicz's sense of melodrama appears to have displaced their politics.

Of course Hearst's life *was* in some sense melodramatic, and writers of the left in the thirties took relish in giving his career the structure of a Hollywood-style morality play. Dos Passos saw Hearst as a "spent Caesar grown old with spending," and Charles Beard, in his introduction to the Lundberg biography, predicted that the old man would die lonely and unloved. By showing Kane as a tragicomic failure, Mankiewicz and Welles were doing no more than what these writers had done, and when they changed the facts to suit the demands of melodrama they were, in principle at least, entirely justified; after all, they were conveying political attitudes through fiction, not through biography. Thus *Citizen Kane* might have been an answer to the plea made toward the end of *Imperial Hearst:*

> Down through the years [Hearst] has played a great and ghastly part in shaping the American mind. He could, more truthfully than any other man, say, "The American mentality is my mentality." This is not because Hearst has become "the voice of the people," speaking their unformulated thoughts and desires. It has been because adequate, widespread and *popularized* criticism of his innumerable deceptions has been lacking.

The italics here are Lundberg's, and they convey his feelings of urgency. *Kane*, however, emphasizes the failures of Hearst more than the deceptions; as Charles Eckert has remarked, the hero dies on a "mystified bed of capital." Harry Wasserman has been more explicit: "It is safe and reassuring," he writes, "to think of Citizen Kane and his sled . . . but unsettling and dangerous to discover the sometimes insidious results of such innocent obsessions. What is more important to remember about a character like Kane is not how the loss of a sled influenced his life, but how the newspapers published by his real-life counterpart Hearst might have influenced a war."

One response to such comments is to say that the film clearly does satirize Kane's public life, and that its "mystifications" are at least partly ironic. It exposes Kane's manipulative interest in the Spanish-American War, it reveals his exploitative "philosophy" of journalism, and it makes several references to his attacks on organized labor. In the election scenes it depicts the corruption of machine politics with the force of a great editorial cartoon. Moreover, it links the press to the politicians themselves, showing Kane hoist on his own petard. In regard to Kane's so-called "progressive" youth, the film is explicit in its denunciation; his democratic aspirations are seen as in reality a desire for power, a means to extend paternalistic benevolence to the "people." We even see Kane on a balcony conferring with Hitler, an image that colors the audience's reaction to everything the character does. What is more radical and more interesting, however, is that *Citizen Kane* brings its own workings under scrutiny, questioning the whole process of popular entertainment, including the "image making" of the movies. From the beginning, when "Rosebud" is introduced as a cheap means of spicing up a newsreel, until the end, when Thompson confesses the futility of searching out the meaning for a single word, *Kane* casts doubt on its own conclusions. Moreover, Welles's brilliant manipulation of cinematic technique keeps reminding us that we are watching a movie, an exceedingly clever and entertaining manipulation of reality, rather than reality itself. This is not, of course, to say that Welles hated Hollywood movies; on the contrary, it was precisely his delight in the conventions of the medium that gave his self-consciousness and self-criticism such poetic force.

Even so, the film is primarily about Kane's private life. It shows that the characters are determined by their material existence, and yet it seems fatalistic about this condition, suggesting that there is no way to radically transform human consciousness. It treats the political issues allusively, aiming relentlessly at "Rosebud" and making Kane a sympathetic, if frightening, character, a tragic failure rather than a living threat. Because of its all-inclusive ironies, its sentimental mythology, and the sheer gusto of its Hollywood craftsmanship, it has always been open to a certain amount of justifiable criticism from the left; indeed the most doctrinaire critics have suggested that *Kane* is a pernicious influence on its audience, leaving us complacently and ignorantly believing that money can't buy happiness.

There are, of course, several possible reasons why the film takes a personal and psychological approach and loads itself with plot conventions from earlier movies—Welles's own ambivalence about the Kane type, for example, or Mankiewicz's methods of working, or the simple wish to stay within the realm of fantasy and entertainment. Doubtless one of the more important reasons why *Kane* is not a more didactic film is that from the time of the modern-dress *Julius Caesar* Welles had contended that the problem with left-wing melodrama was its "cardboard, Simon-Legree villains." But a still deeper reason is suggested by the fact that *Kane* often seems to be very much about Orson Welles himself. It was Welles, after all, who was known as the *enfant terrible*, and this may account for *Kane*'s emphasis on infantile rage. It was Welles, not Hearst, who was raised by a guardian, and the guardian's name has been given to a character in the film. It was Welles who made a famous comment comparing the movies to his own personal electric train set, almost like Kane remarking that it would be "fun" to run a newspaper. According to John Houseman, who worked on an early version of the script, "the deeper we penetrated beyond the public events into the heart of Charles Foster Kane, the closer we seemed to come to the identity of Orson Welles." Houseman, Mankiewicz, and Welles himself deliberately set about filling the script with parallels and private jokes about the film's director; even Raymond the butler was modeled on a suspicious servant who used to lurk around Welles's big Hollywood house. Bernard Herrmann once summed up all the evidence when he noted that the film is "in a way . . . a dream-like autobiography of Welles"; hence, it is no surprise that the film should have been more about psychology than about the structure of an empire, more sympathetic than purely destructive to the central character.

And yet, certainly, the political and even the personal significance of the film was not lost on the man who was the other chief model for Kane. For all its rich poetic sentiment and its mixing of Hollywood convention with iconoclastic social commentary, the most important fact about Welles's first film is that it proved to be a fundamentally dangerous project. Unlike films of the previous decade, it was at least loosely based on a live and kicking subject, a proto-fascist demagogue whose power in Hollywood was second only to his power over a newspaper empire. The dimensions of that power can be assessed by simply glancing through *Variety* for the ten years or so before *Kane* was produced. In November 1928, for example, one reads that "any time the Hearst paper gets in back of a picture it is a box office natural. . . . They did it last week on Marion Davies (*Show People*) and the gross jumped to $33,000." In February 1932, one finds a note on Hearst's interest in movie content: "To avoid trouble with the Hearst papers as in the case of 'Five Star Final,' Warners sent a script of its new newspaper story, 'The Ferguson Case,' to William Randolph Hearst."

In this atmosphere *Kane* was remarkable, and the results were about what could have been expected. Hearst was rumored to have taken it lightly, but the reprisals taken by his press are a matter of record; he even sent a personal note to columnist John Chapman suggesting that anyone who admired the film unreservedly was a "treasonable Communist" and not a "loyal American." As is widely known, the critical response was adulatory, but RKO had difficulty finding bookings. If L. B. Mayer had been successful in buying the rights, the film would never have been shown at all. *Kane* got sensational publicity from Hearst's rivals (probably this was part of

Welles's strategy), but not enough to calm the fears of distributors, who began to grumble ominously that Welles was more interested in courting critics than in selling the picture where it counted. In 1941, *Motion Picture Herald* wrote that "Mr. Welles is showing the picture to almost anyone who might be interested except the showmen who might have to deal with it. . . . It is possible that he has not yet, in his preoccupations, heard about the exhibitor." The condescension in these remarks does not conceal the fact that theatre managers were concerned about Hearst's wrath, to say nothing of what they regarded as the potential artiness of the film. Ultimately, *Kane* was recognized by the reviewers, by certain Hollywood professionals, and even, somewhat reluctantly, by the Motion Picture Academy. It established Welles as a major talent, but at the same time it made his future in American movies problematic.

The paradox—and one of the biggest contradictions of them all—is that Welles had no desire to wreck the motion picture industry. He was a devoted worker who had studied the Hollywood masters and whose film, despite its complexity, was in the best tradition of American popular entertainment. As he himself put it, he was never inclined to "joke with other people's money." *Kane* was held to a relatively modest budget ($749,000) and was praised by journals like the *Hollywood Reporter* for its frugality. Nevertheless, various Hollywood bosses had perceived Welles as an "artist" and a left-wing ideologue who *might* bring trouble. *Kane* may not have been a thoroughgoing anti-capitalist attack, but it was close enough to insure that Welles would never again be allowed such freedom at RKO.

4

The Magnificent Ambersons

As *Kane* was about to appear, the Hearst press made a number of heavyhanded threats, at one point claiming that they intended to expose Hollywood's practice of hiring "refugees to the exclusion of native Americans." Whatever anxiety this sort of publicity may have created at RKO, it certainly had an effect upon exhibitors. On September 7, 1941, for example, the *New York Times* reported that *Kane* had been sold to the Fox West Coast theatre chain, but that it would "not be displayed by any of the circuit's 515 theatres on the Pacific coast, mountain states, and midwest"—this despite the fact that the picture had outgrossed RKO's other new releases when it was shown in San Francisco, Denver, and Omaha. Welles declared that he would sue, but his film had already been kept away from circuit bookings for too long.

Effective as the Hearst vendetta was, the decline of the Mercury group came about for more complex reasons. From the beginning Welles had been disliked in Hollywood, and his problems were compounded by the management at RKO. A month after *Kane*, he was given a "producer-director" contract under which he would bring out three pictures a year. Meanwhile the studio's profits were falling and Floyd Odlum's Atlas Company was gaining a controlling interest. Odlum applied pressure to George Schaefer, who in turn made life difficult for Welles. By early 1942 Atlas was in total control and had replaced Schaefer with their own man; in the process Welles's next three films were sabotaged and his Mercury organization ordered from the lot.

Before the end came, Welles had expressed interest in various projects. The Mexican film described in chapter 2 was announced and then abandoned; according to press releases, Harnett Kane's *Louisiana Hayride*, a biography of Huey Long, was considered and soon dropped, as was Zoe Atkins's *Starvation on Red River*. At some point Welles persuaded George Schaefer to approve Tarkington's *The Magnificent Ambersons*, which the Mercury had done on radio; indeed Welles even played a recording of the radio broadcast to Schaefer in order to convince him. Welles in turn agreed to produce *Journey into Fear* at Schaefer's request. Soon the war began, and Welles immediately involved himself in a noncommercial project sponsored jointly by RKO and the Rockefeller interests within the U.S. government—an ambitious Latin American documentary composed of several interrelated stories and shot in color and black and white, entitled *It's All True*. For this undertaking Welles agreed to waive payment and work in Rio, handling his other film and radio commitments at long distance.

Partly because of RKO's growing desire to be rid of Welles, the documentary turned into a nightmare. RKO had promised to have Robert Wise deliver the rough cut of *Ambersons* to Rio, but Welles never saw it. When the film received bad preview notices in Pomona (where it was shown following a Dorothy Lamour musical called *The Fleet's In*), it was reduced in length by about forty-five minutes and new material was added without the director's approval. The Welles/Norman Foster *Journey into Fear*, scripted by Joseph Cotten and various others (including, according to press reports, Ben Hecht), was also recut by the studio. Meanwhile the new management began circulating rumors that Welles's Rio footage was chaotic and extravagant. With *It's All True* nearly complete, Welles was ordered home; RKO collected its guaranteed money from the government, printed about 13,000 feet of Welles's work (which was never shown), and supposedly destroyed the rest. As for *Ambersons*—a less sensational and less inherently popular work than *Kane*—it was first widely advertised and then downgraded by the studio. In a few big city markets audiences were reported to have laughed at the dramatic moments, and even though the film did respectably at the box office when it was first released, it was soon playing at the bottom end of double-feature programs. *Kane* had been a *succès du scandale*; *It's All True* had become a victim of studio politics; and *Ambersons* had shown no profit. In combination, the three films put an end to Welles's power in Hollywood.

It was the saddest chapter in Welles's career, and it remains a subject of controversy; Charles Higham, for example, has said that Welles "ran out" on *Ambersons* and made *It's All True* a needlessly expensive film, partly because of what Higham calls "a fear of completion." But Welles and virtually everyone else involved with the making of the two movies claimed otherwise. A definitive account of *It's All True* might be constructed from the Mercury archives, but these records, which would make a fascinating book about the interaction between commerce, government, and an individual artist, were not available when I worked on this book. For this reason I have not attempted to write about the film, nor about *Journey into Fear*, which was directed partly by Norman Foster. Instead I have concentrated upon *Ambersons*, a film RKO seems to have resented from the start, but which survives in something close to its original form.

I

Throughout his early career Welles had been fascinated with literature of and about the 1890s. In 1938 alone, his radio broadcasts included adaptations of *The Man Who Was Thursday*, *Sherlock Holmes*, *Around the World in Eighty Days*, *Heart of Darkness*, *The Gift of the Magi*, *Life with Father*, *Seventeen*, and *Clarence*. The Mercury stage performances alternated between the Elizabethans and turn-of-the-century dramatists like Gillette, William Archer, and Shaw; the early sections of *Kane* were filled with an exuberant re-creation of nineties Americana; and when Welles tried to revive the Mercury in 1945, *Around the World* was his first project.

Among all these properties, however, *The Magnificent Ambersons* exerted a special appeal. The novel, which won a Pulitzer Prize in 1918, is virtually ignored today, perhaps because Tarkington clung to an antimacassar style and opted for a popular, sentimental conclusion. The old-fashioned plot conventions, the painfully obvious symbolism, the continually "regional" quality of his work make him seem pale compared to the following generation of American writers, yet *Ambersons* remains intelligent and more readable than many other books with greater reputations. It tells the story of the members of a faintly absurd midwestern aristocratic family who are blind to the coming of the industrial age; pathetically out of date, living side by side in their grand houses, the Ambersons are destroyed by a new economy which eats away at the foundations of their property. Their decline parallels the rise of Eugene Morgan, an automobile inventor who becomes a power in the growing city. (The novel gives the town no name, but in the film it is identified by an insert showing the front page of the *Indianapolis Inquirer*.) Ironically, Morgan has always loved Major Amberson's daughter, but the two are unable to marry because of the Amberson pride. At first Morgan is rejected because he seems a wastrel; Isabel marries the passionless Wilbur Minafer, but when Wilbur dies Morgan is kept away by Isabel's spoiled son, George. Only at the end, in a projected marriage between George and Morgan's daughter Lucy, does the old wealth promise to join with the new. The Amberson era, however, has completely passed, and their houses are bought and divided up by the growing city.

Booth Tarkington had been a friend of Welles's father, and the novel's portrait of a "midland town" passing into the twentieth century was surely reminiscent of Welles's experience as a boy in the quasi-Victorian atmosphere of Kenosha and Woodstock. The book was written at about the time of Welles's birth, so that certain of its characterizations struck quite close to home. The inventor Morgan and the beautiful Isabel Amberson are not unlike Welles's own parents, and Isabel's son George strongly resembles the insufferable young George Orson himself. An overprotected youth, George Amberson Minafer is universally hated by the townspeople, who describe him as a "fool boy with the pride of Satan" and a "highhanded Lucifer." When Isabel dies, leaving this son to become reconciled with a father-figure he has treated as a rival, the possible affinities with Welles's life become even more intimate. In fact, it is interesting that the Oedipal triangle in the novel should be represented in the film by three players who have relatively weak personalities, as if they were simultaneously hinting at autobiographical parallels and defending against them. Eugene Morgan as portrayed by Joseph Cotten is more of a dandy than the Morgan in the book, and therefore presumably bears a greater resemblance to Welles's father; yet Cotten is an actor who seems to have been born middle-aged, and is less sexually threatening to George than he should be. Dolores Costello, an agelessly beautiful silent movie actress who had come out of retirement, makes Isabel into a golden-haired madonna, a woman so abstracted into a com-

placently sweet and self-sacrificing role that she becomes almost invisible (although in the original version, before RKO revised a scene between her and her son, she was a stronger character). Tim Holt, as George, has dark, baby-fat looks that make him a double for the director, but he lacks the appropriate neurotic energy that Welles himself would have brought the part.

Despite the relative blandness of these actors, the film manages to evoke far more sexual anxiety than the novel, chiefly because of Agnes Moorehead's performance as the spinster Aunt Fanny and Welles's own handling of the *mise-en-scène*. After making only a few changes in the ending of the story, Welles used the full weight of a Gothic style to transform Tarkington's bittersweet, undisturbing book into a dark, almost nervous film. The potential mania of George and the hysteria of Fanny are heightened by grotesque visuals, as in the shot shown above, where the shadow of an angry peacock echoes Moorehead's profile. The Amberson mansion itself differs considerably from Tarkington's descriptions of a reasonably pleasant, if ostentatious, manor, and sometimes resembles the house of Frankenstein, as for example when the mansion is shown in a thunderstorm after the death of Wilbur. (See below.)

Everywhere Welles has emphasized the pessimistic qualities of his source, giving the film a sharper satiric edge, a greater degree of sexual frustration and madness. These slight changes of tone, however, are in keeping with Tarkington's underlying social despair.

Throughout the film the inability of the characters to overcome psychological divisions is linked to the split within the society. At the beginning we see Eugene Morgan returning to town after twenty years' absence; a widower with a grown daughter, he longs for the beautiful Amberson woman almost in

the way Gatsby longs for Daisy. When Isabel's husband dies, Morgan seems to have been given a second chance; but history only repeats itself through the intervention of George. In still another repetition, George is parted from Lucy (Anne Baxter), who cannot accept him until his illusions of grandeur have been destroyed. Even the supporting characters are sexually isolated, though not necessarily because of social impediments: Major Amberson is a widower, Mrs. Johnson lives alone in the house across the way, and neither Fanny nor Uncle Jack Amberson has been able to find a mate. The only marriage we see is the companionate union of Isabel and Wilbur, and the web of unrequited loves that make up the plot suggests that loneliness pervades the entire world. Everyone has become a prisoner of class or sex, a citizen of a town Lucy whimsically names "They-Couldn't-Help-It."

Clearly *Ambersons* had permitted Welles to return to the autobiographical material that was one of his obsessions in *Kane,* and to create the same deterministic universe. Although the film covered a shorter time span (1885–1912), it also gave rise to the same notions about the movement of history. Among other things, *Kane* had been devoted to America's passage from one kind of economic organization to another; Charles Foster Kane was a late product of the Gilded Age, a tycoon whose breed was slowly replaced by corporate organizations and faceless newsmen. Because Kane was shown at various stages of his life, we can see his character echoed by all the generations in *Ambersons:* like the elderly Major, Kane becomes an anachronism; like Eugene Morgan, he is the progenitor of a new world, an inventor who creates a monster; like George Minafer, he is an overgrown child with a demonic will. In the purely economic and historical sense, Kane might be said to resemble Morgan most of all, his childlike infatuation with his newspaper being very like Morgan's delight in the quaint little horseless carriages at the beginning of *Ambersons.* Hence just as the newsrooms in *Kane* underwent a transformation from the oak-grained offices of the *Inquirer* to the darkened, smoky theatre of "News on the March," so the midland streets of *Ambersons* are transformed into grimy highways.

Like *Kane, Ambersons* is a lament, even though it regards the passing of the old order as necessary. It sympathizes strongly with the point of view of Morgan, who is at once a progressive, a philosopher, and a would-be poet—a man who seems compelled to invent the auto despite the fact that he is almost grimly aware of the changes it might bring. Also like *Kane, Ambersons* tries to offer consolation by shifting its focus from pessimism over the material world to a saddened, idealistic fascination with the passing of time. There is a speech in the novel—reproduced in the original film but cut by RKO—which both announces this theme and reminds us of the final images of *Kane*. Isabel is speaking to George (in the film it was Eugene who spoke the lines to Isabel):

"[T]he things that we have and that we think are so solid—they're like smoke, and time is like the sky that the smoke disappears into. You know how a wreath of smoke goes up from a chimney, and seems all thick and black and busy against the sky, as if it were going to do such important things and last forever, and you see it getting thinner and thinner—and then, in a little while, it isn't there at all."

George does not understand his mother, but at the end of the novel he comes to believe that "nothing stays or holds or keeps. . . . Great Caesar dead and turned to clay stopped no hole to keep the wind away." This knowledge is revealed only indirectly in the film, though George does become more mature and sympathetic; in its place we are shown—in some of the most striking imagery Welles ever produced—an unremitting movement, an almost ruthless picture of time being lost, like smoke in the air. As Micheal Wood has said, it is this sense "of historical change as tangled and relentless, of the passage of personal time and time of the city, of the intransigence of desire and the uselessness of hindsight," that makes *Ambersons* such a remarkable movie.

Interestingly, Tarkington's vision of everything passing, coupled with his notion of eternal return, seems confirmed by the history of literature, which has always lamented the advent of new societies. In the American novel alone, the middle classes are always rising while the cities are always growing; and in English literature, as Raymond Williams has pointed out, writers mourned the death of an organic, argricultural society as far back as the medieval period. The theme is at least as old as the pastoral, and *Ambersons* is in part a pastoral, an expression of grief not over the loss of a whole and perfect world, but over the change of country into city. And as with any pastoral, it is less interesting as a re-creation of historical truth than as a projection of political and psychological attitudes back upon an imaginary past. We know for a fact that industry created cities at the turn of the century, but the serene world described by the narrator at the beginning of *Amber-*

sons never existed. It is a sentimental memory, and Welles is intelligent enough to acknowledge this fact by the somewhat arch and ironic technique he adopts in the opening montage of the film. He avoids showing what the nineteenth-century town might have been like for ordinary people, depicting it instead as a picturesque village without dirt or poverty. But the falseness, or at least partiality, of this view is not a defect; as Eugene Morgan says in his quiet speech at the dinner table, the coming of the automobile will "change men's minds"; once technology has altered consciousness, we can never fully know the past. The real intensity of the film therefore lies in its autobiographical relevance, in the poignancy with which Welles depicts a scene that partly represents his own childhood, brooding over the way everything passed, turning to chaos. It is a personal theme which has universal application, but also has a more specifically political meaning; at a deep, unstated level, it expresses apprehensiveness over uncontrolled capitalism, that wave of Babbittry which destroyed the old autocratic rule only to replace it with an infernal city.

A similar malaise can be found running throughout American movies of the forties, though it is subtly, almost unconsciously buried beneath the surface. A few contemporary reviewers suggested that Welles's preoccupation with small-town midwestern aristocracy was inappropriate to wartime, but Warner Brothers had released *Kings Row* in the same year, profitable Selznick productions like *Gone with the Wind* and *Rebecca* had been concerned with the passing of great houses, and even that most successful of propaganda films, *Casablanca*, was filled with nostalgia for times gone by. In 1946, Frank Capra's *It's a Wonderful Life* used leftover sets from *Ambersons* to create a drafty old mansion at the center of a town called Bedford Falls, where James Stewart and Donna Reed set up housekeeping; Stewart plays a character who devotes his life to building clean suburbs for the working class, but the place where he lives reveals the film's unconscious ambivalence toward progress. It is a decaying nineteenth-century home for a man of property, more in keeping with the style of the Dickensian villain of the film, a banker played by Lionel Barrymore. Although Capra is clearly on the side of modernity and democratization, he acknowledges implicitly the nostalgic charm of this house, which belongs to another age and another social order.

The major difference between Welles's movie and these others was in its sophistication, its consciousness of its purpose. At the same time it was filled with nearly as many emotional contradictions as *Kane*. Like all Gothic artists, Welles had identified with the very plutocracy whose decadence he shows; a true Roosevelt liberal, he remained aristocratic in his tastes and implicitly contemptuous of *laissez-faire* economics. He intended to show that the tragedy was not limited to the Ambersons alone; at the end, Eugene Morgan would be ironically confronted with the dead world he helped create.

But here a general description needs to give way to a treatment of specific details, for the meaning of Welles's film—to say nothing of its dramatic power—has been muffled by RKO's alterations. It is possible to reconstruct a more faithful version by consulting the final draft of the script (dated October 7, 1941), which may be seen at the Museum of Modern Art's Film Study Center; the draft, however, needs to be read with caution because it bears the same relation to what was actually shot as the published script of *Kane* bears to the movie we see on the screen. A summary of the missing footage, based on the cutting continuity of the original release print, is contained in an appendix to Charles Higham's *The Films of Orson Welles*. In the analysis which follows, I have used both of these sources, and have had the opportunity, courtesy of Richard Wilson, to glance at the last pages of the cutting continuity. Nevertheless, I have been content to describe the studio revisions in very general terms, trying to recover the integrity of Welles's work mainly from the local qualities of the film that has survived.

II

Ambersons is a less self-reflexive, less spectacular film than *Kane*. In form it resembles Welles's radio shows, taking dialogue directly from the novel and using Welles's offscreen voice in place of Tarkington's authorial commentary. But the introductory montage leading up to the Amberson ball is a highly sophisticated example of movie editing, dense with meaning and serving a function rather like the *Kane* newsreel. In less than ten minutes of screen time (slightly longer in the original version), Welles presents the same material that Tarkington had taken three chapters to get through; the town is pictured, the major characters are introduced, and several motifs are established. At the same time, a number of purely visual ironies have been added, so that while this section is true to the novel, it is also one of the most self-consciously "cinematic" moments in the film.

The story begins with a dark screen, Welles's voice remarking that the magnificence of the Ambersons began in 1873, and lasted "through all the years that saw their midland town spread and darken into a city." The screen lightens as Welles says, "In that town in those days, all the women who wore silk and velvet knew all the other women who wore silk and velvet," and the first image is taken from a description of a horse-drawn trolley in the opening pages of the book: we see a charming brick house, framed as if for a portrait, photographed through a vaseline-edged lens; a trolley has momentarily slipped from its tracks at the front gates, and several passengers have stepped off to try and set it right. Faintly on the soundtrack we hear Bernard Herrmann's variations on Waldteufel's "Toujours ou jamais," a wistful, fragile theme that was a particular favorite of Welles's.

Most viewers and not a few critics have assumed that the house belongs to the Ambersons. In fact it is the home of the gossip Mrs. Johnson, and is located precisely across the street from the big Amberson mansion. Although it has no exact equivalent in the novel, it corresponds roughly to a place Tarkington describes as Lucy Morgan's dream house, a bourgeois home at the edge of town which George sneers at because it is "meant for a street in the city." Welles begins with this image partly in order to seduce his viewers into a nostalgic reverie, but also to establish a slightly busy background against which the Amberson magnificence may be placed. Tarkington had given the Ambersons two baronial country estates, one for the Major and one for Isabel, and had made them "as conspicuous as a brass band at a funeral." Welles not only condenses these estates into a single, grotesque example of nineteenth-century eclecticism, he also suggests from the moment we meet them that the city has begun to encroach upon the Ambersons. A road passes their front door, they have neighbors, and we see vehicles passing in every shot—first the horse-drawn trolley and then Eugene with his experimental autos. When the estate is ultimately shown, it will look like a genteel Xanadu, surrounded by walls and hedges, its relatively narrow grounds crowded with shrubbery and ornamental sculpture.

Even before we see the real Amberson mansion, however, a montage of hats reveals the family's standing in the community: first a shot of top-hatted gentlemen crowded into a bar; then a top-hatted, frock-coated young man trying to row a pretty girl in a boat; then Major Amberson's hat being struck by a snowball. (Incidentally, the young man in the boat is recognizable as Tim Holt and the girl is Dolores Costello—a deliberate flaunting of verisimilitude comparable to the way Welles used major players as "extras" in the projection room sequence of *Kane*.) In three shots we have been informed that Amberson fashion influences the fashion of the town, and we have also seen time passing from summer into winter. During his commentary Welles will remark that "in those days, people had time for everything," but on the screen he makes time go by with incredible speed. At first the imagery seems merely a collection of photographs from an old album, yet the more one studies the photographs the more one becomes aware of seasons, sometimes generations, passing with every cut or dissolve, establishing an almost sinister counterpoint to the notion of a slow, easy life. Things vanish almost as soon as they register upon the audience's consciousness; "those days" are glimpsed and then are gone before we know them. The top hats, for example, immediately give way to a newer and slightly more democratic bowler, worn by Eugene Morgan as he studies himself in an oval mirror. As Welles speaks of styles changing, we see a rapid and comic montage of Morgan trying on various boots, pants, and jackets, the calendar turned into a fashion show. Beneath this humor there are still more ironies: Morgan may be foppish and somewhat ludicrous, but he is also a man in touch with new, less conservative times; every change of his costume makes the Amberson top hats recede further into the past.

The montage of clothes ends as Morgan exits from his front door bearing a gift for a lady. Welles returns us to the house pictured in the opening shots—a wintertime view showing a snow-covered roof and a sleigh passing the front gates. As we watch, the seasons change again, moving from a winter day to a spring twilight, then to a summer night in one lovely dissolve. Morgan now enters the frame from a distant point at the lower right corner, running into the foreground and falling unceremoniously into a viola da gamba he has intended to use for a serenade. A closeup shows Isabel Amberson frowning and turning away from her window. Her rejection of Morgan is repeated in subsequent images, where we see the young man coming twice to the Amberson front door and being turned away by a black servant. These scenes will be echoed still later, when George sends Morgan away from the same door: for as time passes inexorably in this film, events also repeat themselves. Eugene Morgan courts Isabel Amberson throughout his life, becoming more prosperous but always being turned away, each dismissal hurting him more than the last. His rival George, on the other hand, is shown first as a child riding madly through the town streets in a cart; in successive stages of the film he journeys down the same streets, first in a carriage and then on foot, becoming more humiliated with each trip. At one point, in a line  of dialogue RKO cut from the completed film, Uncle Jack was to comment on this theme: "I wonder, Lucy," he says, "if history's going on forever repeating itself. I wonder if this town's going on building up things and rolling them over."

As the introductory survey of the town and its manners develops, Welles's commentary alternates with remarks by a chorus of anonymous citizens (among them Agnes Moorehead), who discuss the fancy Amberson dwelling, the courtship between Eugene and Isabel, the subsequent marriage of Isabel and Wilbur, and the arrogance of young George. Like the nineteenth-century narrative tradition upon which Tarkington's novel is based, these scenes contain elements of deliberate artificiality; the settings, costumes, and faces work to persuade the audience that the Amberson world is "real," but the technique is deliberately sentimental, meant to establish a distance between us and the drama. Many of the early shots are fringed with mist, and the actors are posed in rigid tableaux, as in the example shown here, where the Amberson family is arranged in the grounds of their estate, positioned according to their influence and backed by studio artwork that makes them look like figures in an old painting. Welles's gentle, amused voice seems to call these pictures out of a void, manipulating time and the speeches of characters as easily as Tarkington does in the novel. The dissolves and associative editing belong to the illusionist charms of movies, but the pleasure is also that of listening to a raconteur who nudges us gently into a fictional world. Some viewers (Manny Farber, for example) have found all this a bit too coy; to me it seems perfectly in keeping with the rhetoric of the pre-Jamesian novel, a "once upon a time" story that unfolds at the behest of a narrating personality. Welles has caught the tone of this voice exactly, and now and then in the opening sections he adds to the distancing effect by having the actors face the camera and address the audience. Thus Ray Collins turns round in a barber's chair (as Uncle Jack, the bachelor in the Amberson family, he is usually dressed in dapper fashions, surrounded by toilet articles) and looks us in the eye: "Wilbur may be no Apollo," he says, "but he's a good sound businessman." In a similar vein, the actors talk back at Welles, thus enforcing the notion from *Heart of Darkness* that camera=narrator=audience: the narrator remarks that several people wished George might receive his "comeuppance." "His *what!*" a woman asks her husband. "His *comeuppance!*" Erskine Sandford replies, looking into the camera, his words punctuated by Bernard Herrmann's music.

If the opening section is designed to amuse us, it also establishes the dynamics of character which will shape the plot. We are given a complete picture of the Amberson family, and we learn that within this group young George is as sheltered as a hothouse plant. The village gossips announce that his mother, Isabel, has made a marriage of convenience with Wilbur, bestowing all her passion on her one son. The boy we see is not only spoiled, he is a perfect model of aristocratic *hauteur*, and Eugene Morgan will become his rival both philosophically and emotionally. We are therefore prepared for the beginning of the story proper. With George's return from college the Amberson ball is announced—"the last of the great, long-remembered dances that everybody talked about"; the camera tracks through the front doors of the mansion, following Eugene Morgan and his now grown daughter, satisfying at last our curiosity about the interior of the house.

At this point the film begins a new stage. From now until much later the narrator remains silent and the audience enters what appears to be a real world, where time is no longer drastically condensed, where the camera style is less obtrusive, and where the actors behave in naturalistic fashion. The entry into the party is beautifully achieved, a gust of winter wind blowing past Morgan and Lucy while two sets of doors open, warm light and music spilling out into the darkness, the camera tracking forward. Near the beginning of the ball, George encounters Lucy in the reception line; he takes her arm and walks with her across the entrance hall, up a grand oak stairway backed with stained-glass windows, then along the corridors of the second story; in three shots, each a long, fluid tracking movement, we are introduced to the Amberson home—a setting filled with the ornate, highly polished elegance of Edwardian craftsmanship.

As every critic has recognized, the ball is the technical high-point of the film; no scenes in *Kane* involve such complexities of blocking and camera movement, and the results are all the more impressive when one considers that Welles was working with Stanley Cortez, a young photographer whose experience could not compare with Toland's. (The RKO logbooks of daily shooting reveal that Cortez was accompanied by other cameramen, among them Richard Makenzie, Russell Metty, and Harry Wild. Of this group, Wild was the most important. Cortez had been hired from a "B" movie unit because Welles wanted fast, high-quality work; but once he was promoted, Cortez became one of the most beautifully meticulous craftsmen in Hollywood. Rather than stop him, Welles and Richard Wilson hired Wild, who began working on a second unit.)

According to the pressbook issued for the film by the RKO publicity department, the Amberson mansion covered three sound stages and was dressed with more than nine thousand items; Cortez's camera traveled past seven rooms, with more than forty technicians handling the lights and sound equipment. In a later contrasting sequence—tragically cut from the completed film—Cortez made a complete tour of the decayed house, rising up and down stairways, executing 360 degree pans to show all four walls of some rooms. Such expertise is fascinating to contemplate, like the extravagant naturalism of Von Stroheim, but *Ambersons* was not an especially elaborate or costly film, and there were good reasons for Welles's decision to shoot the interiors of the mansion in traveling shots. The point was to make the audience feel the spacious innards of the place, to make them experience as directly as possible the grand solidity of the Amberson wealth—an effect which cannot be achieved by cutting back and forth between relatively static compositions. At the end of *Kane*, for example, it is important that the camera *track* over the assembled possessions rather than simply cutting from one *objet d'art* to another; hence nearly everything at the Amberson party is photographed in wide-angle, deep-focus perspective, with the camera rolling down broad hallways and drifting across ballrooms, traversing the house as if it were the belly of a whale. Actually it is a splendidly convivial home, but the bright party atmosphere cannot hide suggestions of death; the Christmas wreaths decorating the hallways look vaguely funereal, and now and then the camera passes a scalloped archway reminiscent of Xanadu.

The camera movement and the compositions in depth also con-

tribute to the waltzing rhythms of the party; the players move in and out of the frame, sometimes arranging themselves in patterns like the figures in a formal dance, rarely becoming isolated in closeup. (There are two brief exchanges of conventional "head shots": once at the beginning when Eugene Morgan meets Isabel in the reception line, and once at the end of the party when George and Lucy sit on the stairs and watch their parents dance.) The spectator's eye is kept busy, for, as with nearly every film by Welles, the characters are seen in relation to the architecture of the house and in relation to other groups of figures. The contrasting details within a given frame are determined by the story itself, establishing subtle dramatic tensions and a sense of conflict between present and past. The shot shown here, for example, is typical of the way Welles matches a couple in one generation with a couple in another. Obviously the technique has a good deal in common with the technique in *Kane*; we see two sets of figures, one in the foreground and one in the distance, youth being contrasted with age. But there is an important stylistic difference in this film—a far greater degree of movement and instability in any given shot. At the beginning of this scene, George and Lucy sit talking on the stairway, while below Eugene Morgan and Fanny Minafer are walking forward. George has been making derisive comments about the stranger Morgan, unaware that he is talking to the man's daughter. He is about to be rudely surprised, because Morgan is stepping up to claim Lucy for a dance; at the same moment Fanny will move away and Isabel will enter the frame to ask, "George, dear, are you enjoying the party?" In a general sense such instability is perfectly in keeping with the theme of the film: later, Lucy will tell George that they cannot marry because things are "so unsettled."

If parents keep intruding on their children, as in this shot, the reverse is also true. For example, at a later point in the evening the Ambersons stand around a punchbowl with Eugene Morgan. It is a formal, quite static grouping, everyone gathered as if they were having their picture taken. The Major stands with his back to us, toasting the group and saying, "Isabel, I remember the last drink

Eugene ever had." But this attempt to recapture the past is quickly frustrated when Eugene looks offscreen to his left and comments on "the only thing that makes me forgive that bass viol for getting in the way." George and Lucy then cross in the foreground, the camera panning with them and the group around the punchbowl scattering in acknowledgment that times have in fact changed.

Everyone at the party is caught up in a process, a flux of time which is subtly represented by the constant movement of camera and players. A frustration and sadness runs beneath the joy of the evening, affecting both the young and their more anxious but ostensibly cheerful elders. While physical relationships are shifting and changing before our eyes, the dialogue is filled with ironic references to the difference between "old times" and "new times," and in the original version, before RKO senselessly cut a huge section from one of the long tracking shots, Welles had shown the following exchange:

JACK (looking at the young people in the party): Life's got a special walloping for every mother's son of 'em! . . . I suppose you know that all these young faces have got to get lines on 'em?
ISABEL: Maybe they won't. Maybe times will change, and nobody will have to wear lines.
EUGENE (looking meaningfully at Isabel): Times have changed like that for only one person I know.
JACK: What puts the lines on faces? Age or trouble? We can't say that wisdom does it.
EUGENE: . . . The deepest wrinkles are caused by lack of faith. The serenest brow is the one that believes the most.
ISABEL: In what?
EUGENE: In everything.

Beneath Isabel's apparent innocence and Eugene's worship of her, there is a sadness, an implicit acknowledgment that time levels everything. It is a pessimistic moment, but it reveals Welles's admiration for characters who cling to an ideal. Indeed the film's whole attitude toward time suggests feelings of loss and idealistic longing, emotions which are central to Welles's best work.

The relationship of the characters and their attitudes toward time are nowhere more beautifully represented than in the climactic moment when parents and children join together in a dance. We see Eugene and Jack standing before a warm fireplace, backed with a mantel and a pier-glass: Jack remarks wistfully, "Eighteen years have passed, but have they? . . . By gosh, old times are certainly starting all over again!" Meanwhile the camera withdraws as Eugene takes Isabel's hand and dances forward, moving to a tune that blends old waltz rhythms with a newer, more buoyant ragtime. "Old times?" Eugene says. "Not a bit. There aren't any old times. When times are gone they aren't old, they're dead. There aren't any times but new times." Exuberantly, he dances with Isabel in a nearly straight line, passing out of the frame at the right foreground, whereupon George and Lucy enter from the left and stand facing one another in a close two-shot. Lucy asks, "What are you doing in school?" George answers, "I don't intend to go into any business or profession. . . . Lawyers, bankers, politicians, what do they ever get out of life?" He declares his intention to be a yachtsman, and immediately waltzes *backward* with Lucy, joining the movement of dancers on the floor. The movements of George and Eugene have exactly corresponded to their respective attitudes as reactionary and progressive, and as the camera now pans across the dancers Eugene can be seen guiding Isabel in a straight, diagonal movement, dancing in a different style from the other couples. Life, however, will have a "walloping" in store for him, as well as George; if George is wrong in assuming that things are permanent, Eugene Morgan seems equally naïve in believing that the past can be rubbed out or rewritten. Both characters, in their own way, feel an illusory confidence that the remainder of the film will undermine.

The dance is an ideal image with which to close the sequence, because it is movement without destination, labor without pain, stasis within a measured beat of time. For a moment everything seems to be in harmony, but at the very peak of gaiety and light, at the instant when the Amberson ballroom is filled with busy joy, the image dissolves; time has already passed, the house is shrouded in darkness, and Eugene and Isabel are seen waltzing alone to a solitary violinist. The last of the "great, long-remembered dances" is over. When Welles cuts to a closer view of Eugene and Isabel, he underlines the sadness of their lives by posing their children in the distance, in a pool of light. The power of this shot derives from its complex significance. On the one hand it holds out hope that the past can be recaptured; if Eugene Morgan cannot reclaim his "one true love," then at least there is the next generation, represented by the couple in the distance. But even while the image makes us believe that history repeats itself, it also makes us aware of change within repetition. The lighting gives Eugene and Isabel the look of ghosts haunting an old mansion, and we can see the years between them and their children.

The tragic situations of all the characters are glimpsed in the aftermath of the ball, where parallel editing contrasts the Morgans and the Ambersons. Eugene and his daughter are seen driving home, their voices cheerfully shouting above a rattling auto engine, their eyes squinting and tearing in the wintry wind; Eugene clearly loves Isabel, and his daughter smiles indulgently as he talks about her. Meanwhile, inside the darkened mansion, George and his mother whisper in the shadows. Isabel worries about her husband's health and his bad investments—"See here," George asks, "he isn't going into Morgan's automobile concern, is he?" For a moment Wilbur himself (Don Dillaway) appears in a dressing gown, and a single closeup shows that his face has the prim, harried lines of an overworked clerk. As George speaks with his father, Jack and Fanny enter in the background, their fancy dress mocking their age, making them a pathetic couple. Even when George teases Fanny about her interest in the widower Morgan, the comedy turns grotesque. Fanny tries to mock George, but her voice rises to a nervous, off-key pitch; from somewhere in the distance we hear Jack shouting for the couple to quiet down—the first in a series of occasions in this film where an off-camera voice provides an ironic counterpoint to the action. "I'm gonna move to a hotel!" Jack shouts down the cavernous hall; but in a sense he already lives in one.

The evening gives way to the following day and the ride in the snow, further evidence of the beautifully alternating moods and rhythms in the opening parts of the film. Outwardly, this section is cheerful and communal, the most lighthearted moment in the story: George's sleigh speeds past Eugene's stranded auto but then overturns, dumping him and Lucy into a snowbank as the horse Pendennis gallops out of sight. Eugene rushes over and looks on with fatherly amusement as George and Lucy steal a kiss. Isabel, Jack, and Fanny make their way from the car to the fallen couple, their voices mingling like the chatter of a happy family. Eventually everyone climbs aboard the "Morgan Invincible" and putters off down the road, singing "The Man Who Broke the Bank at Monte Carlo." Despite the surface gaiety, however, the essential themes are the same as in previous sequences, and the occasional visual references to Currier and Ives are mingled with dark ironies. The conflict between Morgan's "horseless carriage" and George's sled is both charming and serious, the symbolism carried to the blatant extent of having George push the car and eat its exhaust. (George was to breathe auto fumes at two later points in the film, but RKO's cutting obscures one of these instances and leaves the other out entirely.) Bernard Herrmann gives the sequence a sort of music-box orchestration, evoking the sparkle of ice and jingle of bells, but these sounds are repeatedly disrupted by the squeaky handcrank and sputtering motor of an automobile. Even the countryside is not really idyllic, because it is dotted everywhere with houses, mailboxes, and telephone lines. In the original version, the scene ran longer, showing a brief conversation between Eugene and Isabel about changes and pollution in the town:

EUGENE: I think it used to be nicer.
ISABEL: It's because we were young.
EUGENE: There always seemed to be gold dust in the air. . . .
LUCY (to George, in back seat of car): I don't ever seem to be thinking about the present moment. I'm always looking forward to something.

This dialogue, taken almost directly from Tarkington, makes explicit the interweaving of personal time and social time which can be felt everywhere in the film. In one sense there is no "present moment," because the characters are continually preoccupied with past or future, and every image becomes an intersection of what has been with what will be, a painful joining of regrets and wishes.

Besides these temporal ironies, there is a continuing dramatic tension among the characters. Wilbur Minafer is significantly absent from the fun, and while Eugene compliments Isabel, calling her a "divinely ridiculous woman," Fanny Minafer sits in the back seat of the car with Jack and Lucy, trying to talk loudly enough to make Eugene hear. ("It's so interesting! . . . It's so like old times to hear him talk!") The more Fanny affects girlishness, the more frightening she becomes; Moorehead's voice, hovering brilliantly between delight and mania, injects a note of authentic pain which contrasts with everyone else's happiness. Indeed throughout the film death and madness are never very far away, and the slow, nostalgic iris which closes this section provides not only an affectionate homage to old-time movies, but also a foreshadowing of the next episode: after the circle of darkness closes around the distant auto and the Christmas-card town, the screen lightens to show a dark, circular funeral wreath on the Amberson door.

Though Wilbur Minafer is the most ineffectual character in the movie, his demise is analogous to the explosion which sets events in motion at the beginning of *Touch of Evil*. His funeral (scored by Herrmann with the death music from *Kane*) not only marks a turning point in the economic fortunes of the Ambersons, it also sets the stage for the overt battle between George and Eugene. The first third of the film has been preparation, a cheerful exposition filled with suggestions of impending disaster; the rest, like *Kane*, becomes increasingly somber, with poverty and industrial dirt spreading like slow stains. Unfortunately, however, the remainder of the film has been badly truncated by the studio, and must be discussed in more general fashion. What chiefly survives is Agnes Moorehead's vivid portrayal of Aunt Fanny, and a remarkable imagery of decay.

Wilbur's funeral is shot from inside the coffin, looking up at a stream of respectful but hardly grief-stricken mourners. It closes with a large, impressive closeup of Fanny's tear-stained face—the plain, pinched visage of a true Minafer, expressing not only sorrow but an intense, barely concealed fury. An ugly duckling from the puritanical middle class, Fanny has found it necessary to repress both her sexual feelings and her jealousy of the Ambersons; Jack later remarks that she has nothing "except her feeling about Eugene," but now even that is threatened by Isabel's freedom.

Throughout the film Moorehead conveys Fanny's torment in every birdlike gesture of her body, frequently drawing the spectator's eye into little corners of the frame, where she dominates the screen without saying a word. In the brief scene at Morgan's growing automobile factory, she can be seen bestowing an adoring look on her beloved as he tells Isabel that he feels like writing poetry

again; the glance speaks volumes, but is delivered at the very margin of the playing area and is totally ignored by the other actors. In later scenes Moorehead's depiction of a maddened spinster is so intense that it completely overshadows Tim Holt's performance as George. "I believe I'm going crazy!" George exclaims when Fanny tells him of rumors circulating about Eugene and Isabel; nevertheless he behaves like a dumb child, his insanity reflected chiefly in the settings and in this willingness to listen to his aunt. She pursues him like a harpy ("George, what are you going to do, George?"), her emotions swinging between panic, embittered self-pity, and devilish cunning. The dialogue between the two is staged on the Amberson stairway, where stained-glass windows carry ironic mottoes like "Poetry" and "Music." At one point Welles even photographs them as if they were Iago and Othello, standing at separate levels of an Elizabethan theatre and backed by expressionist shadow.

Fanny, who is the second maternal figure in George's life, is also a predator, as this shot indicates. Without a child of her own, she reinforces Isabel's protective attitude toward the boy, and at the same time manipulates his jealousy toward Morgan. We see her making strawberry shortcake for her nephew and then cautioning him not to eat fast; later she comforts George when his mother dies and remains guiltily beside him until the end of the film, when she collapses on the floor of an empty kitchen in a helpless, childlike despair. Like George, she becomes a mere pedestrian in the town, her sexual frustrations compounded by a motherly instinct and a penny-pinching anxiety which has been bred into her by generations of thrifty Minafers. "I walked my heels off looking for a place for us to live," she tells George in a tearful singsong. "I walked all over this town. I didn't go a single block on a streetcar." In this climactic scene, her back resting against a cold boiler, Moorehead reaches a degree of grief and rage barely suggested in Tarkington's novel; as she dashes out of the kitchen, the camera withdrawing anxiously before her, her performance becomes as extreme as Welles's own directorial style, rising to a pitch of hysteria that makes most Hollywood acting seem pale and mannered.

In defense of Tim Holt, it must be said that he is given a difficult role, with fewer opportunities to express George's mania. The
character he plays is supposed to remain stiff, arrogant, and somewhat ridiculously old fashioned, speaking a language appropriate
to Victorian melodrama. Some of his more powerful scenes—his
confrontation with Isabel after he sends Eugene away from the
house, his solitary recitation of Hamlet's "Tis not my inky cloak,
good Mother"—have been reshot or cut entirely. As a result he
becomes an exceedingly bland presence who is repeatedly mocked
by his environment. His successive trips through the city, for example, are designed to comment bitterly on his decline: as a child
and as a young man he roars through the dirt streets in a horsecart,
the camera photographing him from a low angle when he scatters
passersby and lashes a workman. Later he is seen trotting slowly
through traffic with Lucy at his side; as he speaks of the "Movements" he wants to administer, his horse clatters loudly on pave-
ment and we glimpse mock-aristocratic signboards in the background—"Elite Cleaners," "Barber Shop: Tony Gentry, prop."
Finally, as the last indignity, he traverses the streets on foot, passing advertisements such as "Blaize Credit Co." and "New Hope
Apartments."

But if the film is unable to give George a psychologically rich
characterization, it does not fail in its evocation of death and decay. Major Amberson's ride through the town and the later shot of
Isabel in the same carriage after her return from Europe are photographed as if the characters were in a hearse. In the first shot a
slanting, white-hot light burns through the darkness and falls ruthlessly on the Major's aging face; in the second we see an elaborate,
impressionistic view of the city through the carriage windows, the
buildings magnified on a process screen and tilted at a crazy angle.
Two of the simplest shots—the announcement of Isabel's death
and the closeup of a dying Major Amberson—are among the most
emotionally effective scenes in all of Welles's cinema, despite the
fact that the first was cut in half by studio editors and the second
was reshot at Welles's instructions by Robert Wise. When Isabel
dies the Major is seen reclining on George's bed, fully clothed and
sleeping in the midst of the day; suddenly he wakes for no apparent
reason, glancing around the young man's room in senile confusion;
the camera pulls nervously back and Herrmann plays an eerie,
dreamlike music as George's shadow crosses in front of the lens;
the camera pans quickly to catch the back of George's head as
Fanny bursts in; she grasps him in a tight embrace, her eyes glazed

and staring at the ceiling as she whispers, "She loved you, George, she loved you!" The next scene presents the Major's dying monologue: from a dark screen, Welles's voice speaks slowly, majestically, "And now Major Amberson was engaged in the profoundest thinking of his life." Gradually we see a closeup of Richard Bennett, a silent film star who was in fact close to death when the scene was shot; firelight illuminates his face as he mutters, "The sun. It must be the sun." Offscreen Jack's voice can be heard asking about the disposition of the family property.

Despite such moments, however, the film as a whole becomes less effective as it goes along. Although Welles's associates—including Joseph Cotten and Robert Wise—tried in the director's absence to remain true to the original intent, studio revisions have damaged the film in several ways. First of all, the rearrangement of several sequences and the deletion of others have destroyed the carefully planned dramatic rhythm. The first third of the movie, as we have seen, alternates brilliantly between montage and tracking shots, between light and dark, between comedy and a sense of doom. The rest was intended to be more grim and was shot chiefly in long takes; but the surviving version becomes nothing more than a series of unedited sequences punctuated by slow fades, each segment of the narrative becoming more morose than the last. As Joseph McBride has shown, Welles's original plan for the final third of the film would have maintained a more "fluid" continuity. For example, Jack's farewell to George at the railroad station (where we were supposed to see Jack borrowing a hundred dollars from his nephew) was shot with an unmoving camera, and was to have been followed by an elaborate montage showing George walking down National Avenue, where he tours the decrepit Amberson mansion for the last time. George's prayer at his dead mother's bed was to have been followed by the violent scene with Fanny in the empty kitchen. In the film as it now stands, George's long walk and his final visit to the house have been cut almost entirely, and the slowly paced conversation between Eugene and Lucy in their garden, which was intended to follow Fanny's hysteria, has been moved to the place just after Jack's farewell at the station. Thus at this point, one static scene follows another; the careful contrast between the Ambersons' tragedy and the success of the Morgans has been obscured, and the movie becomes monotonous.

In shortening the film, the studio also cut all sections having to do with economics, preserving only the romance plot. As a result we have very little sense of why the Amberson fortune collapses, and the impoverishment of the family seems precipitous. In the novel, and in Welles's final version of the script, the economic situation is described in detail. In a line cut from the opening montage, Welles spoke of the "sons and grandsons of early settlers," whose "thrift was next to their religion." He had intended to illustrate two economic ideas which were in sharp conflict in the late nineteenth century—on the one hand was a midwestern and southern agricultural society, based on conservative values of labor, thrift, and landed wealth, and on the other was the new, eastern notion of money that makes money. Morgan clearly represents the new wave, not only because he is an inventor and an industrialist, but because he makes shrewd investments; significantly, he has spent twenty years in the East before returning to the last of the Amberson balls.

Both Tarkington and Welles had wanted to show that the Ambersons were pitifully naïve about the new industrial economy. In the surviving version of the film we learn that Wilbur Minafer has made bad investments in "rolling mills," but we were also supposed to see Major Amberson selling off his property in bits and pieces, hoping to maintain his wealth. This property in turn is subdivided and sold by new owners, and the new houses become dirty and dilapidated as the outer boundaries of the city spread. Ultimately the Major dies, leaving no deeds to his remaining property, and the Amberson mansion itself is sold off and subdivided into a rooming house. Meanwhile we were to see Eugene Morgan established in a twentieth-century home, described in Welles's script as "a great Georgian picture in brick with four acres of hedged land between it and its next neighbor."

In both novel and original film, George Minafer's discovery of the eroding family fortune coincided exactly with the death of his father and his own return from college. At the end of the kitchen dinner scene in Welles's movie, George was supposed to look out the back window and shout "Holy Cats!", then rush into the rainy night to discover the grounds of the mansion being excavated for houses. Other scenes had been filmed, taken more or less directly from the novel, showing the Amberson family sitting on their veranda during summer evenings, watching motorized traffic go by as they discussed their money problems. As a result of one of these conversations, Fanny Minafer invests the small inheritance from her brother in an auto headlight factory which collapses; as we see in the surviving film, she is left penniless, sitting on the floor of an empty kitchen.

Tarkington's explanation of the Amberson decline was still more elaborate and had even taken a racist turn. He had spoken of a great change in the citizenry itself, describing a "new American" who came from the European emigrations of the eighties and nineties "in search not so directly of freedom and democracy as of more money." This bizarre argument suggests that the Ambersons were more interested in pure spirituality than their successors, and happily Welles ignored it. He did, however, intend to show the city as Tarkington had described it, run by "downtown businessmen" who believed in "hustling and honesty, because both paid." According to Tarkington "the city came to be like the body of a great dirty man, skinned, to show his busy works, yet wearing a few barbaric ornaments; and such a figure carved, colored, and discolored, and set up in the marketplace, would have done well enough as the god of the new people." Welles had also wanted to preserve the fine historical ironies of the story, in which things like land, livestock, and houses become less substantial than paper money, and in which nature is subdued by commerce. But these ironies are lost almost completely in the final version of the film, which RKO tried to sell as a spicy love story.

By removing the economic sections, the studio sacrificed a series of impressive images. Gone completely, like the house in the story, are the long documentary-style scenes of modern city streets, followed by Stanley Cortez's elaborate tour of the empty mansion. George's last entry into his dead mother's room, which he has kept perfectly preserved, was to be accompanied by Welles reading from Tarkington—a description of how everything in the house is about to be divided into "kitchenettes," with only the ghosts of the Ambersons left behind. George's prayer was originally followed by shots of the exterior of the mansion, its stonework vandalized and smeared with what the script calls "idiot salacity."

Then, too, a number of scenes were reshot, including George's argument with his mother about Eugene (the present version is banal, underscored with sentimental music not by Bernard Herrmann). The most offensive of these revisions is the closing of the film, in which we see Eugene reading of George's accident and then visiting the hospital with Fanny. Charles Higham has defended this conclusion as being more in the spirit of Tarkington's novel, which does indeed end with a reconciliation between George,

Lucy, and Eugene at the hospital (Fanny is not present). But Welles's original version was tougher, more imaginative, and far more true to the tone of the film as a whole. I have reproduced below Bernard Herrmann's recollection of how it went. He has confused the names of two characters, and I have taken the liberty of correcting his mistake; he is probably also mistaken when he says the scene takes place in the "Amberson house," but otherwise his memory is to be trusted:

> The studio got frightened and wanted a more optimistic ending. Some director whom I do not really know and another composer concocted the ending of the film. . . . I'll try to relate what really happened [in the original version]. After the car accident and George's injury, the picture then goes to what we don't really realize until the end has been once the home of the Ambersons. It is now a home for aged gentlefolk. Eugene comes back from the hospital to visit Aunt Fanny. I must describe the room they're in. An old gramophone, a wind-up, is playing a record which was very popular in America at that time, called "The Two Black Crows." . . . through the doorway you can hear the inmates listening to this old record.
> Eugene pleads with Fanny to come look after him, to live with him. And she says, No, I'm very happy here. Remember this in context with the picture. She takes Eugene to the door and opens it, and that's when you realize this has been the Amberson house. He kisses her goodby, he stands at the doorway on the porch, and he looks all around him. Where before in the film it was all surrounded by beautiful country, we see the city. . . . And in every direction the Ambersons are being swallowed. He walks down the stairs, into the city, and in the background we hear "Two Black Crows" getting smaller and smaller, and the sound of traffic getting bigger and bigger, until it finally smothers the whole screen as the film comes to an end.

The "Two Black Crows" recording was actually part of a series of comedy records made in the late twenties by Moran and Mack, a popular vaudeville team (in 1930 they appeared in a movie called *Why Bring That Up?*). A sort of early version of Amos and Andy, their routine consisted of a dialogue between a stereotyped, shiftless black named Amos and a straight man named Willie. I have not been able to locate the specific recording that was used in *Ambersons*, but like all the others in the series it was probably played off against the dimly heard sounds of a blues piano. Amos and Willie encounter one another after a long separation and discuss events back home. It seems a faithful dog has died; in recounting how the death came about, Amos describes a widening chain reaction of disasters, leading up to the destruction of an entire town. The scene inside the boardinghouse was therefore unusually complex, containing several layers of sound, including the gramophone, the monotonous squeak of Fanny's rocking chair, and the noise of boarders. The "inmates," some of whom are eating a meal, could be seen reflected in a typically Wellesian series of mirrors. During their conversation, Eugene tells Fanny that George and Lucy will probably get married, but the mood of the scene is despairing in the extreme.

By any standard this ending to the film would have been superior to the one we now have, in which Joseph Cotten and Agnes Moorehead are seen walking down a hospital corridor wearing silly, beatific grins. As Cotten remarks that he has reconciled with George and has been "true at last" to his "one true love," the wretched music swells and the camera closes in on Moorehead, who is looking blissfully up to heaven. The revised scene (directed by Freddie Fleck and scored by Roy Webb) is not only sentimentalized, it is radically untrue to Welles's intentions. Welles had wanted to emphasize social as well as personal issues, showing Eugene Morgan as a lonely figure against an urban skyline. *Ambersons* would therefore have been far closer to the classic definition of tragedy than *Kane*, its emotional power arising both from the theme of unrequited love and from the imagery of society in decay. Perhaps it is significant that most of the scenes RKO cut from the film were concerned not with the love story nor the midland town, but with the filthy city. By this means they attempted to simplify one of the most sophisticated and morally complex visions of American history the movies have given us.

5

The Radicalization of Style

The Mercury Theatre had grown logically out of the New Deal, and as we have seen all its undertakings were attempts to keep the performing arts reasonably responsive to Popular Front idealism. But whereas the Mercury had tried to remain independent of wealthy communications interests and the studio system, it was in fact tied to these things—at the mercy of reviews, sponsors, box office receipts, and Hollywood producers. Partly as a result of this dependence, it ultimately dissolved, and for Welles and his associates things were never the same again. Even as *Kane* was being filmed, history seemed to be working against such organizations. Here is John Houseman commenting on the period:

> Beginning with *Panic*, through my two years on the Federal Theatre and during the rise and fall of Mercury, I had become accustomed to relating my theatrical activity to the historical movements of the time. On WPA this participation had been immediate and inescapable. . . . Some of this sense of involvement was carried over into the Mercury, where it directly affected our choice of subjects and our methods of operation. Then, gradually, as the Depression receded and international events replaced domestic crises on the front pages of our newspapers, this participation became less satisfying. Germany's persecution of the Jews, the Moscow trials, the Spanish Civil War, the successive threats against Austria and

Czechoslovakia culminating in the enervating suspense of Munich—these formed a mounting tide of tension to which no positive creative response was possible and to which our theatrical activity could no longer be related.

Houseman became disillusioned early, but after the fall Welles himself continued to act as a show business maverick and a social activist, even though he was now a loner rather than the dynamic center of a group activity. In the middle and late forties he directed a couple of fairly topical thrillers (*The Stranger* and *The Lady from Shanghai*, the latter obtained partly because of his marriage to Rita Hayworth), and managed to produce a low-budgeted film of *Macbeth*. He also remained busy as an actor and radio performer. In between *Kane* and *Ambersons*, he rejoined Houseman for a celebrated stage production of *Native Son*, and a few years later, together with his old associate Richard Wilson, he made an abortive, badly calculated attempt to resuscitate the Mercury Theatre in New York, an attempt which will be discussed later. During this time, his political activity was as lively as ever. He campaigned vigorously for FDR's fourth term, lecturing widely and appearing on platforms with Henry Wallace. In 1944, he actually stood in for Roosevelt in a debate with Thomas Dewey at the Hotel Astor. Even more interestingly, he briefly became an editorial columnist for the *New York Post*—a job which paid him fairly little, but which gave him a platform and allowed him to speak like a man with political ambitions of his own. His daily columns began immediately after FDR's inauguration, on January 22, 1945 (the birthdate, Welles observed, of Byron and D. W. Griffith), and continued until June of the same year, just before the atomic bombs ended the war. These columns are a rich source of his opinions about literature, art, and the movies, and are especially valuable as a record of his preoccupation with world affairs—a preoccupation which bears upon some of the films he would make.

"I'm convinced everybody should be interested in politics," Welles declared at the outset. "The disaster of America in the 1920s was that everybody left the practice of politics to the politicians." Even so, he approached the topic somewhat cautiously. The columns began under the title "Orson Welles's Almanac," borrowing their name and format from Welles's radio show of that season, and were at first characterized by a cheerful, homey tone. Random, chatty observations on the day's news were interspersed with playful astrological forecasts ("We are glad to report that planetary aspects today favor thoughts which can be turned into money"), household hints ("Cut stringbeans with scissors"), and notes on the books Welles had been reading. The columns also contained items about celebrities: Welles attacked Westbrook Pegler, "whom Mr. Hearst pays to seek for the truth or something," and defended Frank Sinatra against Pegler's innuendoes; he wrote an open letter to Jack Benny, who had been unable to take Eddie Anderson along on troop shows because of segregation in the army; and he spoke disparagingly of Noel Coward, whom he accused of perpetuating an anachronistic, British public school snobbery. Within a few months, however, Welles had become less discursive, more like a straightforward editorialist. His style remained fairly witty and ironic, but there was an urgency in his voice. On April 13, FDR died, and the title of the columns changed immediately to "Orson Welles Today," in keeping with a growing seriousness of purpose.

After Roosevelt's death, Welles announced to his readers that the president had written him a personal note only a few weeks before, saying that "April will be a critical month in the history of human freedom." Indeed signs of the Cold War were appearing everywhere. The battle against Germany and Japan, which Welles portrayed as the common man's struggle against fascism, was in danger of betraying its ostensible ideals; VE Day left Welles uneasy because he felt that the spirit of Hitler was only dormant, surviving through the old device of the Red scare. (Aspects of this theme were of course explored in *The Stranger*, the film Welles was making at the time, where he plays a Nazi criminal hiding in a New England town. Only when the criminal is discovered and killed does a real VE Day come to Harpur, Connecticut.) "We've been on the move for quite a time now," he wrote, "along a road that's taken us from North Africa . . . to Yalta. The next objective is San Francisco [and the U.N. conference]—and we'd better continue along the same road without a stop. Otherwise we'll find out to our everlasting sorrow that we didn't take the ride at all. We were taken for it."

Welles's columns provided documentary evidence, if any were needed, of his essential liberalism and his intense concern with political affairs. His chief themes were the need to perpetuate New Deal social legislation, and the necessity of translating the Allied victory over Germany into a world democracy. He argued for a fair working relationship between labor and capital, but believed government price regulations should continue after the war; he inveighed against a "certain sort of businessman" who "openly favors a certain percentage of postwar unemployment," saying that such types "don't want any percentage of government control over their affairs. They want to be free as buccaneers, free to encourage a little convenient joblessness." He supported the basic structure of American government and encouraged the two-party system, but at the time he hoped aloud that Henry Wallace would be the next president. When Truman entered the White House, Welles was cautious: "We must reconcile ourselves that the new President will, at least temporarily, do no more than consolidate the social gains of the past twelve years. . . . Harry Truman prides himself in knowing what the little fellow's thinking about. . . . Okay. But if the little fellows of America want to press forward for a better world in the century of the common man, they'll have to let our new Chief Executive know about it again, again, and again."

Though Welles repeatedly commented on domestic affairs, his chief concern from the first column to the last was American foreign policy. The San Francisco assembly was his major preoccupation, and he also attended the Pan American War and Peace conference in Mexico City, writing for several days about the meeting. (It is an interesting coincidence that in the next year *The Lady from Shanghai* would be filmed partly on location in San Francisco and Mexico.) At the Latin American conference, which was sponsored by Welles's old patron Nelson Rockefeller and which has been described by historians as one of the first symptoms of Cold War politics, speakers rose again and again to utter revolutionary slogans and discuss economic reform; nevertheless Welles noted a reluctance to get down to "brass tacks." He remarked on the dark history of pseudo-revolutions in these countries ("Very few of them succeeded without the help of a couple of North American companies you could name"), and was struck by the blatant ironies of the conference itself, where the U.S. "State Department millionaires" made official deals with so-called revolutionary heads of state, many of whom were also millionaires. Most of all he was troubled by divided feelings about the true progressives; he wanted the South Americans to join the war against the European fascists, but he knew that U.S. economic colonialism had made the Latin left as naturally suspicious of the States as the Irish were suspicious of England.

The difficulties Welles found at Mexico City were symptomatic of conflicts he saw everywhere, especially inside the United States. Always there had been a disparity between American ideals expressed abroad and the actual treatment of minorities at home, but toward the end of the war this disparity was becoming especially acute:

Internationalism [Welles wrote] can't be preached in a new government level and practiced on the old states' rights basis. The inconsistencies are just too glaring. . . . Thus, an Atlantic Charter is perused by foreigners with one eye on a lynching in Arkansas. A Crimea communique is studied in reference to a Detroit race riot. A declaration at Mexico City stirs memories of a place called Sleepy Lagoon. . . . That's the connection between the hand of American friendship extended to Haile Selassie, to Farouk of Egypt, to the leader of Saudi Arabia—and the noose around a Negro's neck in Alabama.

Such inconsistencies were enough to belie the country's claim to "moral leadership" at international meetings:

No moral position taken by us against Col. Perón has any meaning for Spanish-speaking America until we break with Gen. Franco. . . . Our attitude towards the policy of the good neighbor matches the rest of our foreign policy. But it doesn't match at all the high principles by which we would justify our leadership in the Americas. We have armed dictators, strengthened unnecessarily the political hand of high churchmen, and everywhere underrated the Democratic aspirations of the people.

The new, more liberalized economic arrangements being made for the world were also being threatened by official hypocrisies. Welles was especially concerned about the fate of the Bretton Woods proposals, which would slash interest rates and allow all countries to borrow from a world bank "without secret, war-breeding deals." The Bretton Woods idea was aimed at preventing the rise of speculators like the "match king" Krueger, who had grown rich after the first world war, but it was being opposed in this country by Senator Taft and the Republican right wing—or, as Welles put it, by "that little Wall St. camarilla who once did so very well by floating foreign loans at fat fees." Taft had wanted to substitute another plan, whereby the U.S. and Great Britain would reach an agreement on the dollar and the pound, extending credits to other countries. What they offered, Welles remarked, was "the old 'key' notion and currency gag—and behind this gaudily altruistic façade one notices that something is missing. Something called the Soviet Union." Even the British, Welles noted, were to become "junior partners in the firm, playing an emphatically minor role, and one bound to get smaller through the years." Welles shuddered at what might result:

We are the world's greatest production plant and the largest creditor nation. Without sensible economic agreements between England and the U.S., Mr. Luce's prediction of the American century will come true, and God help us all. We'll make Germany's bid for world supremacy look like amateur night, and the inevitable retribution will be on a comparable scale.

The mounting anger one senses in Welles's comments about reactionary politics is reflected also in his remarks on current literature and the arts. For example, he wrote at length in praise of Mexico's three famous muralists, Rivera, Orozco, and Siqueiros, but of the three he much preferred Siqueiros because of his manifestly committed, revolutionary subject matter: "It would be easy to denounce Siqueiros as a blind slave, but he is doing the most adventurous and independent work in the world of art. As for his unshackled comrades, Rivera is decorating night clubs, and Orozco is depicting democracy as raddled and bedizened." Somewhat later, in a brief note on John Hersey's *A Bell for Adano* (about to be filmed by 20th Century-Fox), Welles wrote that the popularity of the book was disturbing because of the way it ministered to America's complacent moral superiority: "For those who thought Mussolini was only funny, and who never heard of Mazzini or Garibaldi, for those who like to think that America has a monopoly on the democratic faith, 'A Bell for Adano,' I'm afraid, will be most reassuring." On the other hand, Richard Wright's *Black Boy* needed more readers. White citizens who claimed to "understand the Negro" should be "tied down with banjo strings, gagged with bandannas, their eyes propped open with watermelon seeds, and made to read 'Black Boy' word for word." (Coincidentally, about a year later Welles became involved in a controversy with these same white citizens. On his New York radio show in late July 1946, he charged that black army veteran Isaac Woodward had been taken from a Greyhound bus in Aiken, South Carolina, beaten by police, and blinded. The mayor of Aiken and the local Lions Club denied any knowledge of the incident and threatened to sue, but the issue was never joined.)

By June 1945, Welles was writing from San Francisco, where it was becoming increasingly apparent that the U.N. would become a battleground of Cold War animosities. The American government was already extending official courtesies to known fascists like Nicholas Horthy of Hungary, and the conference itself was rife with backstage politics. Welles could sense a growing propaganda effort against the Russians:

> We are still building our Bulwarks against Bolshevism. The phony fear of Communism is smoke-screening the real menace of renascent Fascism. The red bogey haunts the hotel lobbies and the committee rooms. Near the cigar stand at the Fairmont, Senator Vandenburg growls sarcastically about the 'benediction of Yalta.' . . . Averell Harriman has been talking up the Polish problem to selected groups of reporters in off-the-record cocktail parties. . . . The [anti-Stalin] gossip mill works full time . . . and Rep. Clare Luce declares war on the Soviet Union by radio.

There is a fatalistic note to these lines, which appeared very close to the end of Welles's tenure as a columnist. He had begun his first column by writing about FDR's inaugural and expressing hope for the U.N., but within six months Roosevelt was dead, liberalism was on the wane, and the new international organization seemed doomed by internecine conflict.

I

If I have dealt at length with such matters, it is because Welles's tendency to become involved in controversy, together with his repeated criticism of public life in 1945, has an interesting relationship to his subsequent films. I do not mean that his movies became mere vehicles for ideas, although it is true that his thrillers are filled with topical political references and moral arguments. I mean rather that the mood and style of his later projects were indirectly affected by his alienation from the movie colony and society at large; that the frenzy and unorthodox form of his work for the next ten years may be seen as partly a response to the growth of reactionary politics in the country, and can be related not only to Welles's working conditions but to his growing dissatisfaction with American life.

The continuity between Welles's politics and his situation in Hollywood is fairly easy to detect if one simply considers the few remarks about movies in his columns. "I love movies," he says at one point. "But don't get me wrong. I hate Hollywood." Clearly it had become impossible for him to continue working as an independent, and his sense of dislocation from the industry had coincided with a rise of conservatism in the nation. Welles pointed out that the same money-men who were undermining a liberal foreign policy and arguing for an "acceptable" rate of unemployment were also consolidating their hold on the entertainment business; very soon, he suggested, they would control television communications: "Receiving sets in New York are so adjusted that you can get only ten television broadcasting studios instead of being able to dial anything you want. . . . It's a neat trick, but it shouldn't fool anybody." As for the movies, they had long been dominated by a handful of big operators, in roughly the same way as legitimate theatre had been dominated in the years before the Depression. "I think Jack Warner makes the best movies in town," Welles declared. "But the views of Jack and Harry Warner towards distribution are a good deal less liberal than those expressed in their product. . . . Jack claims that one of his theatres will play one of my pictures as quickly and cheerfully as it will give the time to one of his. I say that's spinach, and I say to hell with it anyway."

Welles had comparatively few observations about the industry product, but on the few occasions when he did turn to specific films, he heaped scorn on Hollywood's establishment. Several times he voiced support for "little" films, and twice used space in the column to recommend William Castle's *When Strangers Marry*. (Within a year Castle himself became Welles's associate producer on *The Lady from Shanghai*.) Welles liked the film because it had the gritty, unpretentious virtues of an intelligent "B" production, making it a perfect foil to the middlebrow sanctimoniousness of Hollywood's award-winning movies:

Did you ever hear of a "B" picture getting one of the prizes or even a nomination? "The Informer" doesn't count as a "B" in spite of its low budget because its director was famous and successful and well-paid. A real "B" is produced for half the money and is twice as hard to make worthy of attention. . . .

Gold statuettes for score and photography aren't enough. The movie industry is the only big business I know of which spends no money on real research. A valid Academy of Motion Picture Arts and Sciences would be a laboratory for experiment, a studio—by which I do not mean a factory building for the manufacture of a product—but a place removed from the commercial standard and reserved for study, for honest creative effort.

Of course Welles's notion of an Academy "removed from the commercial standard" was somewhat naïve, because unless one contemplated revolution, such an Academy would always be influenced at long distance by commerce. Just as the Mercury could not long remain an independent theatre, free of both government dictates and the pressures of a "free" market, so a research unit funded by Hollywood would inevitably face compromises; nevertheless Welles continued to imagine an ideal setting for the performing arts, a place uninhibited by capitalists or commissars.

Welles's suspicion of these twin evils is apparent in his discussion of Eisenstein's *Ivan the Terrible* (part one), which he and Rita Hayworth had seen in May 1945 at the United Nations theatre in San Francisco. He devoted two entire columns to the film, developing a fascinating comparison between it and 20th Century-Fox's *Woodrow Wilson*, which had also recently opened in San Francisco. Here were two major productions by the two postwar Leviathans; both claimed to be portraits of historical figures and both had specific political implications. "The man in the Kremlin," Welles wrote, "is remembered for a certain ruthlessness of action and the man in the White House for a certain chilliness of personality. Eisenstein and Zanuck try to show how their heroes got that way, surrounding them respectively with scheming politicians and scheming courtiers. The Boyars, it seems, did it to the Tsar, and the Republican Senators did it to the President." There were of course certain important differences between the two subjects. Because Eisenstein was dealing with a remote historical period, his unorthodox historical interpretations were easier to accept, whereas Zanuck had problems with even the most discreet adjustments of the facts. In both cases, however, Welles felt the heroes were sentimentalized: "Maybe Ivan and Wilson were good family men, but the scenes to this effect are curiously lacking in significance." Zanuck had attempted to make Wilson a hail-fellow, "but when his impersonator harmonizes 'Down by the Old Mill Stream' we are not persuaded. . . . And as for Ivan, he is still 'The Terrible' no matter how many times in a movie he slaps his friends on the back and chucks his wife under the chin."

Welles implied that both films were propagandistic, suffused with establishment patriotism. The real interest and superiority of *Ivan* as against the American work lay not in its interpretation of history or in its implicit ideology, but in its extravagant, stylized approach to cinema, an approach the Russian audience had apparently been willing to accept:

> Critics and audiences in the English-speaking world, accustomed as they are to the pallid stylelessness of the "realistic" school, are likely to be impatient, even moved to giggles by the antics of Ivan and his friends. This is because the arts and artists of our theatre have been so busy for so long now teaching the public to reject anything larger than life unless it be stated in the special language of glamor and charm that I'm afraid many good citizens who read the comic strips with utmost solemnity will laugh out loud at Eisenstein's best moments. Our culture has conditioned us to take Dick Tracy with a straight face. But nothing prepared us for "Ivan the Terrible."

Welles must have had his own practice in mind as he wrote those lines. From infancy he had been fascinated with Shakespeare, with the European tradition of grand opera, and with the theatrical grandiloquence of large-scale magic shows; the bizarre imagery and deliberately anti-naturalistic acting in the Eisenstein film spoke to his own tastes, but they were doubly attractive because they ran against the grain of studio cinema, giving full expression to the director's personality. Welles praised the Russian film for its "courageously radical stylization," noting how sharply it differed from American movies: "The Wilson picture, of course, has its own stylization and its own conventions. But these are Hollywood habits, not the conscious creation of Director Henry King." In other words, the American film was conservative, built out of a narrow visual and literary code from which the director was not expected to deviate. The Eisenstein film was liberating, allowing the director to make stylistic choices free of a culturally predetermined idea as to what constituted truth to nature.

Both traditions, Welles recognized, had their own peculiar strengths and weaknesses:

> When the American movie-maker becomes aware of a discrepancy between his film and the appearance of life, he corrects the difference in favor of "realism." This search for the direct and literal produces some of our best effects. The Russians go out for the effect

itself—and when they find what they're after—they manage moments of an exclamatory and resonant beauty on the level of eloquence to which our school cannot aspire. When the Russian method fails it is funny; it falls flat on its bottom, and we laugh. When Hollywood fails, it falls flat, the result is merely dull, and we yawn.

Welles did not want to choose between these approaches. "We have much to learn from each other," he said, and the learning process, as he saw it, extended especially to matters of technique. Even the medium-distance, long-take photography which Welles had helped popularize (and had justified in the name of "realism") made an interesting contrast with the Russian montage school: "Because of the inferiority of Russian film stock, lenses, and other equipment, the camera must assert itself by what it selects, and by the manner of selection." The less obtrusive Hollywood camera, Welles said, "has a merchant's eye," and devotes itself to "star-hogging close-ups," or to "lovingly evaluating texture, the screen being filled as a window is dressed in a swank department store."

Hence, just as Welles's politics were progressive and liberal, seeking a middle ground between the White House and the Kremlin, so his aesthetics attempted to find a happy synthesis of two cultures. Where his own work was concerned, he had tried from the beginning to combine what he calls "moments of exclamatory and resonant beauty on the level of eloquence" with the dominant tradition of psychological realism. In both *Kane* and *Ambersons,* for example, he had chosen subjects which had many precedents in the tradition of "well-made" Hollywood films. What was relatively different about Welles was not his subject matter nor even his sophistication, but the degree to which he had brought unorthodox style and autobiography to the fore. In this respect, he had attempted to import something "larger than life" into the main-stream of American movies, a force to countervail what he called the "pallid stylelessness" of studio realism.

Looked at today, the artificial conventions of American movies in the forties are quite apparent, but Welles was correct to say that these films were striving for the "direct and literal." In costume films or in expressionist genres such as the thriller, there was indeed a degree of license, a "special language of glamor and charm," but the tendency of the industry as a whole was toward aesthetic minimalism. Anglo-Saxon critics helped perpetuate this tendency, because they grumbled (as they do today) when they encountered anything unrestrained: it was precisely this quality that made certain reviewers unhappy with *Kane*, and that caused Welles's detractors to portray him as a ham; certainly he took greater risks than most with convention, and when his work failed, it failed on the side of histrionics and silliness, never on the side of dullness. Nevertheless Welles's strengths came from the same sources as his weaknesses—namely what he had called, in speaking of Eisenstein, a "courageously radical stylization," which in his case meant a willingness to challenge not only the habits of the studio system but the limits of popular taste.

Given Welles's position in Hollywood in the mid-forties, however, it would seem his romantic struggle against the studios should have come to an end. After his contract with RKO terminated, he worked infrequently, always in the sort of genre projects which might theoretically have put restraints on his style; even when he ventured into Shakespeare, it was under severe limitations of time and budget under a boss whose biggest star was Roy Rogers. And yet, by staying within genres or B-budgets, Welles managed to retain more individuality than if he had been allowed into the more culturally ambitious, expensive productions. At the level of filmed biographies or adaptations of big novels, Hollywood was controlled entirely by middlebrow producers, devoted entirely to the same conservative "tradition of quality" that Truffaut once attacked so vigorously in France. Conversely, the degree of convention in the standard Hollywood melodrama sometimes worked in the director's favor; producers took less personal interest in the texture of the film so long as the basic plot ingredients were satisfied. Thus the Hollywood movie of this period was at its most exciting when it operated under obvious constraints of money or content, at a moderately low level of respectability. Its meaning lay not in the manifest content of the script, which was usually based on potboiler novels or magazine stories, but in the almost libidinal warfare between a good director's style and the pressures of convention.

I say "libidinal" partly because the Freudian model of id vs. superego provides a good analogue to the system, and partly because the most interesting aspects of Hollywood movies in the high forties and fifties tended to be sexual. The fetishistic, overheated romanticism of the *film noir* became one of the few sources of rebellious energy in the movies, although admittedly it was a fairly timid rebellion. Welles, of course, was especially suited to work in this vein, bringing to it an intelligence and integrity of purpose that kept his films from becoming, like so many others, merely lurid.

And despite the fact that he was seldom able to choose his own topics, he managed to keep his ethical and political themes virtually intact; even the familiar character types recur, sometimes adapted to fit the requirements for "glamor and charm." When he worked at all now, his films became more radically stylized than ever, as if the limitations in subject matter and budget had to be overcome by an utter strangeness of *mise-en-scène*. From *The Lady from Shanghai* through *Touch of Evil* Welles's style became more bizarre and circus-like; his films during this period reflect some of the chaos and uncertainty of his own career, becoming increasingly satiric, charged with self-conscious manipulation of popular sexual stereotypes and visual references to that most private of all Hollywood individualists, von Sternberg. In one sense, therefore, these films were as "personal" as any of his others; and as one might expect, producers and audiences became increasingly unsympathetic.

II   *The Stranger*

The one exception to the trend I've just described is *The Stranger* (1945), about which I shall make only brief comments. (This film is discussed further in chapter 11.) An occasionally silly but nonetheless entertaining picture, it was praised by James Agee for being a "tidy, engaging thriller . . . much more graceful, intelligent, and enjoyable than most other movies." In fact, Agee was being consistent in his dislike for Welles's style, which he had always found pretentious. He had singled out the most uncharacteristic of Welles's films, a picture that barely deviates from industry habits; significantly also, he had chosen a film which was scripted by John Huston, writing without credit with Anthony Veiller.

Actually, *The Stranger* owes more to Hitchcock than to its real writer or director. The themes are ostensibly political, but the dramatic tensions are purely sexual, arising out of a confrontation between a sweet, repressed female (Loretta Young) and a sexually threatening male (Welles). The script borrows heavily from *Shadow of a Doubt* (1942), transforming Hitchcock's psychotic Uncle Charlie into Franz Kindler, an escaped Nazi war criminal who poses as a history teacher in a New England college. Huston and producer Sam Spiegel took most of the crucial elements from the earlier film, down to a scene where the villain sits at a family dining table and breaks into a psychotic monologue; they even include a lush musical score by Bronislaw Kaper and a vertiginous climax atop a bell tower. The only new elements were a dogged war crimes investigator (Edward G. Robinson), who manages to charm audiences despite the relative colorlessness of his role, and a veneer of topical politics in line with Welles's own interests. Thus when Welles takes his protagonists to a high place at the conclusion of the film, he is as much interested in showing the Nazi will to power as in depicting a moral and psychological vertigo: Franz Kindler stands in the clock belfry, looks out over Connecticut, and refers to the people below as "ants"—a foreshadowing of Harry Lime's big speech in *The Third Man*.

The film has a superficially Hitchcockian sense of the absurd, and many of Welles's best moments derive from his ironic treatment of Americana, as if Norman Rockwell were being retouched by Charles Addams. Indeed, given the essentially patriotic tone of the movie, Welles is particularly skilled at avoiding a sentimentalized portrait of the townspeople. Billy House, as the checker-playing proprietor of a local drugstore, is slowly transformed from an unpleasant New England eccentric into the leader of a virtual lynch mob; Richard Long, who specialized in the sort of antiseptic kid-brother role he plays here, is at one point photographed in a harsh light that shows pockmarks on his face; Philip Merivale portrays a rather vapid, silver-haired state supreme court judge who is completely fooled by the fascist at his dinner table; and Loretta Young, giving one of the best performances in the film, suggests a woman driven almost mad by the conflict between her sexuality, her complacent puritanism, and her dawning moral awareness.

The Stranger is quite good at these satiric touches, and it skillfully suggests the class structure of a Connecticut village. Occasionally, too, it rises to a truly Wellesian intensity of style—especially in the scenes involving the drugstore-cum-soda-fountain run by House, where extreme naturalism co-exists with suggestions of madness. The store is re-created in loving detail, and is usually photographed in long takes and subtly distorting deep-focus compositions that emphasize clutter on the shelves. Along the walls Welles has posted mirrors and scrawled notices done in his own hand ("No slugs," says a note in the phone booth). Matrons and shrill adolescent types wander in and out, helping themselves while the proprietor watches carefully from his table near the entrance. Here, and in the brief opening scenes involving the journey of a mad Nazi to Connecticut (scenes which were severely cut by Spiegel), we have all the earmarks of Welles's technique. In most other places, however, the movie is inferior to the Hitchcock original and could have been directed by anybody.

Like the Welles/Foster *Journey into Fear, The Stranger* is a patchwork, but in this case the reasons for the disharmony are not easy to determine. Charles Higham has written that Ernest Nims, the editor, had planned a cutting continuity in advance, and that Welles's contract ordered him to follow Nims's design to the letter. But this does not explain why a number of scenes—including the long, extraordinarily difficult tracking shot of a murder in the woods—are clearly inventions of the director. Probably the film looks the way it does because Welles was lying low, intentionally suppressing his style in order to prove that he, too, could do ordinary good work. "I did it to prove that I could put out a movie as well as anyone else," he said. "I did not do it with cynicism, however." In any case the film was completed under budget and under time, and did fairly well at the box office. It was not until his next project, a vehicle for Rita Hayworth done in return for Harry Cohn's investment in a failing stage show, that Welles was able to follow his own instincts. As a result he produced one of the most radically stylized films of his career in Hollywood.

III   *The Lady from Shanghai*

By many standards *The Lady from Shanghai* is more unorthodox than Welles's previous work, but its strangeness did not result from an early, deliberate plan. The idea for the film originated when Welles entered into an agreement with Columbia Pictures to help save the foundering Mercury production of *Around the World.* This latter show had been initiated by Welles and Mike Todd, and was a fairly expensive musical extravaganza featuring old-time movies, a magic show, and a "slide for life" down a rope from the theatre balcony. When Todd withdrew from the partnership early on, Welles enlisted the help of Richard Wilson and continued as producer/director, feeling a certain obligation to Cole Porter, whom he had persuaded to write the score. (Welles later recalled wryly that Porter, who was born with twenty million, who made another twenty million from his music, and who then married a woman worth fifty million, never contributed money for the production.) With the shakiest financial backing, *Around the World* opened in the dog-days of August in New York, just when wartime gas rationing had been lifted and everyone had left town to escape the heat. The show received mixed reviews and was plagued by one financial disaster after another; ultimately Welles persuaded Harry Cohn to advance him money for doing a movie, in the hope that he could keep the play running until audiences returned in September. His original plan was to film a thriller on a low budget, entirely in the streets of New York, at the same time that *Around the World* was continuing its run. The film would be done in the manner of Castle's *When Strangers Marry*, using no big stars or studio paraphernalia. Almost immediately, however, *Around the World* plunged deeper into debt and was closed. Welles found himself back in Hollywood, where his plans for an offbeat potboiler were transformed into a big-budget vehicle for Rita Hayworth.

The resulting film (originally titled *Take This Woman* and then *Black Irish*) tells the story of how Michael O'Hara (Welles), a naïve vagabond, is seduced by the moneyed glamor of Elsa Bannister (Hayworth), allowing himself to become a gigolo and then a duped accomplice in murder. First O'Hara takes a job as captain of Arthur Bannister's yacht on a cruise to San Francisco, and is then persuaded by Bannister's mad law partner, Grisby, to participate in a supposedly phony murder scheme. Grisby claims that he wants to collect money from his own faked demise and then hide out on a South Sea island, where he can be safe from the atomic bomb. As O'Hara commits himself to this deceitful group, the film becomes increasingly farcical and demonic; from the fantastic love scene with Rita Hayworth in the San Francisco aquarium until the magic mirror maze at the conclusion, the world around O'Hara turns utterly lunatic, with no release until he walks out of an amusement park Crazy House across a pier in morning light. The complex but conventional plot machinations are delivered through hallucinatory visuals, the whole movie becoming a satiric dreamwork or magic show based upon a standard thriller. (This method was natural to Welles, but it was suggested by the repeated references to dreams in Sherwood King's *If I Die Before I Wake*, the novel which was his source; it also has some interesting parallels with Robert Siodmak's less brilliant but highly expressionistic film, *Phantom Lady*.)

The movie was substantially re-edited after the second preview and long held from release, becoming a victim of Columbia's desperate attempt to "save" a story Harry Cohn said he could not understand. (The earlier version is described in chapter 11.) The cutting was turned over to Viola Lawrence, a friend of Cohn's but an enemy of Welles's, and a musical score was added without the director's approval. (Welles later complained, in a letter to the studio, that the music used for Rita Hayworth's dive into a lagoon resembled "a Disney picture when Pluto falls into the pool.") Like *The Stranger* the film is a patchwork, but it is far more energetic and dazzling, its very confusions a part of its fascination. The acting ranges from Welles's phony and inconsistent interpretation of an Irish sailor fallen among the right-wing American rich, to the sublimely grotesque performances of Everett Sloane and Glenn Anders, a pair of unscrupulous lawyers who are scorpions personified. The dialogue oscillates between the bathetic ("Give my love to the sunrise"), the tautological ("One who follows his nature will keep his original nature in the end"), and the downright opaque ("I want you to live as long as possible before you die"); but this goofiness remains somehow in keeping with the general atmosphere of comic delirium. Everywhere the movie is filled with bizarre visual dissonances, Welles's imagery co-existing with scenes or sequences that serve to mock Hollywood. Again and again a brilliant moment will be interrupted with gauzy closeups or over-the-shoulder editing, awkwardly composed and badly acted. The real locales of Acapulco and San Francisco are inter-cut with retakes containing obvious studio settings or process screens, and the student can actually make a game of distinguishing shots that are authentically Wellesian from the ones that are deliberate kitsch. It is a game worth playing, partly because the radical shifts of style in this film take on meaningful implications.

A logical place to begin is with Welles's habit of animating the environment, using it to express the emotions of his players or to comment on their behavior. As we have seen, Welles will seldom do one thing on the screen when he can do three or four. Typically he gives as much information as possible, playing off the most subtle exchanges between characters against two or more levels of action. Even the kitchen dinner scene in *The Magnificent Ambersons* is not so restrained as is commonly supposed: the camera barely moves, but Tim Holt wolfs down strawberry shortcake, a Gothic storm rattles outside the windows of the big kitchen, and the actors keep stepping on one another's lines. Welles depends heavily on this multiplication of artistic stimuli, so that he not only expresses psychology through the settings but gives us the feeling of many actions, visual and aural, occurring simultaneously. It is this richness, this seven-layer-cake profusion, that most distinguishes his work in Hollywood.

The Lady from Shanghai offers many examples of such density, the most obvious being the mirror-maze sequence, which is also the grandest example of Welles's delight in movie illusionism. The gun battle among the mirrors functions beautifully within the plot, compactly expressing the ruthless ambition and the self-destructive mania which has been evoked verbally in the hero's account of hungry sharks; indeed it is such a brilliant moment that it almost transcends its fictional content, turning Rita Hayworth into a series of insubstantial images which symbolize the gaudy unreality and fascination of movie stars. More to the point, however, is the way the sequence shows Welles's love of baroque dynamics; it produces an infinite depth of field and more information than we can absorb in a single viewing.

Not satisfied with the simple phenomenon of reflections in mirrors, Welles complicates the spectacle with a split screen: for example, we see two images of Arthur Bannister (Sloane) and his cane at either side of the frame, in between them two gigantic pictures of Elsa's blonde head. In another shot, two Bannisters are superimposed over Elsa's eyeball. Toward the climax, Bannister lurches to the left and produces three images of himself; the camera then pans and three more Bannisters approach from the opposite direction, the two converging groups separated by a single image of Elsa holding a gun; Bannister now takes out his own pistol, and as he points it his "real" hand enters the foreground from offscreen right. All this time the actors are delivering crucial speeches which are intended to unravel the mystery plot—in fact so much happens so rapidly that only a lengthy analysis can lead to a full understanding of the sequence.

Perhaps the images reproduced here will illustrate some of Welles's methods. These stills indicate how the sequence has been designed to create a montage of conflicts between Everett Sloane and Rita Hayworth. If the ugly, crippled male is reflected many times in a single shot, the unreal sex goddess will usually be seen alone; if both characters are multiplied, one will be larger than the other. Each image has the disturbing quality of abstract expressionism or surrealist art, and yet each is motivated by the plot and the

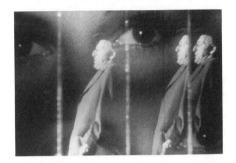

psychology of the characters. In the penultimate shot illustrated here, Bannister tells Elsa that in killing her he will be killing himself, and the hallucinatory image is perfectly expressive of the way the mind can become a hall of mirrors, a distorted, paranoid vision.

The audience does not have to make this sort of analysis in order to appreciate the power of the images, but most viewers feel they have to "meet the film at least half way," as Herman G. Weinberg once said, in an effort to assimilate all the information. Thus, one of the pervasive qualities of this sequence and of Welles's movies in general is *wit*, which means not only a sense of humor but what the *OED* defines as an appeal to the mental faculties, especially to "memory and attention." Of course the typical studio film does not have much to do with wit; its chief desiderata are clarity and simplicity, and that is perhaps one reason why the scenes in *The Lady from Shanghai* waver between a complex satire of manners and a familiar Hollywood gloss.

Keeping to his original intention, Welles shot parts of the film on location, following a practice that was becoming increasingly popular just after the war. Even the interiors, including the sailor's hiring hall, the pierside cafe, the dusty, oppressive courtroom, and the Chinatown theatre, have a harsh surface realism overlaid with a busy, expressive shooting style. In the finished movie, however, many individual shots undercut Welles's expressionism; we catch only occasional glimpses of a startling *mise-en-scène*, usually shot in a real locale. What one recalls most vividly, aside from the trick effects in the Crazy House, are the huge closeups of the four principals: Sloane and Anders are photographed with a mercilessly sharp lens, the camera highlighting every pockmark and bead of sweat on their faces; Welles and Hayworth, on the other hand, become gigantic, romantically blurred movie stars—as fantastic and disturbing in their own way as the ugly characters, so that a glamorous studio portrait photography contributes to the film's aura of surrealism.

In fact, Welles seems to have been quite willing to make studio closeups which disrupt his elaborate blocking of the actors and his fine sense of movement within a frame. Consider, for example, the scene where Grisby calls O'Hara aside to offer a "proposition," and the two men stroll along a hillside above Acapulco Bay. The long shots filmed on location are held on the screen only briefly, but they suggest a conception that is nearly as impressive as the party scene in *Ambersons* or the elaborate track at the beginning of *Touch of Evil*. As Grisby and O'Hara climb the hillside, the whole social structure of Acapulco passes them by, from the impoverished peasants at the bottom of the hill to the American tourists and their Latin retinue at the top. The atmosphere at the bottom is dirty, crowded, and hot, but at the parapet above a sea breeze is blowing and Acapulco sparkles in the sun like a "bright, guilty world."

Welles apparently planned this episode as a series of elaborately choreographed traveling shots that express O'Hara's state of mind while at the same time showing the effects of Yankee capital. As usual, he employs a wide-angle lens, which gives the movement of the camera and actors a dramatic sweep, and he fills the screen with sev-  eral layers of action; the camera spirals up the hill, picking up additional people moving past at different angles, creating a busy, swirling effect. Most of these location scenes are cut on an actor's movement in order to preserve the flow of action and dialogue; Welles tries to evoke a subtly dizzying sensation, which culminates in the final shot—a high-angle, fish-eye view of Grisby and O'Hara standing over the sea. When Grisby steps out of the screen, O'Hara seems to be hanging vertiginously in midair, his image twisted out of shape by the camera to a degree few Hollywood films of the period had attempted.

In the completed film, however, the episode has been substantially revised. Charles Higham has suggested that some of the Acapulco scenes were filmed so clumsily that they "would not cut." It is difficult to believe a sequence so painstakingly blocked as this one could have suffered from an editing problem, but in any case studio shots have been introduced, consisting chiefly of closeups of Welles and Glenn Anders. The lighting in these shots does not match Charles Lawton's strikingly naturalistic photography, and when the closeups are inserted all the restless move-

ment ceases; the two actors are shown as big, static heads, isolated against an artificial backdrop.

A similar intrusion can be seen in the courtroom sequence, which remains one of the funniest in the film. The defendant, O'Hara, who by this time has been made the fall-guy for the villains, is supposed to be completely ignored by everybody; in fact Welles purposely keeps the camera off himself, shooting from a bewildering variety of angles and thus contributing to the maelstrom of activity. The camera leaps back and forth from harshly lit closeups to equally harsh wide-angle views of the room, showing Bannister, the "world's greatest criminal lawyer," parading before the jury on crutches or the audience breaking into spasms. Dialogue overlaps, a juror sneezes, the judge cracks jokes, and nearly everybody deliberately overacts. Now and then, however, the sequence is interrupted by shots of Welles and Rita Hayworth, done in a style which is utterly conventional and radically different from the surrounding imagery. Perhaps someone at the studio felt the trial would make no sense without "reactions" from the protagonists; whatever the cause, the movie seems to have been made by two different hands, or by a director who, out of weariness, contempt, or sheer practical jokery, chose to deface his own work.

I raise the possibility of Welles's contempt because certain defects in the film could have been repaired by any competent technician. For example, after the cataclysm in the mirror maze we are given a shot of Everett Sloane fallen to the floor, curled up, and dying, viewed through jagged edges of glass at the corners of the frame. As Elsa dashes from the room, the camera pans and the "glass" moves with it. The shards in the extreme foreground are revealed as a painting on the front of the camera, and the decision to use a panning movement is clearly a director's error. On the other hand, there is no way of knowing what opportunities Welles had for retakes, and it is obvious that the studio interfered with his more ambitious efforts. Some of his characteristic long takes have been cut to pieces, including the carriage ride through Central Park which opens the film. The long takes that do remain are especially witty moments, indications of what Welles might have accomplished elsewhere. The scene in Grisby's office, for instance, is filmed with a moving camera which snakes around the room, now and then catching O'Hara's bewilderment or Grisby's leer. Later, a complicated and extremely funny shot shows O'Hara learning that he has been framed for a murder: he drives up in Grisby's car, climbs out, and is met by the zaniest swarm of policemen since Keaton's *Cops*. In a lightning succession heightened by the continuity of the shot, the police discover a murder weapon and a signed confession: Officer Peters reads the confession aloud, Arthur Bannister limps into the picture, Grisby's corpse is wheeled under

O'Hara's nose, and Elsa drives up in her convertible. The only cut is here at the end, where we are given a soft-focus closeup of Hayworth, surely intended as a parody of the *femme fatale* (as the earlier shot of her pinned to the deck of a yacht is a parody of cheesecake).

But these interesting moments might have become mere curiosities if the film itself did not retain a certain integrity of purpose. What is surprising about *The Lady from Shanghai* is the degree to which it remains thematically unified, despite the confusing plot turns and the many revisions it appears to have gone through during production. Even as it stands, it is based on some interesting formal ideas. O'Hara's voyage as captain of the Bannister yacht takes him around the continent, beginning with a shot of the New York harbor and ending at San Francisco Bay, as if he were a tourist taking a panoramic view of U.S. corruption. As William Johnson has pointed out, the whole adventure is filled with images of the sea. The lady of the title is of course a shanghaier of sailors, a Sternbergian Circe who lures an Irish Ulysses onto the rocks with her wet swimsuit, or who sings an incredibly bad song which turns O'Hara into a zombie. Again and again Welles combines images of madness with images of water—even the long take in Grisby's office is played off against South Sea islands music coming from a radio.

Furthermore, there is a sense in which all of Columbia's tampering with the film has not been as disruptive as, say, RKO's revisions of *Ambersons*. The reason is that *The Lady from Shanghai* is characterized by a sort of inspired silliness, a grotesquely comic stylization that has moved beyond expressionism toward absurdity. (In one of his best exit lines, Glenn Anders steps close to the camera and whines, "Silly, isn't it?" He then moves out of the frame, leaving Welles sitting there looking as bewildered as usual.) The performances are deliberately exaggerated, so that the sinister moments keep verging on farce—an effect similar to the motel scenes in *Touch of Evil* and K.'s interviews in *The Trial*. Hence the vulgarity of the movie-star imagery only adds to the feeling of satire; for example, the many bad closeups of Rita Hayworth, which seem to have been forced on Welles, often serve as a comment on Hollywood's synthetic sexuality. Welles has added to this feeling by dyeing her hair a fluorescent blonde and dressing her in near parodies of calendar-girl fashion, such as her little yachtsman's suit with white shorts, clog heels, and officer's cap. He poses

her rather like a figure in an advertisement—a smiling woman in a bathing suit, reclining on a rock, her toes nicely pointed and the wind blowing her hair. He deliberately cuts from her awful siren song to a "Glosso Lusto" hair-treatment commercial, or he views her through Grisby's telescope, suddenly lowering the glass and confronting the audience with a full closeup of Grisby himself, who is sweating and leering voyeuristically back at the camera.

These touches are not out of keeping with the mood of the film as a whole. In fact, one could argue that Welles's career during this period had begun to move more and more away from realism to fantasy, from consciousness to subconsciousness, from ports to Crazy Houses. His style, with its fantastic distortions, its complex play of light and shadow, its many levels of activity, had always been suited to the depiction of corruption and madness. But *The Lady from Shanghai*, probably out of sheer necessity, combines the extremes of this style with the extremes of Hollywood convention; in the process it becomes one of Welles's most hyperkinetic films, and his most misanthropic treatment of American life. In a sense it is a dream about typical movie dreams, and can almost be read as an allegory about Welles's adventures in Hollywood, showing his simultaneous fascination with and nausea over the movie industry. Hiding behind a phony Irish brogue instead of the putty nose he would later adopt, Welles enters the film as a wanderer from another country (the very country from which he entered the American theatre), and finds himself in a world of shark-eat-shark individualism. In such a world, which is ruled by what a shipmate calls an "edge," the good characters are powerless; at best they philosophize while the bad destroy each other.

This doomed world is of course basic to the *film noir*, and to most other pictures by Welles; the only difference is that he has cast himself as a naïve idealist instead of a tyrant, a vaguely working-class Jed Leland instead of a Kane. To some extent he is purveying the same left-wing, macho romanticism which characterizes all movies derived from *The Maltese Falcon*; thus his villains are deformed and effeminate men with an unscrupulous woman, and his hero is a proletarian who is trying to write a novel. (Welles was in fact a major contributor to the misogynistic tone of forties melodrama. In this film, made while his marriage to Hayworth was ending, he gives a rather bitter farewell to his wife and portrays her as a woman "kept" by rich businessmen. Later he suggested *Monsieur Verdoux* to Chaplin, and after *The Lady from Shanghai* he turned to Lady Macbeth.) In many other ways, however, Welles has not been content with the mildly alienated fantasies of the tough-guy mystery, and Columbia's revisions have not disguised his intentions. The ostensible hero of this film claims that he is not a hero, presenting himself instead as a confused and likeable fellow who has fallen into a situation over which he has no control. But just as Welles rarely treats his villains without a certain compassion, so his idealists are meant to evoke an ambiguous response. From the beginning O'Hara knows that Bannister is the "world's greatest criminal," and he blithely comments that Elsa comes from the wickedest cities in the world. He recognizes the evil around him quite easily, and the only way to explain his behavior is to say that he is either more foolish or more complicated than we expect him to be. In the introductory voice-over, he says he is "foolish," and adds, "If I'd been in my right mind . . . But once I'd seen her I was not in my right mind for some time." This early comment on insanity prepares us for the distorted style of the movie, and for Michael's voyage to the Crazy House at the conclusion. At the same time, it gives a casual hint of the irrational temptations that underlie the consciousness of the progressive, presumably rational "Hero."

O'Hara is supposed to have murdered a man in the Spanish Civil War, and in the hiring hall the shipmate remarks that "Black Irish O'Hara" can "hurt a guy" when he's angry (we see him do this later, in the funny but terrifying courtoom brawl). Grisby, Iago-like, taunts O'Hara and seems to look right into his past: "I'm very interested in murders," Grisby says. "How'd you do it? No, let me guess. . . . You did it with your *hands*, didn't you?" O'Hara looks dazed, openly conveying the guilt he can barely conceal throughout the film; in fact one suspects that his occasionally whimsical or baffled attitude comes from a reluctance to acknowledge the full extent of his temptations. When he walks the moonlit streets of Acapulco with Elsa, he passes down a long stone corridor lined with open doorways showing the hovels of the poor. When he walks with Grisby above Acapulco Bay, he glances at a peasant woman hanging out clothes, and then at a lady tourist followed by a gigolo who is saying, "Of *course* you pay me." These events are not lost on O'Hara, who remarks that the brightness of the bay can't hide hunger and guilt. The guilt, however, is perhaps as much his own as the Bannisters'.

On the surface, *The Lady from Shanghai* is the story of a contest between Elsa and Arthur, whose reflections we see in the apocalyptic finale. At a deeper level, however, it concerns O'Hara's highly sexual temptation with the bright, rich world—an "exchange of guilt" formula that had interested Welles from the time he arrived in Hollywood to adapt *Heart of Darkness*. Although he was essentially a humane man, Welles was always aware of the perils of humanism (to say nothing of the perils of California); thus O'Hara descends into a nightmare, coming out of it all resolving to grow older, wiser, and perhaps less complacent. The story has been a comedy, a satiric fantasy, and something of a cautionary tale. For all its imperfections, it manages to retain many of the qualities of Welles's best work.

IV The Expressionist *Macbeth*

The financial failure of *The Lady from Shanghai* meant that Welles was out of work in Hollywood for several years until he managed a deal for *Macbeth*, which became what Charles Eckert has called the most controversial Shakespeare movie of them all—"a touchstone to discriminate the *cinéaste* from the Bardolator."

Although *Macbeth* is a decidedly minor film in the Welles canon, it remains interesting because it is a courageous experiment. Welles had always wanted to bring classics to a popular audience, and for over ten years, on and off, he had expended creative energy on this particular play. In 1936 he had achieved major theatrical success with the Voodoo *Macbeth*; a few years later he performed the play on radio with Agnes Moorehead; when he brought the Mercury Theatre to Hollywood, *Macbeth* was on his list of proposed films; in 1947, his fortune much declined, he staged

Macbeth at the Utah Shakespeare Festival; then at last, under an arrangement with Herbert Yeats of Republic Pictures, he turned the Utah production into a film, taking two and a half weeks for the shooting and spending around $700,000. He said later that he did not set out to make a great movie, only to prove that worthwhile work could be done on a shoestring. (Actually, the film was not so cheap by Republic standards, and if one counts the Utah stage show as production time, it was not quite such a quickie as it seems.) The haste and cost-cutting show through in many ways, and yet the film remains both fitfully exciting and revealing of its director's interest in a radical style.

Every time Welles adapted *Macbeth*, his basic strategy was much the same: he gave it a primitive, exotic setting, and tried to eradicate its Renaissance manners. It was precisely this strategy that drew extravagant praise for the Harlem production in 1936. Here, for example, is part of a review by Brooks Atkinson:

> The witches' scenes from *Macbeth* have always worried the life out of the polite, tragic stage; the grimaces of the hags and the garish make-believe of the flaming cauldron have bred more disenchantment than anything else that Shakespeare wrote. But ship the witches into the rank and fever-stricken jungle echoes, stuff a gleaming naked witch doctor into the cauldron, hold up Negro masks in the baleful light—and there you have a witches' scene that is logical and stunning and a triumph of the theatre art.

Welles's film was made with similar ends in mind, even to the point of having the witches (now Druid priestesses) fashion a sort of Voodoo doll out of Scottish clay (a device that is given some precedent in Holinshed's *Chronicles*). Everything in the production was designed to make the play more primitive, so that what Welles gains in melodramatic intensity, he loses in complexity. Macbeth as Shakespeare conceived him is only partly a heathen of the moors—he is also, quite unhistorically, a creature of the Renaissance court, and his machinations are partly a representation of that court's plottings, intrigues, and sophistication. Shakespeare's tragic hero commits his murderous deeds in a reasonably civilized world, where Scottish noblemen are welcome at King Edward's castle, where Macbeth and his lady give housing to their sovereign, where one must "look like the innocent flower, but be the serpent under it." This counterpoint between a highly developed social code and the temptations of ambition gives the play its richness of characterization, its psychological nuance. Welles, on the other hand, chooses to set *Macbeth* in the heart of darkness, emphasizing not psychology but rather the struggle between a ruthless desire for power and a rudimentary, elemental need to maintain order.

Welles announces this theme in a voice-over narration at the very beginning of the film, immediately after the credits, where Jacques Ibert pays homage to Bernard Herrmann by scoring the "power" theme from *Citizen Kane* under Welles's name. We are shown a Celtic cross on the moors of Scotland, a cross which we are told is "newly arrived." The story takes place, Welles says, in a time "between recorded history and legend," when civilization is literally being created out of the primeval gloom. *Macbeth*, in this version, will be a tale of "plotting against Christian law and order" by "agents of chaos, priests of hell and magic," whose "tools are ambitious men." However different this conception may be from Shakespeare's, one can at least argue that it is appropriate to the magic and savagery of the original.

Obviously, however, Welles's approach results in a very different atmosphere from the one we are given in the play. In Shakespeare, for example, when Duncan and Banquo arrive at Inverness they remark on the look of the place:

DUN: This castle hath a pleasant seat, the air
    Nimbly and sweetly recommends itself
    Unto our gentle senses.
BAN: This guest of summer,
    The temple-haunting marlet, does approve
    By his loved mansionry that heaven's breath
    Smells wooingly here. No jutty, frieze,
    Buttress, nor coign of vantage but this bird
    Hath made his pendant bed and procreant cradle.
    Where they most breed and haunt, I have observed
    The air is delicate. (I.vi.1–9)

As we might expect, Welles cuts a large part of these speeches, and when he puts that marlet on the screen it looks more like a stray bat. In Welles's film, when the king and his entourage enter the gates at Inverness, they have to scatter a milling crowd of dogs and swine. The castle itself seems to have been hewn out of solid rock, its battlements vaguely reminiscent of Stonehenge. The artificial sky overhead is always either black or steel gray, while the courtyard looks damp or mottled with ice. Inside, bedrooms resemble the caves of bears, water runs freely down the sides of a wall, and the banquet hall is more suitable to Beowulf than to the Renaissance.

If the decor of the film is deliberately simple and primitive, so are the characterizations. As several critics have remarked, Welles looks more like Attila the Hun than a courtier (although his battle costume in the last scenes is embarrassingly like the Statue of Liberty), and he goes through the entire picture with a crazed, somnambulistic expression. This interpretation is made possible by the fact that Welles has cut extensive passages from Shakespeare's opening scenes, scenes establishing Macbeth as a trusted soldier whose ambitions gradually take control of his better instincts. As a result of the cutting, Lady Macbeth (played by a somewhat matronly but sexy Jeanette Nolan, in her first screen role) enters the film sooner than she does in the play, and we are given very little sense of her as a malevolent, psychologically interesting influence over her husband. The film simply shows the pair as evil conspirators and plunges immediately into murderous barbarism. Macbeth and his wife embrace on his return from battle in the early part of the film; he has informed her by message of the witches' prophecy, and their agreement is already sealed when they kiss. (Behind them, we can see a hanged man dangling from a gibbet.) The opening scenes at Inverness, far from being courtly, are an Eisensteinian montage which mixes welcome to the king, medieval-looking religious ceremony, and barbaric executions. Against this background, Macbeth's intention to murder looks almost ordinary.

Everywhere, Welles has slashed away lines, speeches, whole scenes. He has interpolated his own dialogue, switched episodes around, and even created an important new character. Among his major deletions are the porter scene (there is nothing in this film to break the unity of atmosphere) and the murder of Banquo by three hired killers. Welles has also removed all vestiges of Shakespeare's chauvinism. In the play, Birnam Wood comes to Dunsinane in the company of an English army, and Malcolm makes an ally of the English king. To his contemporaries, Shakespeare was justifying King James's attempt to unify England and Scotland under the title of Great Britain, and by having Banquo's offspring triumph over Macbeth, he was showing his loyalty to the Scottish succession. In place of these political references, Welles substitutes religious conflict, creating a character named the Holy Father (Alan Napier) and giving him some of the lines that are spoken by Ross in the original.

In addition, Welles greatly simplifies the role of the witches. Macbeth's second conversation with them is stripped of Shakespeare's crazy-comic boiling cauldrons, and the character of Hecate (probably not by Shakespeare, anyway) has been dropped entirely. Instead, Welles plays the whole scene as if in a dark pit, with John Russell's camera executing an incredibly slow, almost invisible tracking movement down and in on the tormented hero's face; the witches are not seen, only heard occasionally, like Macbeth's evil thoughts. Even when we see them at other points in the film, they are less like the old hags of seventeenth-century folklore and more like a Wellesian spook show. In Shakespeare, the witches resemble superstitious village gossips, cackling to each other and occasionally throwing a toad or a sailor's thumb into a pot; in Welles, they are three eerie sentinels, half human, half spirit, lost in romantic fog.

All this manipulation of the play may sound as though Welles were striving for greater realism or historical accuracy, but nothing could be further from the case. *Macbeth* is a completely stylized film. It makes very little attempt to conceal the fact that it was shot on a soundstage, and it is so ahistorical that it gives Lady Macbeth lipstick, forties-style shoulder pads, and a dress with a zipper. The setting is like the primordial landscapes of popular fantasy; in fact, as Joseph McBride has observed, the long shots of horsemen approaching the castle early in the film are probably a reference to *King Kong*. The figure of Macbeth, as Welles conceives him, is almost a mini-Kong himself—a stubby-bearded fellow clad in animal furs, often photographed from below with a wide-angle lens. Against this image, Welles opposes a handsome, relatively fair Macduff (Dan O'Herlihy), who has a blonde wife with Shirley Temple curls (Peggy Webber, who doubles as one of the witches). On every level, the film is built out of simple contrasts which have been emptied of any precise historical reference: for example, the major visual motif of the picture is a contrast between the Celtic cross and the satanic forked staffs of the witches. These two emblems are introduced in the opening scenes, and they run through the movie, until the final battle where the attacking armies are represented as a sea of crosses mounted on long poles. In the last images, as the camera retreats *Kane*-style from Dunsinane, we can see the staffs of the witches rising once more out of the mist, symbols of the brutality and lust for power that seem to be overtaking Malcolm's new rule.

The atmosphere of *Macbeth* is so intensely subjective, so much told from the central character's point of view, that at times the movie has a solipsistic quality; this feeling is intensified by the repeated closeups of Welles (including many deep-focus shots of him with his head in the extreme foreground and the other characters arrayed in the distance) and by the fact that he is entirely alone in his castle when Malcolm's army attacks. Often the film is anti-naturalistic to the point that it strongly resembles theatre. Perhaps because of pressures of time and budget, Welles now and then seems to be filming the Utah stage production exactly in its original form, trying to adapt the camera to stage blocking. Consider, for example, the scene where Macduff is informed of the murder of his wife and children. The setting presumes to be a heath of some kind, though it is quite obviously a studio set. In the distance is a huge stone Celtic cross which represents the forces of "Christian law and order." Macduff, the Holy Father, and Malcolm all have speeches in this scene, and as each character delivers his lines he steps "upstage" near the camera, while the others move in a little arc behind him. Except for a couple of cuts at the beginning, the whole scene is filmed in a long take, with the camera tracking a bit to follow the actors in the foreground. Typical of Welles's style is the composition in depth, with three distinct planes of action: a character in the extreme foreground, someone in the middle distance, and the cross in the background.

This depth of composition is emphasized when at one point Macduff walks back toward a small, fork-shaped tree in the distance, stops with his back to us, and cries, "Hell!" Then he turns and crosses to the camera, walking into a closeup while we track with him to the right. The effect of these histrionics is sometimes awkward, and yet something of Welles's talent shows through. The ordinary filmmaker, given a couple of weeks to transfer a stage production to the screen, would have given the actors simpler movements, cutting back and forth between them with "invisible" editing. Welles, however, puts the camera *into* the stage setting, letting the effect of theatre remain but turning it into an artful little ballet. His camera is active, more like one of the players than like a proscenium, the wide-angle lens giving a sweep to even the slightest movements of the players.

Everywhere the movie is characterized by a deliberate, stagy artificiality, as in the scene where Macbeth climbs a hillock and rages at the top of his voice while nature storms around him: the studio lights are turned up and down to represent lightning, a tinny backstage rumble simulates thunder, and on the "sky" behind Welles we can actually see the shadows cast by the phony trees in the foreground. Welles is quite willing to let these awkward effects stand, however, because he is striving for something much like Raymond Durgnat's description of expressionist cinema in *Films and Feelings.* Durgnat says that expressionism is characterized by "heaviness, symbolism and a sense of *haunting."* It represents a "turning away from naturalism" which is reflected in "the German preference for huge studio sets and elaborate technical effects rather than location photography." In addition, he says:

> The relationships of the characters are all reduced to broad, primal attitudes and urges. The acting concentrates, not on the ebb and flow of people's behavior, but on broad, forceful postures and gestures. Thus the film is reduced to a series of *basic* movements each of which is then emphasized and "accordioned out"—giving the characteristic "heaviness" of German silent films.

By this description, *Macbeth* is arguably the purest example of expressionism in the American cinema. It begins with a few highly effective outdoor shots, and then grows progressively less naturalistic as it goes along. It makes use of all the expressionist urges that were characteristic of Welles's style from the beginning of his career: the deep-focus photography, the distortions of the fish-eye lens, the deep shadows, the snaky movements of the camera; but to these it adds an obviously staged, constructed, symbolic environment, to say nothing of an acting style and a conception of the play that is so "simplified" in outline that it actually conflicts with Shakespeare's language. (Language which is further defaced by post-synchronized sound, a flaw one encounters repeatedly in Welles's low-budget European films. Here a number of scenes were shot in the same fashion as a Hollywood musical number, with players mouthing their own pre-recorded speeches, so that a "perfect" reading of Shakespeare could be obtained throughout the complex long takes. When the studio later objected to the Scottish accents Welles had given his actors, much of the film was re-dubbed, creating unfortunate confusion.)

The results are often striking: the bank of clouds that symbolizes "tomorrow and tomorrow and tomorrow"; the shadow of Macbeth's finger crawling along a stone wall to point at Banquo's ghost; the highly artificial, "Nuremberg" style lighting of Dunsinane at night; the misty, heathenish courtyard with a gray cyclorama spread behind it. But in spite of the effectiveness of parts of the film, Welles's methods are often silly, resistant to the photographic realism of the camera, provoking more laughter than Eisenstein's distortions in *Ivan.* Furthermore, one leaves the movie with a feeling of doubt. Can Welles, who appears in public as a sophisticated man of the world, really believe in this sort of elemental, black/white melodrama, this Manichean duel between witches and the church? Has he not accepted the limitations of expressionist drama, along with its virtues?

The answer to the second question is an obvious yes, but the first is much more difficult to resolve. Welles was too complex a man to hold a naïve belief in "Christian law and order"; but on the other hand, his interpretation of *Macbeth* is quite consistent with a theme we have seen in his other films. He repeatedly dealt with the same issue he presents here: a conflict between the will to power and the need for orderly constraints. *Macbeth* is different from the other Welles films only in the psychological simplicity of its conception and the abstraction of its *mise-en-scène.* As Joseph McBride has observed, it lacks the "necessary naturalistic counterpoint," the "documentary verity" that gives many of Welles's other films their social dimension. And yet the "counterpoint" McBride has mentioned is indicative of a latent tension in Welles's work. In most of his films, the division (I would even say conflict) between tragedy and documentary truth is reflected in the style. At one level we have the newsreel in *Kane* or the drugstore in *The Stranger*—sequences that reveal Welles's concrete awareness of American life and his basically progressive social criticism. At another and perhaps more basic level, we have the obviously constructed, symbolic settings like Xanadu or Dunsinane; the remarkable low-key lighting; the highly orchestrated, bravura movements of the camera in the long takes; the dizzy angles of perspective. At this level, we are dealing almost exclusively with the tragic elements in Welles's stories (hence the purely expressionist style of *Macbeth*), and we have entered a realm which has something in common with the demonic, authoritarian bombast of the tyrant hero.

Clearly Welles was a liberal, and yet one could argue that the "expressionist" side of his artistic character is the *sine qua non* of his style. The contradiction, however, is only apparent. It exists because Welles was ambivalent (emotionally, not morally) about power, will, and the so-called "dark-gods." His expressionist style and his penchant for tragedy enabled him to depict characters and emotions he was fascinated with, but which on the consciously moral and political level he found repugnant. In this sense as in others, the filmed version of *Macbeth* has as much in common with Conrad as with Shakespeare: the hero is caught up by what Kurtz calls "the horror"—the primitive, anti-rational world of power which Malraux has described as "everything in man that longs for the annihilation of man." Perhaps Welles himself once felt similar emotions: having come to Hollywood as one of the most powerful young men in the world, and just at the time when Hitler was terrorizing Europe, he must have had firsthand knowledge of "the horror." Therefore the following Nietzschean speech, which he wrote for the unrealized *Heart of Darkness*, might equally have been spoken by Charles Foster Kane, or even Macbeth:

KURTZ: I'm a great man, Marlow—really great. . . . The meek—you and the rest of the millions—the poor in spirit, I hate you—but I know you for my betters—without knowing why you are except that yours is the Kingdom of Heaven, except that you shall inherit the earth. Don't mistake me, I haven't gone moral on my death bed. I'm above morality. No. I've climbed higher than other men and seen farther. I'm the first absolute dictator. The first complete success. I've known what others try to get. . . . I won the game, but the winner loses too. He's all alone and he goes mad.

In the filmed version of *Macbeth*, as in the earlier script for *Heart of Darkness*, Welles is trying to show that the line between barbarous ambition and a civilized order is very thin, and that constraints are needed to hold the will to power in check. At the same time he is fascinated by tyrants like Macbeth and Kurtz, and he gives their downfall a tragic aura. Thus *Macbeth* ends on the very note that is described in the speech above: the "great man," totally alone and mad in his dark castle, is besieged by the millions.

At one level, therefore, Welles did believe in "Christian law and order." And *Macbeth*, whatever its faults and virtues as an *objet d'art*, gives us an insight into the cautious, pessimistic morality which was the underside of Welles's liberalism.

6

Touch of Evil

After *Macbeth* Welles did not make another film in America for ten years, and the work he finally produced is so crammed with sermons, so charged with visual acrobatics, so peopled with celebrity friends dressed as if for a Halloween party, that it might have degenerated into nothing more than an entertaining curiosity. Instead *Touch of Evil* became the most impressive of his films after *Kane,* the one in which all his strengths—the showman, the political satirist, the obsessed romantic, the moral philosopher, the surrealist—are somehow merged.

Touch of Evil needs to be lifted out of chronological order (Welles made two movies in Europe after *Macbeth*) because it belongs with the American work and follows naturally the issues discussed in the previous chapter. Once again Welles is dealing with a thriller which is charged with social satire; once again his style is so outrageously exaggerated that it affronts critics and movie bosses alike. The *Variety* reviewer, for example, labeled *Touch of Evil* a "confusing, somewhat 'artsy' film" with "so-so prospects"—no doubt throwing Universal executives, who had already lost half a million dollars in the first quarter of 1958, into a panic. During the early months of that year trade papers were filled with rumors of sweeping changes within the studio hierarchy, including reports that the film division would fold altogether in order to save their second arm, Decca records. Corporation president Milton

Rachmill announced in April that henceforth Universal would make "the type of picture we think will make money for us." Because of this anxious conservatism, *Touch of Evil* was never given the publicity or theatrical bookings it deserved, and took many years to develop a cult following.

But then it is remarkable that the film should have been made at Universal in the first place. The studio specialized in Tony Curtis/Piper Laurie romances and the "Tammy" series, trying to survive the popularity of television by producing some of the most inane movies of the decade. Certain directors, notably Douglas Sirk, were able to transform Universal soap operas into triumphs of stylistic innuendo over literary content, and the low-budget horror films of Jack Arnold were well scripted and full of sexual intensity despite the relative banality of their direction. *Touch of Evil*, however, was a far more unorthodox movie than any of these, and one of the pleasures of watching it comes from the knowledge of how much it rebels—not only against the general tone of its studio but against the whole fifties concept of artistic respectability. It deals with racism, police corruption, and sexual confusion in an atmosphere so gorgeously sleazy that the very air is filled with blowing garbage. It dresses Janet Leigh in a tight sweater and surrounds her with a gallery of threatening "cameo" players, setting off gifted character actors like Joseph Calleia, Akim Tamiroff, Dennis Weaver, Gus Schilling, and Ray Collins against "stars" in minor roles: Joseph Cotten as an aged police surgeon; Mercedes McCambridge as a butch member of a hot-rod gang; Zsa Zsa Gabor as a madam. Most important of all, Marlene Dietrich plays an old-fashioned Mexican whore who mutters her lines in a Germanic baritone. (According to Welles, Keenan Wynn was to be cast as "a member of the *Lumpenproletariat*." I've never been able to spot him, but a less well-known actor, John Dierkes, appears in a couple of brief shots.) As a result of all this, *Touch of Evil* becomes a brilliant fusion of pulp art with continental sophistication; it has all the energetic cruddiness of a Sammy Fuller "B" picture, and all the self-consciousness of a New Wave melodrama.

Exactly how such a bizarre project came about is still a matter of conjecture. *Newsweek* reported that Welles had been offered the film as a sop for a character role he had played previously at Universal. Charlton Heston has said he suggested Welles as director after reading the film's unpromising script. There is no reason to doubt Heston's good will and influence, but producer Albert

Zugsmith, who was also responsible for some of the Douglas Sirk films, tells still another story. According to Zugsmith, Welles had come to Universal in the late fifties in need of money to pay tax debts, and Zugsmith cast him in the role of the heavy in *Man in the Shadow* (Jack Arnold, 1957); after this film, Zugsmith says, he and Welles became pals over a bottle of vodka, and Welles offered to direct the "worst" script the producer had to offer—the Paul Monash adaptation of Whit Masterson's novel, *Badge of Evil*.

Probably there is some truth in all these accounts. There is also the likelihood that Welles had manipulated everyone into believing the offer to direct was spontaneous, whereas in fact many of the themes and characterizations in *Touch of Evil* were generated out of roles he had been playing in Hollywood during the previous year. I have not seen Paul Monash's original script, but Welles's version has very little in common with the Masterson novel, which is not set in a bordertown, which does not contain a newlywed couple named Vargas, and which makes Hank Quinlan a secondary character. On the other hand, *Touch of Evil* owes a good deal to the appearances Welles had made recently as an actor. Earlier that year he had given an interesting performance as Will Varner in Martin Ritt's *The Long Hot Summer*, and in *Man in the Shadow* had been cast as a southwestern rancher who exploits Mexicans. He had allowed himself to become typed as a fat racist, probably because the character was both colorful and appropriate to the times: the Supreme Court decision on segregation had occurred only four years before, the civil rights movement was under way, and everyone in Welles's audience had a fresh memory of the incidents at Little Rock High, where National Guardsmen were called in to enforce a law that southern politicians and policemen had been unwilling to support. Thus in *Man in the Shadow*, where he was allowed to rewrite his own scenes, Welles developed an embryonic version of the film he would later direct: a better-than-average Universal melodrama, it tells the story of how a demented, tyrannical bigot frames a liberal sheriff (Jeff Chandler) for murder. It is a more political movie than was usual for the studio, even though it doesn't suggest that the police themselves might be racist and corrupt. *Touch of Evil* went further: Welles announced to the press that the point of his film would be "that the policeman's job is to enforce the law, not to write it."

The action which bears this message takes place during twenty-four hours in or near the hellish Mexican border town of Los

Robles, where an influential construction magnate, Rudy Linnaker, has been blown up by dynamite. We learn almost nothing about Linnaker except that he once "had this town in his pocket" and has left behind a daughter who despises him. The film is concerned not with the crime itself, but with a conflict between Captain Quinlan of the American police (Welles) and Mike Vargas (Heston), a Mexico City narcotics agent who, for reasons that are unclear, is spending part of his honeymoon in Los Robles. (One character speculates that Vargas has come to "clean up" the Mexican side of the border—a casual remark that takes on ironic significance when Vargas wades through a dirty river at the end of the film.) Quinlan, who is a racist, tries to frame a Mexican for the Linnaker murder, and when Vargas uncovers this scheme Quinlan conspires with the Grande family, a gang of outlaws, to frame Vargas's American wife (Leigh) in a sex crime. To cover his involvement in this plot, Quinlan murders the leader of the Grandes (Akim Tamiroff), and then dies at the hands of his old friend Menzies (Calleia), who has been forced by Vargas to recognize the extent of Quinlan's corruption.

If these events are sometimes confusing, it is chiefly because the action occurs on a deliberately hazy, shifting borderland, where the audience is prone to lose their bearings. A time-bomb is planted in Rudy Linnaker's car while he is enjoying Mexican nightlife; the car explodes on the American side, and Quinlan goes in pursuit of the killer, blithely ignoring jurisdictional claims and describing himself as a "tourist." The only Los Robles police we see are a couple of ineffectual traffic cops, and the Grande family seem to control narcotics traffic in both countries. ("Some of us live on this side, some on the other," their leader says.) The chief metaphoric and thematic device in the movie is therefore the crossing of boundaries—boundaries not only between nations but, as will be seen, between law and sexuality. As a result the lines of conflict between two countries and opposing sets of characters become increasingly blurred.

A secondary confusion arose because Universal cut the original release print down to ninety-five minutes, creating an even more elliptical narrative than Welles intended. The recently discovered longer version preserves continuity and gives a slightly better sense of day passing in Los Robles—indeed few movies have been as good as *Touch of Evil* at suggesting time by the quality of light, and none has created the various stages in a day's progress with such unobtrusively poetic results. Not all the additional footage seems necessary, however, and there is good reason to believe that the so-called "complete" film actually contains a sequence shot by another director. When Albert Zugsmith was asked to recall how Welles's version of the movie was changed, he replied as follows:

> They reshot, I think, one scene. They didn't think it was clear enough. . . . I think Harry Keller directed it, and they showed me the rewrite. The rewrite wasn't bad. But it wasn't Orson Welles. . . . It was on the road, I believe. I think Chuck [Heston] was in it. I don't remember the exact portion of it . . . , but some people would say that the style clashes.

Judging from these remarks, it appears likely that Harry Keller shot the awkward moment in the longer version where Heston and Leigh drive to a motel, their car backed by a process screen. Hence the original release is probably a purer, if less coherent, example of Welles's work.

I

Whatever changes Universal made, *Touch of Evil* retains its visual fascination and its moral ironies. André Bazin and Joseph McBride have placed strong emphasis on the film's ethics, pointing out the ways it requires us to make a separation between our emotional involvement with the characters and our intellectual commitment to a liberal thesis. Certainly it is a vivid contrast with other social problem films of the time (Sidney Lumet's *Twelve Angry Men*, for example, which was nominated for several awards in the previous year), forcing us to acknowledge the humanity and intelligence of the racist Quinlan even though we see clearly that he is evil. At the end of the movie we are told that the Mexican shoe clerk is guilty after all: audiences usually take this as the ultimate Wellesian irony, but the longer version of the film has still more complications: during the long scene where Quinlan and his men are interrogating Sanchez, the camera exits from the room for a moment and we can hear a punch and a low moan—the sound of police beating their suspect. Sanchez is an unpleasant fellow, as Vargas himself comments, and is a likely perpetrator of the crime; yet given what we know of Los Robles's third-degree methods, it would be a mistake to accept the truth of his "confession." Quinlan's last order to his associate Menzies is an angry command to "break" Sanchez; therefore at the end of the film nothing has really been proved about Linnaker's murder—the point has not been to discover the culprit, but to disclose tensions between justice and pragmatism, between individual passions and social rules, between psychological guilt and legal responsibility.

Doubtless one reason why Quinlan is so sympathetic is that he is played by Welles, in a performance that compares with his work in *Kane* and *Falstaff*. In some ways Welles's acting here is superior, because he gives the role a density which has rather little to do with what the screenplay tells us directly. When Welles uses the script to "explain" the character, as in Quinlan's drunken recollection of his wife's murder at the hands of a "half-breed," the result is disappointingly feeble; indeed Welles's uneasiness about such an explanation is reflected in the offhand, almost unintelligible way the scene is played. The truly intriguing qualities of Quinlan's character arise more from the eccentricities of his behavior than from literary keys to his motives. Largely through acting skills, Welles makes him both a type and an individual, a redneck cop and a bundle of contradictions. To cite a few complexities: he is a shambling, bloated fellow with a game leg, but he has the strength of an ox, and in the scene where he kills Joe Grande, the impossible agility of a psychopath. His face has the puffy, big-nosed plainness of a lower-class W. C. Fields (rarely has Welles's makeup achieved so believable a distortion of his true looks), and yet is capable of expressing a wide range of emotion—everything from misanthropic cruelty, to honeyed charm, to deep grief. Quinlan is a brute, but like most Wellesian brutes he is also a sentimentalist; he uses his one friend with a reckless egocentricity worthy of Charlie Kane, yet his outward appearance bespeaks an inner torment, and he suffers moments of remorse which are supposed to remind us of Macbeth.

Welles has followed his usual practice of making the villain the most fully developed personality in the film, thus forcing a political melodrama into the realm of personal tragedy. We can sense the relationship between Quinlan and the other Welles protagonists in the first remarks made about him, a comment by District Attorney Adair (Ray Collins): "Old Hank must've been the only one in the county who didn't hear the explosion." This casual reference to age and isolation prepares us for the pathos of the man; he is a brooding, introspective spirit, caught in a fat and decaying body, living out his last days on a two-acre "turkey ranch" as remote as Xanadu. But even in his aloofness he retains influence over the town, and from his arrival on the scene of the Linnaker murder he easily dominates the action, moving slowly and with a whalelike power, mumbling in a weary, pained monologue while various officials bob deferentially around him and shout back and forth.

Behind Quinlan's viciousness there is something childlike, almost Falstaffian. During his inquisition of Sanchez, for example, he sends a lieutenant out for coffee; when the man returns Quinlan looks mournfully down at the cup and asks, "Couldn't you get me some doughnuts? Sweet rolls?" Such moments make even his vices seem endearing. He is humanized in other ways, too: he has a good friend in Menzies, whose life he has saved and who admires him next to idolatry, and we learn that he's never used his power to enrich himself. In one of the most compelling images of the film, we gaze up with him at an oil derrick, the camera rocking hypnotically from side to side as the machinery pumps up and down: "Money. Money." Quinlan whispers in time with the movement, acknowledging the power of greed but remaining awesomely detached and self-righteous. "I'm not a lawyer," he tells Vargas. "All lawyers care about is the law." And from the one lawyer we see— Marsha Linnaker's rich, weasely attorney—we can at least understand his anger.

But the most important device of all in gaining sympathy for Quinlan is Tanya, the Mexican prostitute who knew him in the old days, and who is as important to this movie as "Rosebud" is to *Kane*. Welles's work has always oscillated between misanthropy and sentiment, but these extremes are never more apparent than when Dietrich appears in *Touch of Evil*, creating a melancholy humor and bittersweet calm that throw the rest of the film into high relief. A good many viewers are likely to dismiss her entirely as a simpleminded gimmick more patent than Kane's sled—a celebrity posing as an earthmotherly whore. Nevertheless her very artificiality is part of her meaning, and her scenes create many of the same ambiguities as the references to the hero's childhood in *Kane*. In fact, of the many allusions to the earlier film in *Touch of Evil*, one of the most interesting is in a brief bit of dialogue regarding Tanya which was cut from the original release: Adair remarks to a companion that Tanya will "cook chili" for Quinlan, or maybe "bring out the crystal ball." The comment reminds us that, like the glass toy Kane grasps in his dying moments, Tanya's house is a self-

enclosed realm reminiscent of the past; also like the toy it is both tawdry and beautiful, suggesting at one and the same time Quinlan's self-delusion and his idealism. Quinlan's visits there are a pathetic attempt to return to pre-adolescence, a stage in life that Welles's heroes seem unable to transcend, and as always this stage is associated with a pre-industrial past, when things were not so degraded.

The contrast between Tanya's rooms and the city of Los Robles is emphasized when Quinlan stands in the streets, munching a candy bar, and is captivated by the sound of a pianola, while in the distance Adair bids reluctant farewell to the more modern prostitutes of the Rancho Grande; a moment later Quinlan steps dreamily onto Tanya's veranda, drawn toward her parlor as rubbish blows past an oil derrick behind his head. Inside, however, Tanya's rooms create the same ironies as Kane's snowy paperweight, and the emotional power of the scene rises out of a tension in the *mise-en-scène* between romance and cynicism. Tanya herself is both mother and whore, both mystic and cynical realist, whereas Quinlan seems to have stepped into an ironic childhood. In the two pictures here, for example, he is first shown eating candy the way a child sucks his thumb; he is then seen drowsing amid Victorian bric-a-brac, stuffed animals, and the bullfight memorabilia of Welles's own adolescence, all of it thrown together like a junkshop. The effect of these bordello scenes is both funny and sad, especially in the way the present keeps intruding on the past: Quinlan is so aged and fat that Tanya doesn't recognize him; a television set is perched atop the pianola, and even the music of Henry Mancini is synthetically sweet, perfectly appropriate to a place where everything has become "so old it's new."

But while the imagery creates an impressive poetry, the plot

drives forward on its melodramatic path. In one shot (omitted in the original release) Quinlan sees the figure of Vargas moving ghostlike outside Tanya's windows. Welles's symbolism is clear: Quinlan is compared to the noble bull above his head, prepared for the kill by banderillas; meanwhile Vargas, whose reflection we see in the mirror at the extreme lower left, is compared to the matador's photograph on the wall. In his drunkenness, Quinlan assumes that Vargas is a dream, even though it has become obvious, as Tanya says to him in her fortune-teller's voice, that his "future is all used up." Desperately, he avoids the consequences of his acts until the end of the movie, when he shoots Menzies and tries vainly to wash the blood off his hands.

In contrast to this fascinating villain, Mike Vargas is the nominal hero of the film and the bearer of Welles's own political viewpoint. As Charlton Heston has remarked, he is mainly a "witness" to Quinlan's fall, but he remains an admirable figure, torn between his sense of justice and his love for his wife. Heston gives a remarkably believable, unstereotyped portrayal of a Mexican ("he sure don't talk like one," Quinlan says), and because of his strength and virility he becomes the most satisfying of all the antagonists to Welles's tyrants. For all his virtues, however, Mike Vargas is not supposed to be a spotless bearer of the truth. He is a shade too privileged and stiff, so preoccupied with his role as chief of the "Pan American Narcotics Commission" that he actually puts his wife in danger. There is in fact a twisted comedy in the way his job keeps taking him away from his highly sexual mate, so that most viewers regard him as excessively pure. Even when he confronts Quinlan with a ringing statement of the film's thesis ("a policeman's job is only easy in a police state"), Welles deliberately undercuts the power of his line by the way the scene is framed. Quinlan and Vargas are photographed in a tight closeup, facing one another at either side of the screen; as Vargas speaks the important words, Quinlan turns his head slowly toward the camera, his eyes rolling in wonderfully comic derision, commenting on Vargas's self-importance and rhetoric.

In contrast to Quinlan, who is usually shown from low, portentous angles, Vargas is photographed with wide-angle tracking shots that express the anger, intensity, and sexual frustration behind his cool exterior. But in the later part of the film, his reserve breaks and he is forced to imitate his enemy. When his wife is attacked he becomes "a husband now, not a cop"; when he bashes a hoodlum's head into the glass arch of a jukebox, he echoes the scene where Quinlan forces Joe Grande's head through an identical arch in a transom; when he grabs a thug by the neck and carries him the full length of a bar, he makes us recall the scene where Quinlan strangles Grande by lifting him off the floor; finally, he and Menzies entrap Quinlan with a bugging device, and Vargas confesses (in another shot cut from the original release) that his ethics have been compromised. "I hate this machine," he says, but he continues to work out his revenge, insisting that the unmasking of Quinlan is his duty, just as Quinlan has assumed that the destruction of killers is his own "dirty job."

Despite this experience, Vargas never acquires the tortured soul of a Quinlan or a Menzies, who have a more intimate acquaintance with rattiness, sin, and guilt. Perhaps that is why, in the contrast between the chief antagonists, *Touch of Evil* creates an effect vaguely similar to Graham Greene's thrillers—especially to a novel like *Brighton Rock*, where the author's vision of a moral wasteland is contrasted to the simple "right and wrong" of liberal humanism. Welles even evoked Greene for comparison when he began working on the film: "Greene," he said, "is concerned with the plight of the soul. This is about the plight of the citizen." Moreover, in occasionally transcending legalities to emphasize time and the inevitability of death, *Touch of Evil* echoes another famous crime novelist. At the end of the film, two characters—the D.A.'s man Schwartz (Mort Mills) and the prostitute Tanya—stand looking down at Quinlan's body, which has fallen into the shallows of an oil river. Schwartz, who is something of a cool opportunist, remarks that Quinlan was a "good detective." Tanya adds that he was a "lousy cop," and is given the last, most fundamental comment: "What does it matter what you say about people?" she asks, her words and the imagery matching almost exactly the elegiac sentiments in the last paragraph of Raymond Chandler's *The Big Sleep:*

What did it matter where you lay once you were dead? In a dirty sump or in a marble tower on top of a high hill. You were dead, you were sleeping the big sleep, you were not bothered by things like that. Oil and water were the same as wind and air to you. You just slept the big sleep, not caring about the nastiness of how you died or where you fell.

II

But these references to the "human condition" do not fully account for the power of *Touch of Evil*. At some point one needs to deal with the kinky, beautifully lascivious qualities of the movie—with what I've already called its pulpy surface. And here one inevitably talks more about the female characters than about the males. For if the males are vehicles for moral argument, the females are presented largely as objects of sexual fantasy, and are the deepest reasons for the superstructure of legal forms and rules which are guarded by the police.

Like *Psycho*, a film it probably influenced, *Touch of Evil* uses the sexual charms of Janet Leigh for all they are worth, dressing her in silken undies, making her the victim of assault in a motel. At the other extreme from her, of course, is Dietrich, and together these two embody all the stereotypes of female sexuality in popular art. We don't immediately recognize them as a basis for the film's emotional energy, because Tanya is extraneous to the plot and is brought into conjunction with Suzy Vargas only twice: first when Welles cuts from the attack on Suzy to a brief scene in Tanya's bordello, and then at the conclusion, when Tanya crosses in front of the Vargas auto as Mike and Suzy are embracing— "Mike," Suzy cries, and almost simultaneously Tanya shouts, "Hank!" Once they are set together, their importance as a pair becomes obvious.

Together they are perfect examples of the fair lady/dark lady imagery that runs throughout American literature and Hollywood cinema, an imagery which has always suggested latent tensions of race and social class, as well as the underlying American ambivalence about "wildness" versus domesticity. Hence they are in exact visual contrast: one is blonde and youthfully voluptuous, the other is dark and ageless; one is spunky, rational, and naïve, the other is mysterious and world-weary; one is a wife, the other a

prostitute. Between them they account for the film's radical shifts of mood, its movement between violence and quiet, between the rock-and-roll sounds piped through a motel intercom and the wistful melodies of a whorehouse pianola.

In *Touch of Evil* this vision of womanhood is used in an ironic, or at least highly self-conscious, way because one of the obvious aims of the film is to explore the sexual psychology of race hatred. And here, as in the law/police theme, Welles manages to raise social issues while avoiding the trap of rhetoric; he also takes considerable risks, dealing with the most lurid fantasy material without becoming simply opportunistic. To appreciate his success, one must observe the degree to which the film has been made to represent an unstable borderland—an actual border between the United States and Mexico, a social border between whites and Latins, and an even more volatile psychological border between civilization and the libido. Hence the legal, social, and sexual issues are intertwined, as they are in life, and the conflict between Vargas and Quinlan takes place against a background of sexual relations between the races. Marsha Linnaker has been having an affair with a Mexican shoe clerk; Vargas is insecure about the impression Mexico has made upon his blonde, Philadelphia-born wife; Quinlan says that years previously his own wife was strangled by a "half-breed" (even though he now crosses the border to take refuge with a Mexican prostitute); and in the most disturbing scenes of the film, Suzy Vargas is made to believe she has been raped by the greasy-haired, leather-jacketed Grande gang. The whole movie, to borrow one of Joseph Cotten's lines, is a "mixed party."

Perhaps the central importance of this theme will become more apparent if we examine a *locus classicus,* the opening shot; "It's in all the books," an interviewer once told Charlton Heston, but it is worth further analysis. One of the most spectacular moments in Welles's career, it is also functional, establishing the "world" of the film and revealing the social and sexual tensions which underlie the story.

The shot begins with a closeup of hands setting a time bomb, accompanied by Henry Mancini's bongos and the sound of a prostitute's laughter echoing down half-empty streets. It ends, about two minutes and fifteen seconds later, as Charlton Heston and Janet Leigh kiss and we hear the sound of an explosion. In between, the camera executes a complex and beautiful tracking movement, rushing after the bomber as he plants the explosive in the trunk of a convertible, rising in the sky as a couple enter the car, arching over dark roofs and neon signs as the loaded vehicle drives out to the street, then drifting backward ahead of the car to present gradually the town of Los Robles—a type of sin-city that the better Hollywood thrillers have always created with ease, but which Welles has given a special intensity and visual wit.

Universal foolishly printed credits over part of the shot and scored it with a Mancini theme—one of the relatively few times when music originates from something other than a "natural" dramatic source. Despite the changes, however, Welles's skill is obvious, his vision of Los Robles at once more stylized and more specific than the usual studio expressionism. The extreme wide-angle lens opens out space at either side of the screen, giving forward or backward movement a preternatural effect; cars and figures on the street below are blocked in discernible patterns, crossing at diagonals in the near foreground like players on an ever-expanding stage set. Los Robles does not resemble actual places like Tijuana or Matamoros (it is in fact Venice, California, exploited for its pseudo-Venetian architecture, its aging oil wells, and its general decay), yet it is quite true to the essence of border-towns. On the streets we see strip joints and prostitution, a few ragged Mexican poor, and a couple of men trundling fantastic pushcarts. Most of the crowd is made up of tourists, chiefly American servicemen and workers in hardhats who are pumping oil out of the land. The town seems not to have prospered much from this industry; clearly it exists by selling vice to the Yankees, functioning as a kind of subconscious for northerners, a nightworld just outside their own boundaries where they can enjoy themselves even while they imagine the Mexicans are less civilized. (In fact the most corrupt places in Los Robles—the Rancho Grande and the Ritz Hotel—are owned by a man who keeps insisting he is an "American citizen.")

The contrast between the Mexicans and the Americans is made blatant by the passage of Rudy Linnaker's shiny convertible through the streets, impeded now and then by a traffic cop or a herd of goats. But midway through town the camera descends to street level, allowing the car to pass briefly out of sight while it picks up a walking couple (Heston and Leigh) who are equally out of keeping with the environment. Handsome, well-tailored, they seem oblivious to the grotesque background and the time-bombed car which keeps drifting in and out of proximity. Before the shot is over we discover that they are representatives of the two countries whose borders meet here. Significantly, however, they come not from the bordertowns themselves, but from more prosperous worlds to the north and south. Each is confident and possessed of the right moral sensibilities; but as Suzy Vargas remarks toward the end of the shot, this is the first time they've crossed a border together.

Vargas will later tell his wife that Los Robles "isn't the real Mexico." "All bordertowns bring out the worst in a country," he says; and in the closing section of the film he emphasizes the difference between Suzy's immaculate whiteness and the dark, garbage-laden streets of the town. She has to be taken away from this "filth," he tells Menzies. Her name has to be kept "clean, *clean!*" But there is a closer link than Vargas ever admits between border-towns and inlands, which are all part of the "real" country. The border is a zone where the latent corruption and sexual anxieties of the more respectable territories break through to the surface, just as it is a place where the economic exploitation of one country by another becomes more obvious. The dirty oil fields of Los Robles help produce the comforts of Philadelphia, and racial tension in one town has an effect on the unconscious life of another. Thus, immediately after Vargas tells Suzy that bordertowns bring out the worst in a country, he remarks, "I can just see your mother's face if she saw our honeymoon hotel." Here, and in various other places, Welles implies a symbolic connection between the Vargases' marriage and their presence on the border. They've "crossed over" into a sexual contact which, in Los Robles at least, is usually kept surreptitious. As a result their security and complacency will be disrupted.

At the conclusion of the famous trucking shot that opens the film Welles stresses the potential dangers of the Vargas marriage. The couple have just stepped into America, where they pause briefly and exchange affectionate words. The dark, handsome Mexican takes the voluptuous blonde into his arms, and their kiss is timed exactly with an explosion. The shot ends with a cut to a flaming auto dropping from midair, the camera zooming back slightly to convey the impact of the blast. The time bomb concealed beneath the streetlife of Los Robles therefore becomes not only an exciting way to open the melodrama, but a metaphor for the remaining action: it suggests apocalyptic forces ticking away under the streetlife of the bordertown, forces which have been ignited by the violation of a sexual taboo.

With the explosion of Linnaker's car, the film literally shatters into montage fragments. The plot, too, begins to segment as Vargas runs to the bomb site and his wife returns to the "safety" of their hotel. Welles photographs the aftermath of the explosion in a rapid series of tightly composed images which suggest chaos and bewilderment—little groups of players conversing in the darkness, or single heads isolated on the screen, twisted out of shape by the lens and lighted by flames. (The largest portion of the crowd is seen from the point of view of the dead man, in a low-angle shot that recalls the funeral in *Ambersons*.) During the next few moments, a parallel montage begins to set off the encounter between Vargas and Quinlan against Suzy's journey through the raucous streets of Los Robles, where she immediately begins attracting sinister Mexican males.

From this point on, *Touch of Evil* begins shifting back and forth between the legal plot and the sexual plot, between Vargas's idealistic concern for justice and Suzy's gradual descent into the Los Robles underworld. The two strands are woven together with considerable skill, producing a fine sense of emotional contrast and thematic interplay. In fact, *Touch of Evil* seems as much concerned with crossing narrative and visual paths as with crossing borders. In the opening shot two couples move along the same streets, their routes intersecting but never quite touching; during the early scenes, the Grandes trail Mike and Suzy everywhere they walk; at the close, Mike follows Quinlan and Menzies with a tape recorder, moving along a roughly parallel course through a maze of oil wells, barely missing discovery until the denouement. In *Kane* and *Ambersons* the cutting and the elaborate superimpositions had been

designed to give the audience a
sense of *now* versus *then*, but in
Touch of Evil the same devices
make us feel the importance of
here versus *there*. The dark,
cosmic humor of the film derives from a pattern of coincidence and juxtaposition within
a limited time and space, the
Vargases' narrow escape from an
explosion being the first in a

series of near misses: Linnaker's car almost blows up in Mexico;
Quinlan almost succeeds in planting evidence against Sanchez;
Vargas enters his hotel room a moment too late, just after his wife
has been spotlighted by the Grandes; later, he drives right past
Suzy while her screams blend into street noises. Gradually, these
accidents take on the same fatalistic tone one finds in *Kane*.

When Welles isn't using mobile, deep-focus shots to emphasize
fateful mishaps and dual lines of action, he is editing so as to
underline the ironies of his double plot. The most obvious example
of this technique is in a cheesecake shot of Janet Leigh in her
lingerie—where male viewers are given a chance to indulge their
voyeurism. Leigh reclines on the motel bed, her hair down to her
shoulders, her body covered with luminescent silk. But the glam-
our and seductiveness of the image is disrupted when we cut to the
frustrated Heston at the other end of the telephone line—a deep-
focus composition with the pinched face of a blind woman in the
foreground.

We've already seen a similar device in *The Lady from Shanghai*,
but here it foreshadows many other, less ostentatious conjunc-

tions—as when the door of
the Mirador Motel slams on
Suzy's "rape" just as another
door opens in the police hall
of records. And when Welles
uses a slow dissolve in the
manner of his transitions in
Kane, he gives the device a
new richness and power,
stressing thematic comparisons and contrasts. Consider

three images, which take us from one place to another. Here the dissolve is not meant to indicate "time passing," as it usually does, but rather the parallel between Menzies and Suzy, both of them abandoned by a person they love. In the first shot Menzies watches Quinlan and Joe Grande walking away toward a bar, their figures reflected in the window glass. Next, a dissolve shows a desert landscape superimposed on Menzies's face; as this new picture comes into view Suzy raises a window shade, her image appearing at the opposite side of the screen. The desert is revealed as a reflection in Suzy's window, and has been superimposed over both faces. Four separate images have been blended into a single transition, and the effect is heightened further by the soundtrack: in the first shot we hear distant churchbells slowly ringing through the streets, but as Suzy and the desert appear, the bells give way to noisy rock and roll from the motel speakers.

The opening scene of the film has initiated this elaborate parallelism, and has also made the audience an anxious witness to a total picture of which no single character is aware. As soon as Linnaker and his female companion are blown up, we become aware of an impending sexual chaos which threatens to destroy the Vargas couple. At the very moment when Mike debates civil rights with Quinlan, Suzy is being led by "Pancho" (as she calls him) to meet Uncle Joe Grande, whose brother has recently been sent to prison by the Pan American Narcot-

ics Commission. In a scene charged with equal portions of menace and grotesque comedy, Grande threatens Suzy with a gun, pokes a phallic cigar in her face, and then licks his lips as she exits—this last gesture a foreshadowing of the images which will precede and follow her "rape"; "Pancho" will lick his lips before attacking her, and

she will wake from a drugged sleep to find Uncle Joe's head above her face, his dead tongue sticking out of his mouth.

Throughout the early episodes Suzy remains self-confident, her anger edged with a castrating wit. She tells "Pancho" that her husband, a "great big official," is going to knock out his teeth, and when Uncle Joe pokes his cigar at her like Edward G. Robinson she accuses him of playing "Little Caesar." When she returns to her "honeymoon hotel" and finds the Grande boys shining the beams of flashlights through her windows, she responds by throwing a lightbulb at them. Nevertheless the symbolic sexual violence mounts in intensity, and is suggested even in her absence. For example, when a Grande killer throws acid at Vargas the chemical misses its target, sending a poster of Zita (Joi Lansing) up in smoke; the burning poster is an echo of the explosion we have just seen (as Stephen Heath remarks in his commentary on the film, Zita has literally become a "sizzling stripper"), but it is also an indication of what lies in store for Suzy; both she and Zita are bosomy blondes, and we have just heard Quinlan describe them both as "Janes."

During the remainder of the film, Mike and Suzy Vargas live through the worst traumas of racist imaginings, becoming victims of Quinlan's bigotry, Uncle Joe's revenge, and the Grande boys' desire to do violence against Gringo womanhood. Irony is piled upon irony as the many parallels in the plot give the characters a kind of displaced relationship, like figures in a dream. Suzy, the white progressive who has married into the Mexico City bourgeoisie, spends her honeymoon being assaulted by a Los Robles dope pusher (as Stephen Heath has noted, he is played by an actor named Valentine de *Vargas*). Drugged and transported back to town, she is spread out on a seedy hotel bed, where she becomes a surrogate for Quinlan's wife, enabling him to act out the capture

and strangulation of her "killer." Quinlan himself, of course, becomes one of the murderers he hates. Mike Vargas, like Quinlan before him, has to suffer the debasement of his wife by a "mixture" of races (even sexes), and Suzy has to endure a nightmare that might have come straight from her mother's darkest fears. Nearly all the boundaries between good and evil threaten to dissolve, although the film's moral argument remains clear.

The expressionist camerawork during the motel "rape" suggests an even crueler irony: Suzy has been forced to confront her own private demons. We see the beginning of the rape from the woman's point of view, as a succession of hideous, glassy-eyed faces stare down into the camera and whisper to one another. Suzy's WASPish innocence is set off against the vivid stereotypes of a racist and sado-masochist imagination, as if the film were deliberately calling up fears that a respectable marriage between the "good" characters cannot repress. But if the camera represents Suzy it also represents the audience, who are made to experience the nightmare from Suzy's point of view. Here Welles is taking one of his most considerable risks, because despite the fact that the film is made with a progressive attitude, it violates the decorum of nearly all the liberal thesis films of the late fifties. It forces us, through action with a hallucinatory power that almost parodies Griffith, to imagine a white woman being raped by a Mexican thug. Indeed the fish-eye closeup of "Pancho," who gazes into the camera and flicks his tongue like a serpent, has a strong though probably unconscious resemblance to the closeups of Battling Burroughs and Chen Huan in *Broken Blossoms:* in both cases the aggressive male looks directly into the lens, his features distorted wildly; in both cases we cut to a fearful, golden-haired girl who cringes on a bed, in a position rather like Susan Alexander kneeling before Kane. Welles has even changed Leigh out of her seductive underclothes and dressed her in an innocent little girl's smock, the least provocative costume she wears in the movie.

Disturbing as the scene is, there are elements of relief from the tension; audiences usually chuckle uncomfortably when they recognize Mercedes McCambridge as one of the attackers, and the anti-naturalistic exaggeration of the faces results in a peculiar kind of comedy. Stephen Heath has said that the whole scene is "laughably fantastic," as if it were being viewed from the perspective of the neurotic motel "night man" (Dennis Weaver); nevertheless the farcically extreme style is part of the ironic intent, and Welles is far from letting us escape to a safe distance. If we are going to accept the film's vision of a racist society, we first have to rid ourselves of liberal complacencies. Just as we are made to acknowledge the humanity of the bigot Quinlan, so we are made to experience the sexual terror which lies behind his racism. At this juncture the film's eroticism takes on interesting connections with its political argument, requiring us to distinguish between feelings and judgments, never allowing us to fall prey to an easy righteousness. In fact the ironies of the film are so powerful that it is difficult to accept a return to simple good/bad distinctions at the end. Suzy is supposed to be "clean" (she hasn't even been drugged or raped, we are told), while the dead Quinlan floats in an oily lake; but the acceptable limits of melodrama have been stretched so far that nearly all the characters have been touched by the evil of Los Robles. Hence the final embrace between Mike and Suzy looks out of place, too obviously a Hollywood device. "It's all over," Mike says, and they speed off to safer territories. Their convertible, however, looks very like the one Rudy Linnaker was driving at the beginning of the movie. It may be that the parallel between the two cars is a simple case of studio economics, especially since Universal had a merchandising agreement with Chrysler Corporation; but then again, economics sometimes reveals latent meanings that no one consciously intended. Whatever the cause, *Touch of Evil* never quite restores its world to a comfortable equilibrium.

III

These many dramatic and psychological ironies result in a kind of maliciousness, a satiric vertigo which is as much a matter of style as of script. Indeed the vertigo becomes a literal physical property of the film, and what is most difficult to convey in either static images or words is the continual movement of the scenery. Russell Metty and John Russell have provided Welles with the technical expertise he needs, and Welles in turn has never seemed more conscious of the peculiar dramatic rhythms created by the wide-angle lens; for example, the closing sequence of Vargas pursuing Quinlan and Menzies, which is shot from every possible angle, makes no spatial sense whatever: it is unified by a dizzying, nearly unceasing swirl, the camera and actors turning, rising, falling in the night air as if they were swept along by a maelstrom.

The melodramatic plot also gives Welles plenty of excuse to photograph action; this is easily his most brutal picture, filled with references to explosion and obliteration that are entirely true to the atmosphere of the South in the late fifties. Frequently the camera "acts" along with Vargas, as in the scene where he is informed that Suzy has been charged with murder: an extremely large telephoto closeup is at the left of the screen, the right side of Vargas's face masked by the back of Schwartz's head; "Murder!" Vargas says, and the camera zooms in, the screen going black and then opening on a wide-angle traveling shot which moves down the corridors of the Los Robles jail; Vargas's shadowy figure is in the foreground, the camera slowing as he runs down the hallway, fusing two separate mechanical operations and the blocking of an actor into one continuous movement. Earlier, when Vargas lifts one of the Grandes by the scruff of the neck and carries him down to the end of a bar, the camera makes the audience directly experience the force of his rage: it tracks suddenly back and away from the two figures, as if sucked by a vacuum; for a moment Vargas is lost in the smoky gloom of the nightclub, but before the camera movement has ended he starts forward out of the haze, carrying his victim toward the lens with superhuman energy, the whole room scattering in front of him.

What is still more interesting about *Touch of Evil* is the way it frequently explodes the notion that style ought to imitate "content," creating an "organic" vision. For even while the story and the fetishistic imagery work to stimulate the audience's involvement, the sheer eccentricity of Welles's technique and casting often demands to be appreciated for its own sake, as the "author's" artifice. If, as Andrew Sarris has said, *Touch of Evil* is a "movie that makes you rethink what a movie should be," that is not simply because it has a complicated morality and psychology; what is most impres-

sive is the way it uses a fairly unorthodox form to convey its meanings. Except in his preference for location shooting, flat lighting in the daylight exteriors, and music which usually emanates from realistic sources, Welles has ignored most of the rules of movie naturalism. His idea is to make a world that is both grittily accurate and surreal, characters that are both plausible and weirdly out of key, a film that maintains a level of serious intent even while it calls attention to itself as a grotesque joke.

In his previous American work Welles had shot at least a few scenes with a quiet, eye-level camera, but here virtually everything is photographed from radical angles, with a lens so extreme it resembles a funhouse mirror. This extremism often becomes deliberately silly, particularly in the acting, which is sometimes exaggerated to the point of hysteria. One could cite many examples— Uncle Joe and his boys dashing through the early morning streets and squabbling like the Three Stooges (Joe loses his wig, which is turned into a comic prop); Menzies expressing grief over Quinlan by dropping his head flat down on a table and speaking in operatic despair; the hot-rod gang twitching around, snapping their fingers

like the chorus in a television skit. But the most obvious instance is Dennis Weaver, whose performance as the crazy Mirador Motel nightclerk begs to be contrasted with Tony Perkins in *Psycho*. Consider, for example, the scene from the Hitchcock film where Perkins first encounters Janet

Leigh. The shot has an extraordinary number of things in common with *Touch of Evil*. Leigh is featured in both movies, and the basic plot situations are much the same; Welles's camera operator, John Russell, had become Hitchcock's photographer, and Robert Clatworthy helped design the sets for both pictures. But the differences are equally striking, so obvious as to become perfect indexes to the contrasting temperaments of the directors. Hitchcock wants to create an atmosphere of normality which will be disrupted by horror; as a result Perkins behaves like a shy, slightly nervous young man, and his encounter with Leigh is shot in classic symmetry. There are, to be sure, many subtleties in the image—for example Leigh is repeatedly photographed against mirrors; nevertheless the acting and photography seem perfectly natural, never obtrusively "dramatic."

In contrast is the way Welles and Dennis Weaver have chosen to stage a roughly equivalent scene: Weaver's behavior is pushed as far out of proportion as Welles's wide-angle photography. He has been allowed to use a whining accent rather like the one he made famous as Chester in *Gunsmoke*, but Welles told him "never let anyone get in front of you." As a result he plays nearly every scene on a diagonal with the other actors, usually dashing about in quickstep, his head jerking from side to side in what Manny Farber once described as "spastic woodpecker effects." In this scene, he expresses his fear of women by clinging to a wall, and in a few moments, unable to control his panic, he will dash outside and speak to Leigh through an open window. Later, when he is confronted with the Grandes, he has an attack of heebie-jeebies, and he screams in terror when he discovers a leftover joint in Leigh's abandoned room. Outside the motel after the rape scene, we see him in the most stylized pose of all, embracing a windblown tree and babbling like a Shakespearian fool.

Nearly all the performances in *Touch of Evil* are done in this broad, roughly expressionist form; only Heston and Leigh use the techniques of "normal" movie acting, partly because they are meant to be out of place, like unwilling witnesses who have chanced into a crazy house. (Even they, however, are extravagant presences—Heston cast against type as a Mexican and Leigh made so sexy in her role as a sweet wife that she becomes unreal.) Elsewhere the film offers a heyday for character actors, who have been allowed to defy the notion that they should not emote but simply "be." As we have seen in earlier chapters, Welles is almost alone among American moviemakers in his love for a theatrical intensity, a "hot" style of acting which has more in common with Griffith or Eisenstein than with the tradition of talking pictures. Consequently he relishes the opportunity to people his film with an assortment of international types in offbeat costumes, players who scurry about making broad gestures and yelling their lines. He has a keen sense of how these various bodies react against one another within the frame of an individual shot, and he tries for an exaggerated, highly choreographed effect that produces a surreal comedy.

The best example of the technique is the pivotal episode in Sanchez's apartment, which is photographed in three elaborate shots, the action broken only when Vargas exits to cross the street and telephone Suzy. Throughout, the actors are in continual motion, the camera drifting in and out of three rooms. Sanchez's apartment sometimes threatens to become as crowded as the shipboard room in *A Night at the Opera*, yet the camera movement remains fairly unobtrusive, the compositions changing in size with the fluidity of invisible editing. The wide-angle lens enables Welles to take in a broad playing area, even while it distorts space and gives the feeling of giant heads swimming in and out of closeup. Everywhere the lighting is relatively simple, lacking the romantic chiaroscuro of the ordinary studio film: it originates from a few sources, usually from a low angle which casts the shadows of the actors on the ceiling and gives their faces sallow, demonic looks.

Welles and Heston dominate the space in the room, their movements slow and powerful, their voices held to a low key until they confront one another in a tight composition and Vargas shouts, "You framed that boy, Captain! *Framed* him!" Heston is ramrod stiff, his head cocked slightly, his chin jutting out, trying to remain a neutral "observer"; Quinlan, on the other hand, is weary: he moves with great effort ("I'm an old man," he tells Marsha Linnaker) except when he suddenly deals Sanchez a vicious slap. One of these two kingly presences usually occupies a central spot in the frame, surrounded by tinier figures who rush nervously about, speaking at a higher volume. Sanchez (Victor Millan) is angry and distraught, wringing his hands and virtually jumping in frustration; Menzies is wiry and puppylike, moving urgently at Quinlan's suggestion; Uncle Joe Grande is a chubby, quick little figure who tries to stay out of the picture, always talking with his hands. Now and then one of the smaller players will insert himself between Quinlan and Vargas, gesticulating wildly, as in the image shown on page 170.

The actors bite at one another's lines, their speeches contrasting in pitch and tone so that they take on a strangely rhythmic, musical counterpoint. For example, the dialogue which accompanies the picture (see below) goes as follows:

SANCHEZ *(gazing wide-eyed at Quinlan, who avoids his stare)*: Where did you find this?

QUINLAN *(pained and weary, in a low voice)*: Right here in your love nest.

SANCHEZ *(shrill)*: Where?

MENZIES *(offscreen, shouting in a child's derisive sing-song)*: Right where you had it stashed, of course!

SANCHEZ *(more shrill)*: What are you trying to do?

QUINLAN *(low, tired)*: We're trying to strap you to the electric chair.

MENZIES *(at the top of his voice)*: We don't like it when innocent people are blown to jelly in our town!

QUINLAN *(quiet, almost dreamy)*: Yes, an old lady on Main Street last night picked up a shoe . . . The shoe had a foot in it . . .

SANCHEZ *(pleads with Vargas in Spanish, his voice whining)*.

VARGAS *(overlapping Sanchez)*: You'll have to stop him yourself . . .

QUINLAN *(to himself, overlapping Sanchez)*: He can talk Hindu for all I care.

The scene is vividly overwrought, like a bad dream. It even generates an obsessive, darkly comic *motif* involving shoes and feet: Sanchez works in a shoe shop ("the best shoe clerk that store ever had"), and has met Marsha Linnaker in the course of his job ("I've been at her feet ever since"); he is charged with a crime that left an old lady's foot and shoe on Main Street, and the evidence has been planted in an empty shoebox in his bathroom. Jokes like this give the film part of its crazy energy, a delirium which is intensified by the distorting lens, the continual movement of actors and camera, the array of strange facial types, the fantastic interplay of voices.

It is remarkable that Welles was able to give life to expressionist theatrics so late in the fifties, when a great many movies were being shot on location, and when dramatists like Chayefsky and Inge were being praised for their "realism." In a sense, *Touch of Evil* is the last flowering of artful crime

melodrama from the forties, a style that survives in our own day only in the form of nostalgic imitations. Debased as the world of the film is, the actors seem driven by beautiful demons, and the shadowy rooms and buildings retain a certain voluptuous romanticism. (Welles may be the only German Expressionist who is also authentically attracted to Latin cultures, and who is able to appropriate their "feel" to his style.) In another sense, however, Welles is breaking with the *film noir*, making Los Robles too decadent by far, extending the artifice of the film to such a degree that it becomes a new style, a foreshadowing of depressed, bombed out landscapes of movies like *The French Connection*. Perhaps because he has never taken thrillers very seriously, he exaggerates everything to the point of absurdity. He uses "cameo" players to break the surface of the illusion, and he enters the film as "our local police celebrity," having Joseph Cotten look offscreen to announce his arrival. Even when he is creating his strongest emotional effects—as in the scenes with Tanya—he loads the movie with references to himself and Dietrich. It doesn't matter that both characters wear makeup; in fact Dietrich's black hair and dark skin are meant to resemble one of those fantastic costumes she wore in the von Sternberg musical numbers, and Welles has photographed her in soft focus amid wreaths of smoke, in the manner of her earlier films. She keeps her German accent, and when she looks at Welles and remarks, "You're a mess, honey," the players separate from the fiction altogether.

In other ways, too, the bordello scenes are self-referential; for example, Tanya says that her business has become so diversified that "we show movies." Such moments might be regarded as indulgence (to an extent they are), but the film's surface is so exciting that the director has earned them. Hence the scenes work at two levels, as if Welles were speaking out of his own age and thwarted idealism, acknowledging that the film is an expression of his own psychology and his desire to make fun of Hollywood. He sets the audience in an odd relation to the events, making us aware of the spectacle even while we are immersed in it. When Dietrich walks off into the darkness of the Los Robles oil fields at the end of the movie, turning back to the audience to say, "Adios," we are asked to regard everything as a magic trick, a form of play. It has been only a movie, Dietrich suggests, and she has noted that it doesn't matter what you say about people. But the very casualness of the gesture tends to heighten the wit, the satiric insight, and the imaginative power that have gone before.

7

The Gypsy

Ironically, Welles's departure from Hollywood and his fitful, hectic career on the continent were precipitated by the stage musical entitled *Around the World*. At the end of that show's financially beleaguered two-month run, Welles had gone $350,000 in debt and had been forced to commit himself to three movies (*The Lady from Shanghai, The Third Man,* and *The Prince of Foxes*). The Internal Revenue Service refused to allow him to deduct his losses, and for the time being no important offers came from U.S. movie producers. Partly to raise extra money, partly out of his growing alienation from America, Welles sought out work in Europe, living in France, Spain, and England, filming in locales from Morocco to Yugoslavia. In 1973, looking back over his career in the States, he gave a Spanish interviewer a bitter summary of the facts: "During the twenty years that I worked in or was associated with Hollywood, only eight times did they permit me to utilize the tools of my trade. Only once was my own final cut of a film the one that premiered, and except for the Shakespearian experiment only twice was I allowed to give my opinion in the selection of my subject matter."

Welles's subsequent European movies were financed largely from his own pocket, and are a testimony to his resourcefulness and ingenuity. In the main, he had to work under worse conditions than celebrated "art" directors like Bergman, Fellini, or Wertmüller. Frequently his backers were in financial difficulties themselves, or caused problems similar to the old Hollywood moguls. For example, when the original producers of *Othello* went broke, Welles spent four years of intermittent work on the film, stopping now and again to act in *The Black Rose* (Henry Hathaway, 1950), until he could gain enough money to continue; it is said he even "borrowed" equipment from the Hathaway movie to shoot parts of *Othello* in North Africa. In September 1961, Filmosa S.A., the production company for *Mr. Arkadin (Confidential Report)*, charged Welles with a breach of contract because they were infuriated with the almost chaotic form of the film's narrative. Welles seemed in trouble until about a year later, when Michael and Alexander Salkind, two energetic entrepreneurs without much money, approached him to play a bit part in *Taras Bulba*; "Are you kidding?" Welles is reported to have said, "I *am* Taras Bulba!" He refused their offer, but persuaded them to arrange financing for *The Trial*, a project he had been contemplating for fifteen years. The Salkinds raised $1,300,000 and hired a well-known international cast, only to find themselves in financial and legal troubles midway through the picture. Just as the production was about to fall apart, Welles conceived a way to shoot scenes in an empty rail station across from his Paris hotel, avoiding higher production costs and speeding up the work; in addition to writing, directing, and acting in the film, he also worked as second cameraman, editor, and dubber, completing everything within the original budget and a week ahead of schedule.

A good deal has been written about whether Welles's move to Europe was a self-destructive act. The decision, however, was not entirely voluntary. Possibly Welles could have managed his career so as to become a prosperous character actor, occasionally able to find theatrical or film work in America; on the other hand, the 1942–43 campaign against him at RKO had made a lasting impression in Hollywood. He was typed as unreliable, extravagant, and poor box office; his style was outrageous and idiosyncratic, and except for *The Stranger* he had never made a picture which audiences could watch with an easy, passive involvement. He had therefore gone where he could find the best chances of making films, and in the next twenty years he was able to direct two distinguished adaptations of Shakespeare and two other films that are completely in his own style. In between these projects Welles acted in a variety of other people's movies, usually bad ones, but sometimes he was able to influence lesser directors in interesting ways.

The Prince of Foxes (1949), for example, is ostensibly directed by Henry King, but parts of it bear the marks of Welles's style as vividly as the Robert Stevenson *Jane Eyre* had done in the early forties.

As an actor in these films, Welles was usually a "character" in the worst sense, and was frequently miscast by directors who did not understand his essential immobility or the fact that he was best when he played a vulnerable or childish figure of power. He appears to have chosen roles casually, out of immediate need for cash, but he does fine work as Cardinal Wolsey in Zinneman's *A Man for All Seasons* and as Bresnavitch in Huston's *The Kremlin Letter;* he also makes a nice parody of himself as Le Chiffre in *Casino Royale*, and a clever imitation of Alex Korda in *The V.I.P.'s.* On the other hand, he seems to me hollow and disappointing as Father Mapple in *Moby Dick;* and as General Dreedle, the pure monster of *Catch-22*, he is too much like a movie celebrity playing a cameo. Of all these roles, the one for which he is most famous— Harry Lime, the villain in the Carol Reed/Graham Greene production of *The Third Man*—is also the best. Here Welles not only steals the film but makes its success possible, largely because of the strategically clever places he appears, the beautifully sinister compositions in which he is photographed, and the use he makes of his own spoiled-baby face. Actually he has little to do, but has been given the title role and is the subject of everyone else's conversations; therefore his brief, tantalizing appearances are supercharged, bringing just the right amount of Luciferian dramatics to the bleak, downtrodden backgrounds of postwar Vienna. There is in fact a good deal of the young Charles Foster Kane in his performance. Joseph Cotten plays a man not unlike Jed Leland, and the famous scene between him and Welles atop an empty ferris wheel has many of the same psychological dynamics as the newsroom encounters in *Kane*. Welles's "touch" is everywhere apparent in that scene: poised high above an amusement park reminiscent of the one in *The Lady from Shanghai*, he looks down on the people below and calls them "dots," an echo of Franz Kindler in *The Stranger*. A moment later he makes a bravura exit speech, disarmingly confessing his ruthlessness with a joke that Graham Greene has said Welles invented: "In Italy for thirty years under the Borgias they had warfare, terror, murder, bloodshed. But they produced Michelangelo, Leonardo da Vinci, and the Renaissance. In Switzerland they had brotherly love. They had 500 years of democracy and peace. And what did that produce? The cuckoo clock." (A few years later Welles told André Bazin that while he was responsible for putting the gag in the film, he had in fact stolen it from "an old Hungarian play.")

The films Welles directed during these years were infrequent and sometimes technically crude, but as the *auteur* of *Chimes at Midnight* he can hardly be said to have lost his powers. In retrospect, his best work was done inside the studios, where he was able to take full advantage of an elaborate machinery for creating fantasy and a series of technicians who could bring his ideas to life. The bitterest irony of his career is that he had the potential of bringing so much imagination to an inert studio technology, but was regarded as too romantically individualistic to be supported by the American system. Hence in the European films one sees all the old ingenuity, but nothing to compare with the sumptuous illusionism in *The Lady from Shanghai* or the viscerally effective camera movement of *Touch of Evil*. The dazzle is gone, if not the intelligence.

Of course in some ways the European films are more satisfying than the American ones. They are free not only of Hollywood formulas but of the aestheticism and tendentiousness of the worst of the avant-garde. Frequently they gain in interest and charm because of the contradictory impulses in Welles's personality—his old-fashioned love of the "classics," plus his youthful instinct for motion picture spectacle. And yet something is always missing, and not only at the superficial level of technical resources. The deepest problem with these films as a group—a problem barely suggested in serious criticism of Welles's work—is that their director has lost touch with the social and cultural environment he knows best. It is true that Welles was always an internationalist, and, as Andrew Sarris says, he "imposed a European temperament on the American cinema"; nevertheless his best work was always grounded in contemporary American mores, politics, and popular myth. His purely European films, by contrast, are set in nonspecific dreamworlds, or they are adaptations of "classics" from an earlier age. Hence what Welles gains in seriousness, he loses in vitality and the shock of recognition. To a large degree, his talents were those of the satirist and the moralist, the sort of artist who needs to maintain a constant relation with manners and national types, or else his humor goes flat and his anger becomes merely rhetorical. Outside America, Welles quite simply lost the roots of his art, his work growing more introspective and generalized. He retained his brilliantly surreal imagery and his gift for narrative, but except in *Mr. Arkadin* all the manic satire and punch of the Hollywood films was lost. Splendidly constructed and mature in outlook as some of these later pictures may be, they have never been able to generate the sheer excitement of the more populist American work.

The complexity of such issues will, I hope, become evident in subsequent chapters, but for now let us consider Welles's first two European films, which illustrate some of his difficulties. Of the two, I have chosen to give more space to *Mr. Arkadin*; relatively little has been said about it, and for all its obvious flaws it seems to me the more interesting.

I *Othello*

Of all Welles's films *Othello* is the one for which the adjective "beautiful" is most justified. Given the series of pictures he made before and after it—*The Lady from Shanghai, Macbeth, Mr. Arkadin, Touch of Evil*—it seems almost classically proportioned. The story is lucid, the acting naturalistic, the visual compositions relatively simple and pleasing to the eye. Welles's characteristic lens distortions and long takes have given way to a crisp, somewhat muted photographic expressionism, and, despite the occasionally garbled and poorly dubbed soundtrack, most of Shakespeare's verses are audible. It is odd that so many writers—including Welles himself—should have described the film as if it were another exercise in operatic bravura.

Of course *Othello* is hardly anti-Wellesian. It has all the *Stimmung* of his earlier films and takes several liberties with its source. When costumes failed to arrive on the first day of shooting, Welles decided to stage the attempted murder of Cassio in a hastily improvised steam bath, where Roderigo could be dressed in a towel and the air filled with atmospheric mist. The brawl between Cassio, Roderigo, and Montano took place in a foul Arabian cistern; actor Micheál MacLiammóir was impressed by "the macabre sorcery of the place, which I suddenly realize would probably, in the hands of any modern director but Orson, be utilized for mystery-farce starring Abbott and Costello." The film also has Welles's typical plot structure, beginning with the funeral of Othello and Desdemona, then showing how their deaths came about, then bringing the story full circle by returning to the funeral. A heavy sense of determinism hangs over everything, and Iago's reference to the "net that shall enmesh them all" provides a key to the visual design. Welles told MacLiammóir that the costumes should be "Carpaccio," which meant "very short belted jackets, undershirt pulled in puffs through apertures in sleeves laced with ribbons and leather thongs, long

hose, and laced boots. Females also laced, bunched, puffed, sashed and ribboned." At every opportunity, Welles has used images of confinement. Near the beginning, for example, he shows Iago being dragged through the streets of Cyprus in a dog-collar and chains; a subjective camera sees a guard forcing him (us) into a tiny iron cage, which is then hoisted above a jeering crowd. Welles repeatedly situates the same cage at corners of the action during the story proper, reminding the audience of Iago's fate but also of the way the other characters are imprisoned by their passions. The players are often separated by gates or pillars, and are photographed amid bar-like shadows or masses of ship's rigging. Even the bedchamber of Othello and Desdemona is designed like a cell, with a heavy metal hatch at the top through which Lodovico and several others gaze down at the doomed Moor. (As an example of the technique, note the closeup of Iago shown here.)

The film's style is never self-effacing—indeed, as I hope to show, the camera tends to serve as a substitute for acting. On the whole, however, Welles appears to have decided upon a reasonably calm effect, trying to hold his natural tendency to exaggeration in check so that *Othello* would be different from the ill-fated *Macbeth*. In the advertisements he told audiences, "None of our settings were built in the studio. They are all real." Technically speaking it was a false claim, since some of the castle interiors were designed by Alexandre Trauner (art director for *Les Enfants du Paradis*, among others), and a few brief shots were made in an Italian studio. Nevertheless Welles was being essentially truthful; he had gone to the other extreme from the stylized, rudimentary settings of the studio-bound *Macbeth*, choosing real locales in the Mediterranean. The early scenes with Desdemona and her father were photographed in Venice itself, principally at the Doge's palace, where Welles emphasized the sensuous, twilit canals and the cultivated, almost fussy Renaissance decoration. Othello's military domain was "played" by a sixteenth-century Portuguese fortress near the North African seacoast town of Mogodor, its mammoth and impressively functional walls surrounded by rocky beaches and baked in a hot, clean sunlight. The one artificial element here—and it is a good one—is the ship used to carry Othello home from the wars; its shadow is seen bobbing up and down against the walls of the fort like a surreal toy.

The opposition between the two worlds of the play is emphasized throughout: in Venice the male players dress in gilded robes and pillowy hats, whereas in the African setting they wear simple tights and light armor; in Venice flocks of pigeons scatter from the façades of crowded buildings, while in Africa the sky is filled with clouds and wheeling gulls. As usual, Welles was supremely aware of how the environment expresses character, and used his locations to show that Desdemona and Othello are as different socially as they are physically. She is a fair Botticellian girl (nicely played by the Canadian actress Suzanne Cloutier) whose father has kept her sheltered in an ultra-civilized society; he, on the other hand, is a dark, nobly direct man of action, a slightly aging veteran of "big wars that make ambition proud." Each is partly a stranger to the other, this strangeness accounting for their mutual attraction as well as their vulnerability to Iago's manipulation. Welles's settings disclose these facts, even while they give the film a sense of natural air and architectural solidity: indeed a few of the exteriors at Mogodor have such a windblown naturalness that they conflict with the artful rhetoric of the language.

In *Macbeth* the acting had been as artificial and exaggerated as the stage sets. In *Othello* the approach is just the opposite. Welles restrained several of the performances, and sought out a psychologically "realistic" explanation for Iago's villainy. Here again the interpretation runs slightly counter to Shakespeare, but in still another direction from the method Welles adopted in *Macbeth*. In the play Iago gives reasons for wanting to undo the Moor, but they are afterthoughts, rationales for a motiveless malignity. "I am not what I am," he says, suggesting that he dissembles even in the moments when he seems to lay bare his soul. He has a protean quality, an evil so resistant to categorization that ultimately it must be confronted for its own sake. Welles, however, has made "I am not what I am" imply schizophrenia, and has given the character the kind of subconscious motives that were cheerfully ignored in *Macbeth*. He decided, in fact, that Iago suffers from impotence. The malady is never specified in the actual performance, which retains many of Shakespeare's ambiguities, but it becomes a "subtext" for Micheál MacLiammóir's behavior. Welles and MacLiammóir agreed to dispense with all traces of "Mephistophelian villainy," and most of Iago's soliloquies—those fascinatingly repellent visions of a truly evil mind—have been cut from the play. There must be no "passion" in Iago, MacLiammóir wrote in his diary, "no conscious villainy." On the outside, Iago would be a kind of "businessman dealing in destruction with neatness," but to avoid monotony in the peformance, MacLiammóir would always remember "the underlying sickness of mind, the immemorial hatred of life, the secret isolation of impotence under the soldier's muscles." Because of his affliction, Iago would develop a hatred of life, a hostility directed as much against Desdemona as against Othello.

The resulting portrait is an interesting one, accomplished with a high degree of technical skill and underplayed to the point that Iago becomes more of a revolting presence than a passionately vivid force. The "soldier's muscles" are nowhere in evidence, MacLiammóir conveying instead a smallish, sometimes rather epicene quality; his hooded eyes and the thin beard along the line of his chin give his face a mask-like appearance, as if he were utterly detached from his inner pain. But despite the fact that MacLiammóir himself contributed to this conception of the role, he was left with vague dissatisfactions about movie "realism":

> Only thing that depresses me [he wrote] is the camera's inability—
> or unwillingness—to cope with the great organ-stop speeches, the
> "Othello's occupation's gone" one, for example, which [Welles] de-
> livers so far with caution as if afraid of shattering the sound-track.
> . . . this feeling accompanied by a longing to see Orson himself, or
> Gielgud, or Hilton [Edwards], or any fine speaker of verse stand up
> on an honest wooden stage and let us have the stuff from the wild
> lungs and in the manner intended. This I know Orson tried in his
> film *Macbeth* and people didn't like it, a verdict possibly shared
> by the camera, so there maybe is the answer.

Welles seems to have decided, somewhat uncharacteristically, that the movies were too intimate, too "modern" for Shakespeare's lavish stage conventions; he reasoned that the camera's tendency to exaggerate an actor's behavior must be taken into account—

good enough logic for most movies, but inimical to Welles's temperament and his best work. Therefore MacLiammóir was right when he sensed something lacking in Welles's performance, which is not so muffled as MacLiammóir's own, but which does have a controlled, even guarded quality in the "organ-stop" moments. Welles is at his best when Othello is trying to repress his feelings, or in the relatively quiet, determined mood just before the murder of Desdemona; the "put out the light, and then put out the light" speech, for example, is superbly delivered and genuinely moving. On the other hand, Welles as actor never captures Othello's splendidly romantic self-confidence and hubris, his ability to charm Desdemona and the audience with tales of his exploits. The great speech to the Duke explaining how he won the girl ("She wished she had not heard it; yet she wished/That heaven had made her such a man") is delivered in a near monotone and photographed in soft focus, and Othello's calm put-down of an angry mob—"Keep up your bright swords, for the dew will rust them"—is virtually tossed away. In the later mad scenes, where we ought to see the easy destruction of all this strength, Welles is equally restrained. Othello's epileptic seizure, the foaming at the mouth described by Iago in Shakespeare's text, is nowhere to be found. The attack on Desdemona before a group of senators from Venice is delivered with a fine visual shock, but the camera literally becomes Othello: Desdemona walks into a closeup, looking into the lens as if it were a character, and Welles's hand suddenly enters from the left to slap her face. Because he is so intent on visual effect, Welles has left Othello's violence, his incoherent reference to "goats and monkeys," to a disembodied offscreen presence.

"When I love thee not," Shakespeare's Othello tells Desdemona, "Chaos is come again." But Welles's performance, for all its intelligence, lacks chaos and true terror. When Othello falls into a passionate swoon beside the ocean, a series of dissolves and tilted camera angles are used to convey his agony. What is needed, however, is a naked intensity comparable to Agnes Moorehead's depiction of Fanny in *The Magnificent Ambersons*, or perhaps comparable to Welles's own terrifying destructiveness in the bedroom scene in *Kane*. The film wants a dramatic climax in which camerawork does not substitute for human behavior. In the murder scene, for example, Welles is reminiscent of Charles Foster Kane *after* the tantrum in Susan's room; when he approaches Desdemona's bed, he does so with the somnambulistic stiffness of Kane going past the mirrors in Xanadu. But nowhere have we seen a sufficient release of the character's festering madness, a moment of crisis when everything breaks loose, leaving him with this stunned, almost resigned determination. Instead Welles has chosen to make the camera project emotions that speakers of verse were meant to deliver.

Few would deny that the film succeeds admirably at the visual level. The punishment of Iago—"The time, the place, the torture; O! Enforce it!"—has become an image instead of a mere allusion. The shots of a funeral cortege bearing Othello and Desdemona equal the stylized, heroic montages in any one of Eisenstein's late films, and they have a far greater sense of dramatic movement—as when Desdemona's body is drawn past the camera at a slow descending angle, her death become a chilling fact. The scenes showing Iago's destruction of Othello's confidence in Desdemona are photographed in two brilliantly contrasting moods: first a long walk in sunlight across the castle battlements, where, in the uninterrupted flow of a single shot, we see Othello disintegrating before our eyes. Next, a more fully edited sequence inside the castle, the bright air and the steady fortifications replaced with a descent down a serpentine stairway into a narrow, murky tower. Iago remarks, "I see this has a little dashed your spirits," and Othello, whose face is seen in a small distorting mirror, hastily replies, "Not a jot! Not a jot!" The Moor has become psychologically unmanned, a fact which is emphasized when, during their discussion, Iago helps him remove his steel armor and his huge cloak. Even in these expressive scenes, however, Welles has held back a little. When Othello murmurs the line, "and yet how nature, erring from itself," we see his face in a small "Carpaccio" mirror; but the hideous distortion of his features comes from a mirror, a naturalistic source, not from the extreme lenses Welles would later use in *Touch of Evil*. *Othello* therefore breaks fewer rules of plausibility and coherence, and for all its beauty it is a less fundamentally daring film.

When Welles employs unorthodox techniques here, he does so in subtle ways, chiefly at the level of editing. For example, as Noel Burch has observed, he created a "deliberately jerky" rhythm for the film by introducing a slightly illogical ellipsis between some of the cuts. To cite one instance: in the scene where Desdemona pleads with Othello on behalf of Cassio ("Good love, call him back"), we see Welles and Suzanne Cloutier in a large two-shot, the camera located behind Cloutier's shoulder. "Shall I deny you? No," Welles says, and Cloutier exits, moving out of the frame to the right. Instantly we cut to a reverse shot of her, seen from Welles's point of view as she walks away; but she seems nearly a block down the street, having moved much farther than the ordinary time between a shot/reverse shot combination would allow. Most viewers who are aware of such things will notice that this slight discontinuity is typical of the later sections of the film, where Welles gives the feeling that Othello's world is falling apart.

Like most of Welles's films, *Othello* is fascinating to watch; it is even more remarkable when one considers that its high degree of formal control was obtained under the poorest of circumstances, with Welles periodically suspending production while he sought money to continue. The beauty and rigor of his style indicate that he had seized upon a clear, forceful conception from the very beginning, and was able to maintain a vision of the whole despite numerous delays and hardships. What results is a distinguished film, but not a great one. Jack Jorgens, in his fine essay on Welles's imagery, has said that *Othello* should be regarded as "poetry of the screen," which in many cases it certainly is. The early reviewers who claimed that the film was arbitrary and excessively stylish were incorrect; if *Othello* ultimately falls short of greatness—and I believe it does—it fails not as visual poetry but as drama. Welles, MacLiammóir, and Cloutier are physically effective in the leading roles, but they lack fire. Welles has been a bit too wary of his own romantic inclinations, and never generates an acting intensity equal to the drama itself. He is the last director one would accuse of taking an "academic" approach to Shakespeare, but in this case, for all the liberties he has taken with the source, he comes very close to a well-made, passionless gloss, a Gothicism in good taste.

II *Mr. Arkadin*

Welles's next project makes an interesting contrast. It is even less effective as human drama, but the difference in subject matter liberates him in many ways. From a respectful adaptation of a classic, he moves to a burlesque of his own earlier work, producing a more chaotic but more truly adventurous film.

Mr. Arkadin opens with a legend printed in typescript capitals: "A certain great and powerful king once asked a poet, 'What can I give you of all that I have?' He wisely replied, 'Anything, sir, except your secret.'" The legend fades away to reveal a single-engined aircraft winging across a clear sky. Welles's voice announces that "on December twenty-fifth, an airplane was discovered off the coast of Barcelona. It was flying empty. Investigation of this case reached into the highest circles and was responsible for the fall of at least one European government. This picture is a fictionalized account of the events leading up to the murder, and the appearance last Christmas morning of the empty plane." The credits then appear (according to Peter Cowie, Welles intended to show them against a background of frightened bats flying in all directions, which would have been a perfect metaphor for the rest of the movie), and at their conclusion we see a young man (Robert Arden) crossing a snowy plaza in Zurich. He walks up an old stairway while the camera tracks back and away from him.

Upstairs in an attic filled with decaying mementos of Nazi Germany, the young man encounters a consumptive Jew named Jacob Zouk (Akim Tamiroff). Identifying himself as Guy Van Stratten, he tries desperately to make Zouk come away with him; first he babbles about a man named Arkadin and then pauses to explain what has happened in recent months. The movie now becomes a series of flashbacks within a flashback, narrated by Van Stratten's offscreen voice.

It seems Van Stratten is an uprooted American who has been earning a living smuggling cigarettes in the European black market. One evening in Naples, he saw the police shoot down a man on the docks and heard the dying man whisper the name "Arkadin." Hoping to use this flimsy evidence for blackmail, he sought out the fabulously wealthy armaments king, Gregory Arkadin (Welles), at a castle in Spain. To gain an audience, he romanced the man's daughter, Raina (Paola Mori, Welles's third wife). Although Van Stratten's blackmail attempt was a clumsy failure, Arkadin gave him a job anyway, devising a fantastic quest that would keep him as far as possible from the girl. Claiming to remember nothing before 1927, when he found himself on a street in Zurich with two hundred thousand Swiss francs in his pocket, Arkadin proposed an investigation into his own past, a search that would ultimately take Van Stratten to three continents. But Van Stratten was more competent and determined than Arkadin realized. Gradually he uncovered the tycoon's secret history as a white slaver in Poland. When Arkadin learned of this discovery, he set about murdering everyone who had known him in the old days, and as a last stroke he planned to kill Van Stratten himself.

At this point we return to the loft in Zurich, where Van Stratten tells Zouk that between them they are the only ones left who know Arkadin's true identity. There follows a series of darkly comic attempts to hide Zouk from his potential killer; the attempts fail, and Zouk is knifed. Realizing that he will be the next to die, Van Stratten flies to Arkadin's daughter in Spain, where he plans to tell her the whole story. By luck he arrives ahead of his pursuer. Believing that Raina has been told the truth, Arkadin commits suicide by leaping from his private plane. Van Stratten is left standing in a Barcelona airport, as penniless as he was at the beginning of his adventure, while Raina drives disconsolately back to town.

I have summarized these events in some detail because *Mr. Arkadin* is an unusually frenetic and bewildering movie, its labyrinthine plot further obscured by awkward dubbing of the actors' voices, its continuity disturbed by Welles's blithe refusal to obey the laws of classical editing. In many ways it is a deliberately confusing, low-budget version of *Citizen Kane* and *The Third Man:* against the background of postwar Europe, a search is conducted for the secret of a rich man's life; we begin with a mysterious death and return to the same point, having discovered, through flashbacks, a tycoon's crimes and the identity he has tried to keep hidden. But Arkadin as a character is profoundly uninteresting. He lacks the psychological fascination, the contradictory personality, the historical validity of a Charles Foster Kane or a Harry Lime. In outward form his story follows the same "tragic" curve as theirs, yet the scenes of his discovery and death are emotionally empty. He seems hardly more than a bombastic figure in costume who gives Welles an excuse for the rest of the movie, and if one admires *Mr. Arkadin* as I do, then one looks for its power in something other than conventionally realistic characterizations or even a plausible story. In its own way it is as unorthodox a film as the Welles *Macbeth*, but it is photographed in real places and takes itself less seriously. An effective but often tongue-in-cheek variation on the psychological thriller, it reduces the *Kane* plot almost to the level of archetypes, becoming a sort of hallucinatory fable; even more interestingly, it links its quasi-Freudian theme to a vision of society, a satiric portrait of the world after the war, showing a flotsam of international gypsies living in the ruins of Western civilization.

One of the impressions *Arkadin* registers most strongly is of a dizzying montage, a kaleidoscope of exotic settings and grotesque cameo performances. Slightly ahead of his former associate Mike Todd, Welles created his own perverse *Around the World*, a mad journey which leads us past a series of well-known performers: Misha Auer as a flea trainer in a Copenhagen circus; Peter Van Eyck as a fastidious black marketeer in Tangiers; Michael Redgrave as a homosexual fence in Amsterdam; Suzanne Flon as a Polish aristocrat reduced to working as a *vendeuse* in Paris; Katina Paxinou as the poker-playing wife of a government official in Mexico; and, most impressive of them all, Tamiroff in the role of the former dope-peddler Jacob Zouk. According to the script, all these characters were once in Poland, most of them having been witnesses to Arkadin's criminal life there in the twenties. When they appear, however, they produce a crazy-quilt of accents in wildly different settings, and Welles has created a still more disjointed effect by occasionally dubbing his own voice in place of theirs.

The protagonist of the film, Van Stratten, is an American ne'er-do-well who speaks movie gangsterese, his dialogue filled with mispronunciations like "aminesia." His investigation into Arkadin's past introduces him to nearly a dozen minor characters, whose faces keep looming like apparitions in a nightmare. Consider, for example, the small gallery reproduced on p. 186. In barely concealed mythical terms, Van Stratten is a knight trying to rescue a fair lady from an ogre in a castle, and these faces are the monsters he encounters on his quest. In an equally displaced but more clinical sense, the faces are cathected objects, symptoms of sexual anxiety, and the movie plays indirectly on the theme of a "confidential report" into the unconscious. Van Stratten is a young man caught up in a contest of masculinity with the powerful Arkadin; the two are rivals for power and for the love of Raina, and by working his way back to a sort of primal scene Van Stratten hopes to replace the kingly older man. "Maybe I'll be an Arkadin some day," he says, in one of the many places where a parallel between him and his opponent is stressed. Hence one of the most powerful shots in the movie—actually it appears twice—is designed to suggest a journey into a psychic heart of darkness: Van Stratten crosses a snowy street in Zurich, walking up a stairwell while the camera retreats backward into a dark corridor, as if into a cave or a womb. The lighted archway of the stairs becomes a tiny square of light at the corner of the screen, resembling the old-fashioned iris which closes the snow scene in *Ambersons*, except that here the entire image shrinks into sinister blackness.

Of course the "primal scene" turns out to be rather banal, the

movie generating its most impressive effects at the level of imagery rather than content. As with most of his other films, Welles uses Freudian expressionism in a teasing, half-conscious way, constructing the story as a devious, defensive puzzle, a conjuring trick which plays upon certain anxieties without naming them directly. The characters are so broadly drawn that they suggest various symbolic possibilities: Arkadin and Van Stratten resemble the antagonists in a "family drama," and because one is American while the other is Slavic, they also vaguely connote figures in a Cold War allegory. In the most general sense, they are like the scorpion and the frog in the little fable Arkadin tells his party guests. One day, the story goes, a scorpion persuaded a frog to carry him across a river; midway across, the scorpion stung the frog and drowned himself. When the dying frog complained that "there is no logic in this," the scorpion replied, "I know . . . it's my character." The moral, as in Welles's other films, seems to be that life is determined by irrational principles. In this case the frog manages to survive, but toward the end his antagonist tells him, "You didn't know know what you were asking for."

Like any assault on the surface logic and reasonableness of things, *Mr. Arkadin* generates a nervous humor. It resembles *The Lady from Shanghai* in being narrated by a frog-witted, sometimes dumbfounded protagonist whose reactions height-

en the zany unreality of events. Nearly always there is a tension between Van Stratten's clipped, world-weary commentary—which falls squarely in the tradition of the private-eye story—and the surreal quality of the imagery. For example when Van Stratten remarks that Arkadin spied on him and Raina, we see the couple cycling through a forest in Spain; Welles then cuts to the shot reproduced here, showing one of the tycoon's well-dressed minions peeping out from behind a slender birch tree. Much of the film is played in this farcical style, as if the world were making Van Stratten the victim of a practical joke. He bumps into a stuffed armadillo in Trebisch's junk shop, where the proprietor keeps trying to sell him a rusted "teleoscope"; he is peeped at through a magnifying glass by a flea-training "Professor," who tells him (in the voice of Orson Welles), "after twenty-thousand years murder is a business that is still in the hands of amateurs"; he is quizzed by a silly German policeman (Gert Frobe), who shouts in broken English, "It's very interesting to learn how you that knew!" In the midst of his desperate attempt to escape Arkadin, he is blackmailed by Zouk, who insists on being given a hot goose liver for Christmas dinner; at that very moment, a cuckoo clock chimes on the wall behind Van Stratten's head.

Some of the richest humor is reserved for the darkest, most pathetic scenes, especially the ones involving Van Stratten's attempts to hide Jacob Zouk from Arkadin. Zouk is a ravaged figure intended to remind us of the persecution of the Jews, but he is also a good example of what Shakespeare would call "unaccommodated man." Despite his age and illness, there is a human comedy in his wish to be left alone, his intransigent, donkey-like refusal to heed warnings of danger. When he is literally dragged from his bed, he grabs his blanket and starts a tug of war. After he and Van Stratten have inched halfway across the room, Zouk shouts, "But this ain't the way out, Mister!" Van Stratten then whirls around in the other direction and hauls away at the blanket, while Zouk scoops up his clothes with a free arm. Outside, Van Stratten suddenly realizes that Arkadin is about to appear, so he opens one of the apartment house doors and shoves the pantless old man into the presence of a lady in curlers. The lady takes money and agrees to hide Zouk under the covers of her bed. Meanwhile, a band outside in the street begins playing "Silent Night":

ZOUK: I ain't heard that piece in fourteen years.
LADY: Get into bed!
ZOUK: That's something else I ain't heard in fourteen years.

Later, Van Stratten rents a hotel room as a hiding place, and Zouk turns into a sadistic tease: "If I dunt get dat goose liver I'm going *ho-ome*," he sings. Sitting primly on a chair at the far end of the room, he chuckles, "I'll give you an hour," his laughter turning into a diseased cough. As a clown he is all the more effective because he is in such pain, and he causes Arkadin to laugh hollowly. "What are you laughing at?" Zouk asks. "Old age," Arkadin says.

In the scenes with Tamiroff, *Mr. Arkadin* has a more truly Shakespearian feeling than *Othello*, generating a bigger-than-life energy and moving effortlessly between broad comedy and images of death. But these scenes are relatively quiet compared to the rest of the movie, which seems bent on creating a restless confusion. The interviews with Arkadin's former associates are interspersed with montages showing Van Stratten talking with people in streets all over the West; Paul Misraki's Slavonic dance music plays on the soundtrack, and each shot ends with a rapid pan to the right, the camera stopping in a new country. The world spins out of control, and when the film pauses to allow exchanges of dialogue we are kept in a state of vertigo. In one scene aboard Gregory Arkadin's yacht, where we are given important information about his politics and his past, the entire set rocks wildly to simulate a storm at sea. The camera rolls at different angles from the cabin, and the two players, who are dressed gaudily for a shipboard party, literally stumble from one corner to another.

This frenzy is reflected also in the editing. *Mr. Arkadin* is the most fragmented of Welles's movies, every scene split into multiple facets, with a variety of camera setups for even the most static dialogue. And if Welles gives us little time to orient ourselves geographically, he uses the editing to confuse us in regard to local space. A typically baffling moment occurs in Mexico, where Van Stratten has tracked down the mysterious Sophie, who knew Arkadin in Poland. We see Van Stratten walking across a sunlit, white-columned parapet above the sea; suddenly, inexplicably, a telephone rings and Van Stratten steps behind a column to answer it. Arkadin's voice comes from the other end of the line, and we assume that the call is long distance. But Arkadin is playing a joke and has come to Mexico himself. When Van Stratten hangs up the phone, he walks to the edge of the parapet and sees his employer down below, seated in a portico and surrounded by an entourage of servants and bathing beauties. We cut back and forth between the two men as they speak to one another, and then, as Van Stratten leaves the parapet, we shift to a wide-angle, over-the-shoulder view photographed from behind the tycoon; Van Stratten can be seen approaching down a huge stairway, from a distance so vast that the two men could hardly have held the converation we have just seen.

Welles repeatedly uses lens distortions, radical camera angles, and shifting perspectives to give the film a jagged, out-of-kilter appearance. In one of the early scenes between Arkadin and Van Stratten, the two men are shown concluding their business arrangement as they drink brandy in Arkadin's curiously spartan office. Welles makes the spatial relationship between the two actors slightly confusing by shooting their heads from several angles and by cutting from one extreme viewpoint to another—for example he shows Van Stratten as a small, distant figure in a wide-angle shot from over Arkadin's shoulder, then cuts to a tilted, middle-distance closeup of Arkadin. Sometimes the eyelines of the players—the directions of their glances in respective closeups—do not match; in one exchange Van Stratten looks almost directly at the camera while Arkadin stares a bit off to the left.

The soundtrack is also disorienting, often creating a split between words and actions. Undoubtedly because of revisions and the chaotic, make-do circumstance of the production, Welles has created an unusual blend of offscreen narration and dramatic speech, using Van Stratten's voice to summarize events during scenes which appear to have been shot and edited for dialogue.

The technique resembles the sort of speeded-up, economical exposition one frequently encounters in novels, where scraps of dialogue are blended with an authorial voice. But the effect is more complicated because we are given a "present tense" of actions and sounds at the same time that we are being told about them in the past—a simultaneity and multiplicity of detail that is possible only in the movies. (In some cases the visual track has been blended with at least three separate levels of sound, in a difficult and meticulous process of recording.) Now and then Van Stratten's narration is redundant of the visual presentation, as happens frequently in a film like Wilder's *Sunset Boulevard,* but more often the commentary is modified by what we see. The narrative is both extremely dense with information and extremely rapid, the action usually standing in ironic relation to the voice-over. The audience must therefore strain to catch the auditory implications, even while they struggle to orient themselves in space.

Welles's bewildering, shattered style owes something to the conditions under which the film was made, but it is also appropriate to one of his underlying themes—the decay and metamorphosis of Europe after the war. *Mr. Arkadin* fits rather nicely Raphael Pividal's description of modernist works by Artaud and Beckett: these two, Pividal says, are witnesses to "a world that has fallen apart, to a mankind that is homeless and terrorized by a faceless master." The delirium in these works, Pividal writes, "cannot be reduced to the simple Oedipal triangle," chiefly because it has more to do with the State than with the family. In the same way, *Mr. Arkadin's* disequilibrium and its sexually obsessive imagery are combined with references to a more specifically historical madness—for example, in the poster advertising Milly as a "striptease atomique"—and if Gregory Arkadin is partly a Freudian bogey-man and partly a lonely child, he is also a political figure, whose fall brings down a government.

The political theme is treated so lightly that at first glance it is difficult to see. At one point Van Stratten reads aloud a written report he has received from one of Arkadin's rival financiers: "In another epoch this man might have sacked Rome or been hanged as a pirate," the report says. "Today we must accept him for what he is—a phemomenom [*sic*] of crisis and dissolution. " This is as close as the film comes to passing explicit judgment on Arkadin, who is never believable as a historical type anyway; he has as much in common with oriental despots as with modern capitalists, and can be regarded as a symptom of the times only in the most abstract, symbolic sense. Nevertheless there was some factual basis for the character. In 1951 Welles had toured Italy and occupied Germany, recording his impressions for the British journal *The Fortnightly*; among the people he met was a tycoon he describes with cinematic relish:

Herr Fritz Mandel, presently of Buenos Aires, smoked in silence. Everybody watched him do this, waiting for the oracle to speak again. Finally it did. "If the Russians should march west today—they'd cross the Rhine tomorrow."

In Germany you were almost blinded by the glare of that political reality. Still blinking from it, you'd journeyed down from Berlin, and, in a break in the journey, you'd come upon this real, live munitions maker. How it brought back melodramas of a pre-war pacifist past! There he was, with a flower in his button-hole, an Argentine girl at his side, a respectful ring of Swiss bankers all about him, smoking an Havana cigar on the banks of an Italian lake. The eyes in the sharply drawn, solid-looking head are set in a questing expression, . . . like the vacuum in the heart of a tornado.

"Wait and see what happens this time," Mandel again. He took the cigar from its holder, carefully extinguished it, and sat back, staring across the Lake of Como at nothing. An Italian prince roared by in a speedboat towing a mannequin on water-skis. Some Americans at the next table were wondering if their 'plane reservations for home were soon enough. . . .

What was he thinking about? It's no use saying it doesn't matter. It matters that he makes the guns and tanks for Perón. Perón matters. And Mandel's thinking, wrong as it may be, is somehow related to the queerly changing shape of our world. He still had the cigar in his mouth and seemed to be looking for a match . . . maybe he was brooding over the third war.

Brooding is the word, not gloating. Zaharoff used to gloat. But then those were different wars. . . . I gave him a box of matches. He thanked me and we smiled at each other. After all, why not? We've got something in common: We've both been married in our time to movie stars.

The passage suggests *Mr. Arkadin* in its surreal mixture of nationalities. Swiss bankers, an Argentine girl, Havana cigars, and American tourists are blended together with an Italian prince and an English model on water skis. At the center of it all is an outlandish figure left over from pre-war melodramas, a man devoid of personality but interesting nonetheless because of the power he represents. Gregory Arkadin is a more colorful fellow than this, but he has the same anachronistic flavor, the same empty expression

"like the vacuum in the heart of a tornado," the same brooding attitude. Welles seems to have regarded him as a savage, a total pretender to a radically changing European civilization and therefore a slightly different type from charmers like Kurtz, Kane, and Harry Lime. Like them he is a sort of hollow man, but he is seen chiefly in costume: first in a grand cape at a masked ball, then wearing a yachtsman's suit and dark glasses, then dressed as Santa Claus. Even when he appears in normal dress he wears a false face, his closeups showing the artificial lines of an ill-fitting wig and spirit gum holding his beard in place. We never see what lies behind the disguise, a fact which Welles emphasizes in the credits, where the camera zooms in on Arkadin as he is about to remove one of his masks, and then fades to black. Arkadin is so blank, so rudimentary, that he seems to exist outside time. We are told that he profited from the Russians, from Mussolini, and from the Nazis, and that he is presently interested in air bases the Americans plan to build in Portugal; thus he seems to exist outside nations as well. He is almost a mythical creature, a man of animal ruthlessness and lusty appetite, made quirky by his obsessive love for his daughter. (Like the ancient pharaohs, he is isolated to the point of becoming incestuous.) "It's as if he had come from some wild area to settle an old European civilization," Welles told André Bazin. "He's the Hun, the Goth . . . who succeeds in conquering Rome."

But he is not the only invader. Over against this modern Attila, this doomed Gothic rebel, Welles has placed a more believable type—Van Stratten, the minor savage. Robert Arden's portrayal of the role has been criticized, but his slightly brutish, hirsute looks and his repellent air are exactly in keeping with the barbarian theme; in fact, quite by accident, he bears an uncanny resemblance to a young, athletic Richard Nixon. Certainly he is very different from the urbane narrator of Welles's novel, *Mr. Arkadin* (which Welles has disowned as an unauthorized translation), and he gives a stronger impression of an interloper from another culture. Welles concentrates mainly on the way the two men clash with their surroundings: we see Arkadin's plane whizzing over the turrets of his castle, while Van Stratten and Raina dodge in and out of a herd of goats on the streets of San Tirso. Later that evening, a procession of mendicants makes its way through the village, the huge peaked hoods of medieval costumes creating a disturbingly surreal spectacle; suddenly Van Stratten steps in between the line of monks, his

flowered sportshirt flashing out in the dark. Joining Milly and a group of tourists beside the road, he explains that the men in the procession are paying for their sins. Milly (who has posed in kinky black leather underwear in an advertisement for her striptease act) takes one look at the parade and cocks an eyebrow: "They must be awfully sorry," she says.

Inside Arkadin's castle, which has been photographed against stormclouds that make it resemble El Greco's painting of Toledo, the same cultural ironies are visible everywhere. Van Stratten wanders about amid papier-maché reminders of Spanish art (designed by Welles), all of them jumbled together into a nightmarish costume party. In his bewilderment, he asks a guest about the strange masked faces that fill the room:

THE MARQUIS OF WADLEIGH: All these people are supposed to represent the painters. Now some of us have come as the visions and monsters . . . Goya.

VAN STRATTEN: Who?

WADLEIGH: You know, Goya.

VAN STRATTEN (assuming he is being introduced to a passerby): Glad to meet you.

Arkadin, of course, is not so dense nor quite so alien as Van Stratten, although his desire for moral respectability in the eyes of his daughter leads to his suicide. He is what Raina calls an "expensive gypsy," a new, sometimes rather pitiable barbarian. He seems most human when he is seen through the eyes of Sophie (Katina Paxinou), a maternal, world-weary female rather like Tanya in *Touch of Evil*; she carries one of his old photographs and remembers him from another age, when he called himself Athabadzie. It is Sophie who gives the film its only moment of nostalgia, offering Welles another occasion for lament over the twentieth century, another opportunity to show the link between a restless egocentric and the mania of a society.

As a whole, *Mr. Arkadin* is too confusing, too lacking in a plausible dramatic center; it is weakest in those moments when it strives to create emotional interest in Arkadin—as when the tycoon is shown pleading for an airline ticket in a crowded terminal. As satire and spectacle, however, it seldom fails, and of all Welles's European works it comes closest to the rebellious tone and the historical immediacy of his Hollywood days. It is in fact a Hollywood thriller seen from the vantage point of a European intellectual, foreshadowing the rise of "personal" art films in the early sixties. Sometimes it has the dreamlike power of a Fellini film, and sometimes the abstract, rhetorical tone of Godard's *Alphaville*. No wonder it was greeted with such enthusiasm by the critics of the *nouvelle vague*, who hailed it, in the words of Bazin, as "completely the work of Welles."

8

The Trial

From the start of his career Welles alluded to Kafka, with whom he had obvious affinities. One could hardly imagine two men of more dissimilar backgrounds or personalities, but both are artists of nightmare, their occasional lyricism mediated by a love for grotesque, satiric visions, their characters inevitably shown as victims of sexual and institutional torment. The Gothic political rally in *Kane*, the furtive conversations on a grand oak staircase in *Ambersons*, the mad courtroom in *The Lady from Shanghai*, the police inquisition in *Touch of Evil*—all these celebrated moments are made possible by Kafka, or at least by the modern sensibility that Kafka largely created. They are all examples of comfortable reality becoming as absurd as a dream, of recognizable daytime life beginning to turn into a hopeless, centerless labyrinth.

But note that I have said "beginning to turn," for however angst-ridden and fatalistic Welles's stories may be, however irrational and sexually charged his images may become, he continued to insist, both inside the fiction and outside, that his characters are morally responsible agents in a society of their own creation. The Welles who was fascinated with the subconscious and the demonic was also the Welles who wrote political editorials for the *New York Post*; he may have been pessimistic, but he was never truly despairing, and in that sense if in little else he maintained a link with the dominant ethos of Hollywood cinema. It is not surprising, therefore, that when the Salkind brothers gave him a free hand to adapt *The Trial* in 1962, he felt a need to make basic changes in the text. Consequently he produced a work of great cinematic intelligence and some Kafkaesque terror, which nevertheless seems divided against itself.

The divergences between film and novel are most interesting in those areas where Welles and Kafka would seem to have something in common. For example they are both fond of introducing fables or parables into the midst of dreamlike narratives, and Welles was naturally attracted to Kafka's parable of the Law. He has in fact moved this little story to a place of honor at the beginning of the film, telling it in the form of a slide show illustrated by Alexeieff's "pin-screen" technique—a process whereby images are created from shadows cast by pins inserted in a mat. The drawings thus produced serve not only as an introduction to Kafka's world but also as an indirect commentary on the nature of movies: one by one they are flashed on the screen, flipping upward like pages and then becoming shadowy, three-dimensional figures. We are shown a massive stone wall with an arched doorway resembling a primitive version of RKO's art work on Xanadu, while Welles's voice begins to recite the parable offscreen. "Before the Law there stands a Guard," he says, and with each successive statement another image flips upward, transforming the sentences into "shots." A man from the country appears, begging admittance to the Law. But the Guard cannot allow him past the door. Can he enter later? Perhaps, the Guard replies. Timidly peering beyond the open arch, the man sees another doorway, the first in a whole series of entrances, each more august than the one before. Respectfully he waits, growing old in the process. Seasons pass, but the Guard remains at his post. The old man tries bribery and obsequiousness, even making friends with the fleas in the Guard's fur collar in hope that they might have influence. Nothing helps, and when the old man nears death he asks the Guard a question: Why in all these years has no one else come to the door? "No one else could enter this door," says the Guard. "This door was intended only for you, and now I am going to close it."

The tale ends on a note of cosmic irony, and is a superb instance of an effect Welles was hinting at in Michael O'Hara's account of hungry sharks or Arkadin's story about the scorpion and the frog. But there is a crucial distinction between the way the exemplary parable of the Law has been used in the novel and in the film, and it is here that Welles's particular viewpoint becomes apparent.

In Kafka's novel, the story appears in the penultimate chapter, where it is told by a priest as a way of illustrating a "particular delusion" about the Court. At the conclusion, Joseph K., who has been respectful and attentive, immediately deduces a lesson: "So the doorkeeper deceived the man," he says. "Don't be too hasty," replies the priest. "I have told you the story in the very words of the scriptures. There's no mention of deception in it." Then for the next half-dozen pages the priest and K. become entangled in an elaborate exercise in hermeneutics, a debate which might be read as a dizzying satire of Talmudic scholarship and literary criticism. "But it's clear enough," K. remarks. Not so, responds the priest, who lists various possible interpretations, alluding to several commentators and methodically undermining K.'s every effort to reach a judgment. "It is not necessary to accept anything as true or false," the priest says at last; "one must only accept it as necessary." "A melancholy conclusion," says K. "It turns lying into a universal principle." But K. can no longer really object to anything: "He was too tired to survey all the conclusions arising from the story, and the trains of thought into which it was leading him were unfamiliar, dealing with impalpabilities better suited to a theme for discussion among Court officials than for him."

The method is deliberately comic, the priest's interpretation dissolving all meaning, leaving K. with an "explanation" as maddening as the Court itself. Welles appears to have recognized this quality in Kafka's handling of the parable, and in his final script for the film he tried to acknowledge it by having the narrator walk forward to the audience and make the following announcement:

This is a story inside history. Opinions differ on this point, but the error lies in believing that the problem can be resolved merely through special knowledge or perspicacity—that it is a mystery to be solved. A true mystery is unfathomable and nothing is hidden inside it. There is nothing to explain. It has been said that the logic of this story is the logic of a dream. Do you feel lost in a labyrinth? Do not look for a way out. You will not be able to find it. There is no way out.

In the completed film, however, the address to the audience does not appear, Welles remarking instead that the story we are about to see has the "logic of a dream . . . of a nightmare." The parable of the Law is presented without comment at the beginning and then alluded to near the end, where Welles, in the role of the Advocate, begins to retell the story only to be cut short by an angry Joseph K. (Anthony Perkins). The painfully comic explications of the parable have also been excised, partly because they are talky and uncinematic, but also because in the last analysis Welles recoils from Kafka's absurdist view of life. Instead we see Joseph K. walking through a church and into an empty theatre where the Court uses "visual aids" to instruct the populace. The Advocate flashes the Alexeieff drawings onto a movie screen, assuming the role of a Court-appointed lecturer-cum-producer. Almost as soon as the slide show has begun, K. stops it, remarking, "I've heard it all before. We've all heard it." The "we" links him with the audience, which in turn becomes a generalized human community. When K. accuses the Advocate of turning "lying into a universal principle," he does so with anger and conviction, refusing to accept the connections between himself and the accused man in the parable. The remainder of the scene, invented wholly by Welles, serves not only to give K. heroic dimension, but to attack the presumably nihilistic vision Welles senses behind Kafka's work:

K.: I don't pretend to be a martyr. No.
ADVOCATE: Not even a victim of society?
K.: I am a member of society.
ADVOCATE: You think you can persuade the Court that you're not responsible by reason of lunacy?
K.: I think that's what the Court wants me to believe. Yes, that's the conspiracy. To persuade us all that the whole world's crazy, formless, meaningless, absurd. That's the dirty game.
PRIEST (entering as K. searches for an exit): Can't you see anything at all?
K.: Of course. I'm responsible.
PRIEST: My son . . .
K.: I'm not your son. (Exit.)

Thus Kafka's ironic, impersonal vision of despair has been transformed into a Wellesian morality play. An audience without prior knowledge of Kafka cannot be aware of the change, nor can it recognize this moment as an explicit criticism of the film's source, but the effect is much the same in any case. The scene amounts to an attack not only on Kafka but on certain tendencies in modern art which by the early sixties had spread widely into the public consciousness. It is in fact a revision or self-criticism of the film we have been watching, a sudden lifting of K.'s nightmare to the level of conscious analysis. At the very least, it reveals Welles's ambivalence toward the abstraction and absurdity he has been trying to render, and it follows from this scene that he should have chosen to revise the end of Kafka's novel. Instead of making Joseph K. die "like a dog," he allows the condemned man to fight back.

Joseph McBride has observed that a closer filmic approximation of *The Trial* is to be found in Hitchcock's *The Wrong Man* (1957). The comparison is appropriate, not only because Hitchcock provides a rough stylistic equivalent to Kafka, but also because the story contains the same vision of petit-bourgeois character. Manny Balestro, the protagonist of the film (played by Henry Fonda), is an innocent accused of crime, a good father and husband who sees his home collapse and his wife go insane under the weight of an impersonal legal system. When at the end of the film the "right man" is accidentally discovered, Manny shows only one expression of anger, which is directed at the criminal rather than at the court. "Do you realize what you've done to my wife?" he says to his lookalike, and then he thanks the police for doing a good job. Hitchcock, ever the cool craftsman, leaves us free to interpret this scene ironically if we wish; nevertheless he gives the impression that absurdity underlies ordinary life, that while "good citizenship" may be no guarantee against chaos, it is the only chance available.

Such a view derives from the fact that Hitchcock, not unlike Kafka, remains a victim of the fears his film describes. Welles, on the other hand, is something of a patrician, a man who has always been more interested in the psychology of the oppressors than in the anxieties of the oppressed. He therefore stands outside ordinary life, vaguely contemptuous of the Manny Balestros and the Joseph K.s. This may explain why he draws from Anthony Perkins a curiously mixed performance, making him a cross between a Norman Bates and a Promethean rebel.

The scenes involving K.'s defiance of the Court are improbable, given the Kafkaesque world with which the film begins; nevertheless they are consistent with Welles's description of himself (in an interview with Kenneth Tynan) as an "Edwardian" rather than a "modern" intellectual. He clings to the nineteenth-century belief that literature ought to hold out some hope for humanity, and interestingly his alterations of the original story imply a reasoning similar to Georg Lukács's attack on Kafka in *Realism in Our Time:*

Ought *angst* to be taken as an absolute, or ought it to be overcome? Should it be considered one reaction among others, or should it be a determinate of the *condition humaine?* These are not, primarily, of course, literary questions; they relate to a man's behavior and experience of life. The crucial question is whether a man escapes from the life of his time into a realm of abstraction—it is then that *angst* is engendered in human consciousness—or confronts modern life determined to fight its evils and support what is good in it. The first decision leads then to another: is man the helpless victim of transcendental and inexplicable forces, or is he a member of a human community in which he can play a part, however small, toward its modification or reform?

Welles is not, of course, a socialist realist like Lukács, even though the words he gives K. near the end of the film are very like the ones just quoted. His uneasiness with Kafka is an example of an internal quarrel which has grown up within liberal democracy and which conducts a battle within Welles's own consciousness— a conflict between what Lukács would call "bourgeois modernism" and "critical realism." On the one hand is the kind of art which submits to abstraction, to angst, to the notion that life is absurd; and on the other hand is the kind of art which, however much it may be influenced by the modernist tradition, retains an essential humanism. It is this latter view which Welles is trying to assert, despite the fact that it nearly breaks his film apart.

Welles's difficulty is created not only by his personal dislike for the novel's conclusion but by historical circumstances, some of which he acknowledged in an interview with *Cahiers du Cinéma* after the release of the picture. Explaining why Kafka's original ending could not be tolerated in 1962, he remarked, "To me it is a 'ballet' written by a Jewish intellectual before the advent of Hitler. Kafka wouldn't have put that after the death of six million Jews. It all seems very much pre-Auschwitz to me. I don't mean that my ending was a particularly good one, but it was the only possible solution." Kafka had created a nightmare vision of ordinary life under the Hapsburg monarchy, a proto-fascist society in which people are transformed into objects or "cases," and where a vast, enigmatic bureaucracy envelops everything. In this atmosphere Joseph K. is arrested by a bizarre tribunal, tried, and then punished without even knowing the charge against him. At the end he watches the faces of two weird executioners bending over him, twisting a knife in his heart, and he cries out in despair, "as if the shame of it must outlive him." The reference to "shame" is a crucial instance of the attitude Welles finds so troubling; it hints at K.'s guilt and masochism, his unconscious acceptance of the authority of the Law. By feeling this shame, by hoping in his last moments to find "the Judge whom he had never seen," K. participates in his own dehumanization.

As Welles has said, Joseph K. "belongs to something which represents evil and which is a part of him at the same time. He is not guilty of what he is accused of, but he is guilty all the same: he belongs to a guilty society, he collaborates with it." Naturally Kafka's vision of social alienation and sexual repression remained a valid artistic subject for Welles, who attempted to transform it into a symbol of "big brotherism" in the post-industrial age; but to leave K. a passive collaborator at the end of the film was, he believed, to suggest that Hitler was necessary, even to imply unconscious complicity between Kafka and the Nazis. Welles felt it necessary to insist that K.'s madness is not part of an abstract human condition, and in so doing he took a position far more hopeful than Kafka's own. Kafka's friend Janouch is supposed to have remarked once in conversation that modern bureaucracy and automation were "progress towards the end of the world," to which Kafka replied, "If that, at least, were certain! It is not certain . . . the conveyor belt of life carries you on, no one knows where. One is more of an object, a thing, than a living creature." The ending of Welles's film is therefore closer to Janouch than to Kafka; when K.'s executioners lead him to a pit in the ground and throw dynamite after him, he picks up the bomb and throws it back, the world ending with a bang rather than a whimper.

Historically speaking, there were other good reasons for Welles to feel dissatisfied with the detachment and absurdism in modern art. By the early sixties, the avant-garde had become qualitatively different from their predecessors. The Cubist and Expressionist paintings of the early modernists had created an environment for a later abstract expressionism, and the literary experiments of Joyce and Kafka had given way to Beckett and Ionesco. One notes during this period a steady loss of historical specificity in art, and a consequent loss of social perspective. The awareness of time and place that had made Joyce's Dublin and Kafka's Prague such vivid settings had been replaced with a kind of literary no-man's land—a landscape of the moon. Lukács had described this phenomenon as

a loss of "authenticity," a retreat into abstraction which had resulted from the nuclear age and the Cold War. "As the crisis of modernism deepens," he wrote, "critical realism grows in importance."

One problem with Welles's adaptation of Kafka, however, is that it is less completely critical than it needs to be, and it lacks the "authenticity" of the original. In various ways Welles has tried to update the novel, making it a vehicle for contemporary social satire; for example, he introduces a giant computer into Joseph K.'s office, and he has K. speak out against the currently fashionable artistic notion that life is "absurd." He even implies that the slavish court artist Titorelli (played by William Chappell but dubbed entirely with Welles's own voice) has been influenced by trendy, abstract "action painting." Yet, ironically, Welles's film is a product of the very abstractionist tendency it has chosen to attack. Welles had in fact directed a stage version of Ionesco's *Rhinoceros* in London in 1960, and the influence of "theatre of the absurd" can be found everywhere in *The Trial*. Consider the scene where K., having just returned home with a cake he has bought for Miss Burstner, encounters the crippled Miss Pittle (Suzanne Flon) dragging a heavy trunk along the ground. In an exceptionally lengthy tracking shot we see him walking along behind the woman, trying to help her. She refuses assistance and accuses him of being responsible for Miss Burstner's eviction; on and on they walk together, holding a protracted argument. (See above.)

The landscape, filmed in Yugoslavia, is barren and filled with anonymous public housing. K. juggles his little white box, nearly skipping with nervousness and guilt, while the woman lugs away at the black trunk, her braced leg clanking heavily with each step. It is an eerie, darkly comic moment, which has no equivalent in Kafka; on the contrary, it has much more in common with the absurdist drama of Beckett or the early Edward Albee. Welles's aim, here as elsewhere, appears to have been to establish the existentialist atmosphere of contemporary theatre while at the same time showing that absurdity is the product of a "guilty society." Unfortunately he is never able to find a satisfactory dramatic realization of this aim, as he had in thrillers like *The Lady from Shanghai* and *Touch of Evil.* The world he creates is altogether too artful; it is a nonspecific totalitarianism, a generalized "human condition" represented by those vast apartment houses; it has little concreteness, few vestiges of a real social context, and therefore the satire is blunted.

To see how much difference there is between *The Trial* and Welles at his best, one has only to contrast the opening moments of the film with the interrogation of Sanchez in *Touch of Evil.* Both scenes take place in drab apartments, both are photographed in long takes with a distorting lens, and both are characterized by a surreal comedy. In both, public officials have forced their way into the most vulnerable areas of a man's private life, police authority literally extending into bedrooms, where we see burly men examining Sanchez's love letters or investigating K.'s relations with the lady next door. The earlier film, however, is clearly the more fascinating, and not only because it is more formally complex, with a more interesting group of players and a soundtrack which does not inhibit the acting. What is also missing in *The Trial* is some reference to an actual milieu. As K.'s landlady tells him, "With your arrest I get the feeling of something abstract." In the opening scenes the dubbed voices of Hollywood-type police seem oddly out of key with Kafka's Czech names, and Anthony Perkins's distinctly American energy is set off against Jeanne Moreau's European languor. A similar mélange of nationalities can of course be found in *Touch of Evil,* which was certainly not intended to represent "the real Mexico"; nevertheless the crazy, nightmarish distortion of that film was an *interpretation* of a real place, and the various accents are wittily appropriate to the bordertown. In *The Trial,* by contrast, the setting has become nearly as generalized as the cast: the government architecture of Zagreb, intimating a gray, Iron Curtain socialism, provides background for the early scenes; but then the abandoned Gare d'Orsay in Paris is used for K.'s encounters with the Courts of Law. Whereas *Touch of Evil* had been a dream about America, *The Trial* has become a dream about everywhere; and to paraphrase Andrew Sarris's remark about Murnau, a film devoted to no place in particular cannot hope to represent everyplace in general.

Welles himself has commented somewhat defensively on the differences in tone between his film and Kafka's novel, focusing especially on the unusual settings, which were criticized by Anglo-American reviewers for their giant, baroque quality. Because of his producer's financial difficulties, he was unable to use specially designed sets in Yugoslavia; consequently he improvised in the empty Paris station, doing the best he could in typically desperate circumstances. His original premise, however, was even more abstract than the picture he actually made. "In the production as I originally envisaged it," he said, "the sets were to gradually disappear. The number of realistic elements was to gradually diminish, and to be seen to diminish by the spectators, until only open space remained, as if everything had been dissolved away." One can detect traces of this concept in the completed film, which begins in K.'s narrow apartment and then takes us through a series of rooms without walls: K.'s office, for example, is a raised platform at one end of a hangar-sized building, overlooking hundreds of secretaries who sit typing at identical desks (a favorite image of the expressionists, appearing first in the days of Lang and Murnau, then in Vidor's *The Crowd*, and ultimately in Wilder's *The Apartment*). The Advocate's quarters are represented by a maze of huge, partly enclosed, candlelit rooms in the upper reaches of the Court; the roof is a skylight, the "bedroom" a raised platform echoing the one in K.'s office, and the "kitchen" a refrigerator and sink placed at the extreme end of a cavernous loft. At the climax of the film, the boundaries between one setting and another become even more tenuous. The artist Titorelli lives in a slatted cage with a back door that leads directly into the Court; as K. flees out the front exit, a church seems to materialize in an empty plaza, and a curtained wall behind the pulpit leads him into an empty theatre. Finally, the pair of executioners seize K. and march across open fields, where dynamite shatters the rocky landscape. The modern government structures and the massive public buildings reminiscent of an earlier age have given way entirely to a wasteland, the story closing with what is perhaps the most depressing image in all Welles's cinema—a dark cloud of smoke hanging in the sky, with hardly a breeze to indicate life.

As the foregoing description may indicate, Welles's ideas for staging *The Trial* were at least coherent, even if the results are sometimes flat or overly abstracted. In fact, despite the lack of authenticity in the settings, the film is as technically interesting as anything Welles has done. He has forsaken the out-of-kilter editing style of his previous three pictures, using a movie syntax as lucid and correct as Kafka's own prose. In *The Trial* it is the *mise-*

en-scène which has become irrational, K.'s peregrinations taking him through a world nearly as shocking and bewildering as the funhouse at the end of *The Lady from Shanghai.* The camera repeatedly tracks with him as he moves from one weirdly different locale to another, Albinoni's *Adagio* forming a sad, yearning musical leitmotif that enhances the continual gliding rhythm of the shots. Space seems logical and all of a piece, but K. has only to open a door or cross a hallway to find himself in a new environment. From the moment he leaves Mrs. Grubach's rooming house, the world is transformed into a deceptive, protean, increasingly menacing place. When he tries to penetrate the Courts, he moves through gigantic open areas which are filled with passive crowds; when he tries to escape, he finds himself always inside the Court's boundaries, running down tunnel-like corridors that lead him to new confrontations with the Law.

The unhappy influence of the contemporary avant-garde does not obscure these formal beauties, nor *The Trial*'s dramatically effective qualities as sexual nightmare. Indeed at this level it becomes a more intriguing work—certainly very different from the self-indulgent adaptation that Welles's reviewers once made it seem. The opening scenes, for example, are carefully designed to establish a relatively normal setting from which the rest of the film will depart, even while they define K.'s psychology and foreshadow the structure of the remaining events.

From the beginning we sense that *The Trial* will be the psychodrama of a troubled bureaucrat, everything in the story being generated from the subconscious of the central character. The story proper opens with a tight shot of Perkins's head, upside down like the faces that introduce *Othello* and the funhouse section of *The Lady from Shanghai.* His long, rather feline lashes flutter awake. From a low angle, we see one wing of a double door opening, and a dark-hatted man entering a room. We return to Perkins, who sits up in bed. The camera trucks left, swinging around behind his shadowed head, as if the scene were being projected from his mind. The strange man, a police inspector, walks forward from the door, which is situated directly across K.'s room; in the ensuing action, photographed in a single take, other policemen casually enter and leave while K. tries to wake up and change out of his pajamas. He is accused of having a clandestine relationship with his neighbor, of wanting to "dress in the hall," and of concealing an "ovular shape" under his rug. Nervous and confused, he denies having any "subver-

sive literature or pornography," then he inadvertently calls his record-player a "pornograph." His specific crime is never mentioned, and the mysterious police make no formal charge, claiming only that "proceedings have been started." Nevertheless it is clear that K.'s guilt is mainly sexual; Welles has the chief investigator enter from doors leading to a lady's apartment—doors which have been placed nearly at the foot of K.'s bed. One notes also that K.'s room is institutionally white and functional, except for an unframed print of Van Gogh's "Sunflowers" hanging near his dressing table, the mad blossoms suggesting an inner torment.

This bedroom scene makes the connection between State and superego nearly explicit, and shows K.'s anxiety growing out of his willing participation in a repressive social hierarchy. "I am a man of regular habits," he tells the police as he dresses in gray pants and a vest. In a subsequent conversation with his mousy, somewhat maternal landlady (Madeline Robinson), he becomes petulant, boasting that the police could never have broken into his office, where "people sometimes have to wait for weeks before they can speak to my secretary." Later, when he talks with his sultry neighbor Miss Burstner (Jeanne Moreau), he confesses that he has always felt guilty when confronted with authority figures, including especially his father and his teachers: "It's even worse," he says, "when you haven't done anything wrong and you still feel guilty."

The early parts of the film also establish the formal "rules" of the remaining action. The interior of K.'s rooming house is photographed with a number of tracking shots that move through different rooms, creating the effect of a tiny maze which echoes the larger maze to come. Significantly also, the initial long take in K.'s bedroom ends as he moves up to the double doors leading to Miss Burstner's apartment and swings them open, confronting a bizarre scene. (See above.)

In the remainder of the film K. repeatedly approaches similar entrances and suddenly opens a door to confront an unexpected sight. The four shots reproduced here will help indicate how often the doorway imagery recurs: in shot one, K. has marched down the

hallway to tell Miss Burstner that the police have been in her room; he knocks, abruptly opens the door, and sees that she is undressing. Frightened, he quickly swings the door shut and returns to his own room, where, in shot two, we see him pacing anxiously back and forth between the double doors connecting his apartment with Miss Burstner's. Shot three takes place somewhat later in the film, when K. has walked down a huge silent corridor in search of the Law Courts; he swings open a pair of double doors similar to the ones in his own apartment and is met by a rush of noise and light from a jammed "courtroom." Shot four appears very near the end of the film, explicitly linking the various doorways to the most important entrance of them all—the gateway to the Law, which we have seen illustrated in the parable at the opening of the film. Here K. is standing between a slide projector and a screen, his shadow falling at the center of the huge arch to which he has presumably been forbidden entrance; subsequently he denounces the Advocate and walks forward toward the projector, but as he does so, his shadow shrinks, as if he were walking *into* the maze of gates on the screen behind him.

The various doors are among the chief symbols of K.'s dream-world, and are one of the principal methods of achieving transitions from one stage of the action to the next. Always they open onto bewilderingly different places. In the opening scene Miss Burstner's quarters are at the opposite extreme from K.'s own—tiny and dark, covered with flowered drapes and cluttered with memorabilia from her mother's vaudeville routine ("Burstner's Birds," she calls it, in one of Welles's more puckish attempts at humor). Later, the tribunal to which K. is summoned makes a striking contrast to the lonely corridor outside; actually it is a European-style political rally—an exaggeration of the one Kafka describes, echoing *Kane*—with hundreds of men packed in the rafters and the air thick with smoke. Still later, K. makes his way through a sea of typists in his office and opens the door to a tiny storage closet, where, in one of the most brilliantly edited and disturbing moments of the film, he finds a man in leather whipping two corrupt policemen. The huge corporate workroom has given way to a claustrophobic torture chamber, an ugly little space lit with a naked bulb and filled with cringing figures. The offending officers cling to the walls, shirtless but with their hats on, submitting to a beating while K. pulls back in horror to avoid being lashed himself. Welles cuts rapidly between the Gestapo-like torturer raising his strap and the pathetic, middle-aged flesh of the victims; the lamp sways wildly with every blow, creating a strobe-light effect, a shattering violence which is further increased by the tempo of the cutting. Meanwhile Anthony Perkins conveys K.'s terror with the bodily skill of a good dancer; he forces himself out of the room the way he came, fighting to get free of a man who pleads for help, then paces nervously back and forth in the hallway outside. Once out, he bites his fist and hunches his wide bony shoulders, twisting into a humiliated near-crouch, then quickly forces himself upright as a secretary enters to announce that he has a visitor in his office.

The "next room" in *The Trial* always suggests a repressed psychic horror—either a forbidden sexual desire, as in the case of Miss Burstner's apartment, or a hidden guilt, or a fear of retribution. Every entranceway portends some kind of shock; when K. crosses one of these he commits a psychic as well as literal transgression, and his anxiety inevitably increases. In the concluding scenes, however, his entrances and exits become more purposeful, reflecting his transformation into an angry, more active character. Near the climax, after he has witnessed the debasement of the Advocate's client Bloch (Akim Tamiroff), he leaves the room by defiantly breaking down a locked door. At the conclusion, the inhibiting walls and boundaries have become more fragile, at last yielding to an open space.

Perkins's movements through doors and ultimately into a field indicate the progress of his character; he does not actually get anywhere, but he does change. The film has begun with K. having all the respect for officialdom that his accusers could desire. He arranges his life methodically, he cowers before his boss, and he acts like a martinet to underlings in his office. He somewhat unsuccessfully fights back sexual longings, all the while boasting of his efficiency on the job. "Don't be surprised if you hear any day now that I've become Deputy Manager of my department," he tells his cousin. "Why, all I've got to do is apply those same abilities to this case of mine." His every conscientious effort to defend himself against the Court makes him more and more a cog in the system of institutional horrors; even his complaints about the violation of his "civil rights" result in his becoming a guilty, frightened witness at the torture of low-level policemen. Gradually, however, he begins to show flashes of anger. Standing before an old man who waits patiently outside the Courts of Law, he becomes testy and aggressive: "I'm under arrest [also]. You don't see *me* putting up affidavits. What makes you think this kind of thing is necessary?" He even commands respect from the Court's Guard, a weakling who regards him as a kind of hero. At the end of the film K. continues to insist that "I've got to catch up on my work at the office," but he has become progressively more defiant, finally dismissing his attorney and sneering at the authority of the Court.

If K. never becomes a sympathetic character, he is at least given a chance to assert himself. And as K. becomes bolder, his accusers visibly weaken. At first the police are bullies and Advocate Hastler is a demonic presence—indeed Welles has devised a typically theatrical entrance for himself: rising from a bed like a baroque exaggeration of all the invalid father-figures in Kafka, he removes a hot towel from his face, steam floating in little clouds around his head. As usual, however, Welles tries to convey a softness and vulnerability behind the powerful façade. He makes Hastler into a childish, sometimes rather funny villain—for example when he confides to K.'s uncle Max (Max Haufler) that there is a hole in the

floor of his room at the Court: "Not quite big enough to fall through, but if you stumble into it you find yourself with your leg hanging down into the corridor below—the very place where all your clients have to wait." He pats his mistress on the bottom with all the ostentatious but somehow charming vulgarity of a Hank Quinlan, and he mischievously hides under the covers of his bed in order to play sadistic tricks on visitors; he puts on a show of authority, making his client Bloch humiliate himself while K. watches, but the display only makes K. more determined to rebel. The same ineffectiveness is seen in all the other legal officials; in the final episode, for example, the executioners do not even have the strength to put a knife into K., and are last seen running in fear from their own dynamite. At best, Welles suggests, the Court's power over its cases is dependent upon the cooperation of the accused.

But K.'s progress through the labyrinth leads him to only a partial release from frustration, only a pyrrhic victory. Moreover, even though he becomes an angry member of a "human community," he is less fortunate where women are concerned. His qualified moral triumph is obtained against what appears to be a purely masculine institution, a bureaucracy which is concerned with the abstractions of the "law." It is worth noting, however, that females always hover at the edges of this institution, and they represent an unresolved conflict. Repeatedly they offer K. favors or comfort, their charms luring him away from obsessive preoccupation with his "case." In K.'s own offices and in the archives of the Court one occasionally notes prim ladies with their hair fastened in buns and their dresses buttoned to the neck; but just outside, K. encounters a whole gallery of more fascinating, threatening types. First there is Mrs. Grubach, the maternal landlady; then Miss Burstner, the prostitute; then Irmie (Maydra Shore), K.'s cousin from the country; then Hilda (Elsa Martinelli), the *hausfrau* who washes and sews outside the courtrooms; then Leni (Romy Schneider), who acts as nurse and sexual companion for the Advocate. As a group, they seem to prove the Advocate's notion that a defendant in a trial is always more "attractive" than ordinary law-abiding citizens.

"It can't be a sense of guilt," the Advocate muses, trying to explain why his own mistress likes to seduce his clients. "We can't all be guilty, hmm?" Yet the officials of the Court are as driven by secret desires as K. himself; thus the lawbooks have dirty illustrations in them, the official proceedings are interrupted by perverse sexual byplay, and the Examining Magistrate lusts after the Guard's wife. Everywhere the rigid structuure of the Law seems threatened by Eros, the women often becoming sinister manipulators of the higher authorities. It is typical of Welles, in fact, that the males who are connected with the Law and the public world of social responsibility are weak, disorganized, and even impotent. Throughout his career one finds the same theme recurring—weakling fathers like the elder Kane or Minafer being set off against strong, dominating women, and the legal structure (as in *Touch of Evil*) being undermined by sexual passion. It might be said that the typical psychological difficulty of Welles's protagonists lies precisely in the futile attempt to assert masculine control, to pass out of infancy and sexual chaos, to identify with a "father" who is ultimately not strong enough.

As a sign of the threat women embody in *The Trial*, Welles usually poses them at the other side of a doorway or a subtle visual barrier. Notice, for example, the compositions in the four shots reproduced on pages 212-13. In the first, K.'s cousin Irmie stands outside the glass partition of his office while K. talks with the Deputy Manager; K. wrings his hands, trying to ignore her. Meanwhile his boss gives a wry look and makes an insinuating remark: "We'll have to keep an eye on you, old man." In the second, Hilda pulls up her dress to show K. her new stockings; "Do you wanna see?" she says, but the shadow of a crossbar in the foreground suggests that K. is psychologically forbidden to look. In the third, Leni holds out a key which opens the door to the Advocate's house, but at the same time she stands behind the bars of a partition. Finally, we see one of the urchin girls outside Titorelli's room, peering through a slat in the wall. Images like these, which contain both an invitation to contact and a prohibition against it, help to illustrate K.'s divided consciousness. They also turn the women—who are not so much characters as enigmatic objects of desire—into potentially dangerous creatures. By provoking K.'s desire to transgress, the females stimulate guilt, anxiety, and hostility. He attracts them, but he is also irritated and fearful, uncertain whether they are influential parasites—like the fleas in a guard's coat—or an actual menace to his "case."

The more K. becomes angry at the Court, the more appealing he becomes to the women, who have been arranged in an increasing order of aggressiveness. Mrs. Grubach, dressed in curlers and housecoat, plays the role of a respectable matron, so devoted to K. that she becomes jealous of Miss Burstner; Miss Burstner, in turn, allows K. a free kiss despite her need for sleep and her wish to be left alone; Irmie trails K. around and remarks that "cousins get married"; Hilda says that K. can do with her "whatever you want"; Leni fixes K. in her eye from the moment he enters the Advocate's house, luring him into a room piled with tons of papers, where, after swaddling him in a judge's robe and lying down amid the chaotic residue of legal "order," she tries to seduce him; finally, a horde of teenagers—the mirror image of cousin Irmie—chase K. up a spiral staircase, pulling at his coat and squealing in sexual frenzy.

These women are slightly different from the ones in Kafka. They are wittier, usually authentically attractive, and lacking in what Walter Benjamin called Kafka's "dirty voluptuousness." We see Leni spreading her hand to show a web of flesh between the fingers, but on the whole Welles seems either unwilling or unable to provide a truly Kafkaesque imagery of sexual unhealth. (Romy Schneider is, in any case, altogether too beautiful for the character she plays.) On the other hand, Welles has echoed Kafka by making the women in K.'s world become more unpleasant and threatening as they become increasingly erotic. At first they are only mildly annoying, but they become associated with a mounting perversity and violence as the nightmare deepens. Mrs. Grubach's smothering solicitude angers K., who unsuccessfully tries to close a window shade in her face; the promiscuous Miss Burstner throws K. out of her room when she suspects that he has committed a "political"

crime; Irmie embarrasses K. at his office and follows him around the streets; Hilda brings him face to face with a terrifyingly sadistic law student who picks her up and carries her away; Leni, a vixenish woman with a "physical defect," deceives and manipulates K., at one point trying to seduce both him and the client Bloch at the same time. In the most frightening scene of all, the swarm of urchins gather outside Titorelli's garret, peering at K., reaching through cracks in the walls to pinch him, begging to be let inside. Titorelli calls them "dirty-minded little pussies" and threatens to punish them with an ice pick. When K. leaves the garret he first tries to avoid the girls by taking an exit that leads him into the Court; realizing the futility of this course, he goes back the way he came, running a gantlet of squealing females who chase him through an obviously symbolic sewer.

All this ambivalence toward sexuality is perfectly in keeping with Kafka's novel, but it may also be a reflection of Welles's own much-mentioned reactionary attitude toward women. "I hate women," Maurice Bessy quotes him as once saying, "but I need them." In fact his female characters are often predatory types—suffocating mothers or sexy, conniving prostitutes. *The Trial* brings the psychological implications of this recurrent fantasy closer to the surface than any of his previous films, and it leaves K. imprisoned within the terrible dream. The original script contained a passage in which K., being led away by his executioners, catches sight of Miss Burstner: trying to run toward her, he cries, "Miss Burstner! Marika! Will I never be able to reach her?" It is difficult to say whether the scene, which was suggested by the novel, was intended as an indication that freedom might be obtained through love, or whether it was simply another instance of a mysterious temptress lingering outside the grasp of the Law; in any case it was never shot, and an atmosphere of isolation and sexual pessimism hangs over the film until the end.

By contrast, K. has been allowed to speak out against the idea of absurdity, and he achieves a sort of "manliness" when he attacks those who stand timidly before the doors of the Law. Against the patriarchal authority of the court he is reasonably effective; in a sense he cuckolds the Advocate by dallying with Leni, but he refuses to pay the penalty imposed on other "clients." Soon afterward the executioners take him to a pit in the ground where they bid him lie down and remove his shirt; in his last moments he refuses to collaborate in a ritual which suggests castration, and he dies while making a rebellious gesture. The psychoanalytic message of his nightmare seems pretty clear: an oppressed child turns against a weak but menacing father and deposes him. But the victory is obtained at the cost of extinction, and the sexual malaise which provoked the original anxiety remains unabated.

A similar pessimism is suggested in Welles's earlier films, even in the ones that preserve the optimistic formulas of Hollywood melodrama. In *The Lady from Shanghai*, for example, Welles had closed on a highly qualified note typical of the *film noir*. Michael O'Hara is as much a "collaborator" with an evil society as is Joseph K., and he, too, suffers from a dangerous attraction to a female. The last shot of the film is wonderfully lyrical and ostensibly liberating, the camera rising on a crane while Michael walks toward a sunny horizon; at the same time, however, he is shown as a brooding, isolated figure, reminiscent of the loners Bogart usually played, and in his final words he suggests that he will spend the rest of his life trying to forget the woman he has left behind. *The Trial*, if only because it remains adequately faithful to its source, follows this problem to a darker resolution. We see K.'s executioners lighting a bundle of dynamite and tossing it at him; a rapid series of shots follow, showing K. laughing hysterically, the fuse burning down, and the executioners running away. Very briefly, K. is seen bending to pick something up. Cut to a long shot of the empty field, K.'s laughter heard across the vast space. Then a series of explosions, leaving the dark cloud in a dirty sky. Albinoni's *Adagio* begins to play softly while Welles's voice reads the credits to the film. We do not know whether K. has succeeded in destroying his persecutors or not, but the last shot conveys an utter desolation, as if death were the only escape from sexual paranoia.

9

Chimes at Midnight

When an artist admires Shakespeare as much as Welles did, he seems to identify strongly with the plays and his comments on them are likely to be a helpful guide to his own work. Here is Welles speaking to André Bazin about Shakespeare's temperament:

He was very close indeed to another age, if you understand me. He was standing in the door which opened onto the modern age and his grandparents, the old people in the village, the countryside itself, still belonged to the Middle Ages, to the old Europe. . . . His humanity came from his links to the Middle Ages, . . . and his pessimism, his bitterness—and it's when he allows them free rein that he touches the sublime—belong to the modern world, the world which had just been created.

If the historical terms are changed, this becomes a fairly accurate description of the man who made *The Magnificent Ambersons*—a film that draws its "human" qualities from a nostalgia over the nineteenth-century Midwest, and its lyric pessimism from a bitterness over the modern age. Thus Shakespeare's links to "the countryside" are very like Welles's own attachment to a vanished Wisconsin, and the bard's "sublime" is very similar to the director's romantic quarrel with industrialism.

In Welles's films this historical myth is nearly always tied to personal concerns. All his major characters—Kane, George

Minafer, Captain Quinlan—are imprisoned by their past, destroyed not only by the aging process and the inexorable march of "progress," but by the sheer difficulty of becoming adult in a new world. And given his obsession with this kind of story, it is only natural that Welles should have had a lifelong preoccupation with Shakespeare's history plays, which treat the same intersection of public and private problems in the context of the Wars of the Roses. The two parts of *Henry IV* in particular are devoted to the transition from a medieval, chivalric code to a modern empire, from a kingship of heredity to a kingship of power politics; and they depict this theme by means of a personal *rite de passage*—Prince Hal's exchange of childlike revelry for adult responsibility. Moreover, the prince's abandoned friend Falstaff is the exact embodiment of a type Welles dealt with again and again: an adolescent caught in an aging body, a living contradiction of spirit and flesh, who suffers banishment under the new order of things.

The very plots of the Henry plays confirm Welles's notion of Shakespeare as a man caught between two ages, because they are a blend of medieval folklore and hymns to renaissance imperialism. The character of Hal is at least as old as the prodigal son, and Falstaff, the tempter and "father ruffian" who partly substitutes for Hal's true father, is an updated version of the vice figure from the Morality plays; at the same time, Shakespeare gives us a fairly specific account of how Hal and his father manipulate public opinion in order to gain power, subduing the Percy family and creating a rule which depends more on political craft than on legitimacy. It is as if the playwright, with one foot in the Middle Ages and the other in a secular and skeptical time, had deliberately sought to create a dialectic between past and present. As C. L. Barber has noted, Falstaff is "a Lord of Misrule ... brought up, so to speak, from the country to the city, or from the traditional past into the changing present," who becomes "the mouthpiece not merely for the dependent holiday skepticism which is endemic in a traditional society, but also for a dangerously self-sufficient everyday skepticism." When the old medieval Vice is thus brought into contact with the new politics, his meaning alters slightly; he is, as always, a creature of anarchic libido who gives a necessary release from too much pious social authority, but he has also become a skeptic among skeptics, a charmingly honest rogue who acts as a critic of the state. To quote Barber again, he is "set in an environment of sober-blooded great men behaving as opportunistically as he," and "the effect is to raise radical questions about social sanctities."

Welles was aware of this tension in the history plays, and had tried to document it as early as 1938, in the failed Mercury production of *Five Kings*. The idea of combining the history cycle into one unified piece stayed with him until the early sixties, when at last, under the usual catch-as-catch-can circumstances, he made a film about Falstaff, called *Chimes at Midnight*. It is a brilliant editing of scenes from *Richard II*, *Henry IV* parts one and two, *Henry V*, and *The Merry Wives of Windsor*, spliced together with offscreen narration spoken by Ralph Richardson from Holinshed's *Chronicles*. Quite a free adaptation, it does no violence to Shakespeare's text and actually improves the story of an heir apparent and his dissolute friend by making it more unified. The acting, particularly by Keith Baxter as Hal, John Gielgud as Henry IV, and Welles himself as Falstaff, is virtually flawless, and the script serves to heighten a quality that Welles's best movies have always had in common with Shakespeare: an architectural mastery of double plots and multiple characters by means of which, as Barber says of the history plays, "everything becomes foil to everything else."

By condensing the story into an account of the Falstaff-Hal relationship, Welles forces the audience to make repeated contrasts and comparisons between the characters, who are quite paradoxical in themselves. "The interesting thing about the story," he once told an interviewer, "is that the old king is a murderer, he has usurped the throne and yet he represents legitimacy." Hal, the "legitimate" prince, "must betray the good man in order to become a hero." Falstaff's public and private selves do not conflict so much, but he, too, is an ironic figure; an old man who stands for youth, he continually makes jokes about the difference between appearance and reality: "My Lords," he tells the bishops, "you that are old consider not the capacities of us that are young."

One has only to consider a few closeups of Falstaff, such as the two reproduced on page 218, showing him in a burlesque of kingship, to see what complexities he brings to the story. To some degree Welles seems to have been influenced by the nineteenth-century romantic notion of the character, turning him into a true friend of the prince and a wise man among politicians; he has called Falstaff "Shakespeare's good, pure man," whose faults are minor compared to the rest of the world. In the film as a whole, however, the portrait is rather more ambiguous. If Falstaff is not quite a rogue, neither is he the source of all virtue. Physically he is

the opposite of John Gielgud's monastic king, resembling a filthy Santa Claus who has carried "gourmandizing" to a dangerous extreme; but at the same time his sly behavior is like an "honest" version of the king's opportunism. The furthest thing from a clown, he is in fact a man of very high intelligence, an alcoholic in the same way as Welles's idol John Barrymore was, whose playacting in the scenes above or whose behavior during the battle with the rebellious Percys is an intentional commentary on the selfishness behind kingly idealism. Yet he is also something of a child, and like a child he sometimes overreaches, his very wit becoming self-destructive. Consider, for example, the later scene where he drags Hotspur's dead body across the battleground, dumping it between the king and the prince while boasting of his valor. On the one hand the scene parodies Hal's ambitious, calculated attempt to obtain "honor" by killing Hotspur; but on the other hand it becomes a hollow joke, robbing a dead man of his dignity and derisively capitalizing on the bloody sacrifice that has gone before. Clearly Falstaff is out of his element when he is brought into actual proximity with the king, and his attempt to carry on the joking of the tavern badly misfires; thus when he delivers his encomium on "sherris sack" in the wake of the battle, the prince turns away, drops his cup, and wanders off across the field toward his real father.

Although Falstaff is the center of the film, the true dynamics of the story are created by Hal, who in some way resembles everyone else and seems to profit from their mistakes. He is partly like Falstaff, the carousing publican; partly like the king, who is burdened with responsibility and cursed by his own drive to power; and partly like Hotspur, who is capable of a beautifully aristocratic, if misguided, courage. In Shakespeare, Hal somehow absorbs the best traits of these characters into a healthy synthesis, becoming an ideal figure of state; but in Welles's more left-wing and pessimistic view, the dialectic breaks down and the synthesis never develops. Hal is a tragic figure who deliberately chooses power and responsibility over friendship, keeping an eye always on his future. Welles never suggests that he ought to have avoided his destiny, and never completely sentimentalizes Falstaff; the dilemma of the film is simply that youth and age cannot be reconciled, any more than lovable, sometimes dangerous anarchy and needful, sometimes self-regarding social order.

At a deeper level, this contest between youth and responsibility contains the same sexual dilemmas we have seen in Welles's work from *Kane* to *The Trial.* The connection is difficult to see at first, because *Chimes at Midnight* presents its major conflicts in the form of a "family drama" of king and heir, taking place in an exclusively male world of camaraderie, politics, and power, where the nearest thing to a romantic relationship is the rough-house between Hotspur and Kate. There are no mothers in sight—only Doll Tearsheet (Jeanne Moreau), who offers brief comfort to Falstaff in his old age, and who is passed freely among the men. In a sense, however, Falstaff acts both as a substitute father and as a displaced mother, being associated throughout with softness, earthy affection, and nourishment. Perhaps because he is a male, and a "rounded" Shakespearian character, he is not treated in the same abstracted, ambivalent way as the mothers in Welles's early films. Nevertheless he has the same affective power as they do, and many of the same functions within the drama. He is the figure who stands for the child's need of love, intimacy, and human contact, whereas the king represents the need for public control and an autonomous adulthood. As usual in Welles's films, the two needs are never integrated, leaving human personality torn between infantile hedonism and a role-playing manipulativeness. Just as Charles Foster Kane is a character who never grows up, so Prince Hal is a character who never seems to have been young; behind the two types is the same problem, the same psychological split between private and public that inhibits the development of personality.

To the extent that the film is about fatherhood, it shows that state to be exceedingly fragile; and here again the pattern is the same as in the previous films, where male authority is uncertain and dependent. Although Falstaff and the old king have an anxious vulnerability that is typical of parents in Welles's work, it is interesting that Falstaff has more vitality and even physical agility than the prince's true father. Falstaff clings hopefully to the prince, like a doting mother, trying to manipulate but being manipulated in turn, while the king withers away, always suspicious of his son. As for the prince, he lacks any clear identity beyond the cold, practical purposefulness he has learned from birth. Keith Baxter is particularly good at conveying what William Empson called the character's "parasitic" absorption into whatever world he encounters: in the tavern scenes he seems slight and rather boyish, like a sensual Tony Perkins; on the battlefield against Hotspur he is resolute, heroic, and a model of chivalry; in the closing moments he begins to take on the chilly demeanor of his father. He is, furthermore, systematically destructive to his various "hosts." He breaks Falstaff's heart, of course, but he also kills off Hotspur and literally takes the crown from a dying king. Having outgrown them all, he is grimly isolated, walled up in a castle like so many of the frustrated wielders of power in Welles's earlier movies.

But if Hal has many faces, he is also ruthlessly forthright about his true intentions. Never a hypocrite, as several critics have called him, he pauses amid the gaiety of the tavern to tell Falstaff that he will "banish fat Jack"; he announces to his father that he will henceforth "be more myself"; he sends a message to Hotspur confessing that he has "a truant been to chivalry" and will redeem his honor with a "single fight." The problem is that the other characters never quite believe him, and for understandable reasons. Even Poins (Tony Beckley), his rather sinister, perverse companion in revelry—and the true hypocrite of the film—cannot accept the prince's confessions of weariness and grief on the days just before he assumes the crown. This, too, Poins assumes, must be a kind of dissembling, but in fact Hal has never concealed his feelings. He is an honest pragmatist, burdened by neither his father's guilt, nor Hotspur's sometimes crude machismo, nor Falstaff's cynicism about power. In a way he is paler, more cryptic than these others, who are more obviously ruled by their passions. Thus when the king broods on the way he got the crown, or when Hotspur promises to die bravely in the act of rebellion, or when Falstaff drifts into melancholy, there is a vivid, irreconcilable conflict between the nature of the man and the nature of the world. Hal, on the other hand, seems always perfectly aware of his capabilities, just as he always knows what time it is. The only thing that keeps him from becoming an utterly callous figure or a pure egoist like Kane is that he expresses an authentic sympathy for the men around him who are outmoded and dying: he speaks in awe of his father's crown; he gives a moving eulogy for Hotspur; and he grieves inwardly and promises to "enlarge" Falstaff from banishment. It is precisely because he has these personal emotions that his fate is so sad. He is led by hereditary ambition to outstrip everyone else, finally becoming a purely public man, surrounded by plotting courtiers, whose inner pain has been subordinated to the need for powerful rule.

The two sources of the film's tragic view—the passage of youth and the necessities of politics—are most apparent in the opening and closing images. At the beginning, before the credits, we see Falstaff and Shallow (the latter played by Alan Webb) moving across a snowy landscape, the whiteness in the air recalling both *Kane* and *Ambersons,* where snow is a multivalent symbol of innocence and death. The two aged men resemble pathetic clowns, one huge and swollen, the other tiny and thin; as they amble painfully toward an empty inn and sit before a fire, they discuss old times, Welles's booming voice contrasting with Webb's fluty tones:

SHALLOW: Is Jane Nightwork alive?
FALSTAFF: She lives, Master Shallow.
SHALLOW: Doth she hold her own well?
FALSTAFF: Old . . . Old, Master Shallow.
SHALLOW: She must be old. She cannot choose but be old.

A tight closeup of two faces in firelight shows the lines and pocks of age, like the closeup of a dying Major Amberson. "Jesus, the days that we have seen!" Shallow cries, and Falstaff slowly replies, "We have heard the chimes at midnight, Master Shallow." Stirring music and a montage of military scenes provide backdrop for the ensuing credits, but the basically elegiac tone of the film has been established with force. Clearly this will not be a purely comic, saturnalian version of Falstaff, but rather a story about a charmingly unscrupulous bohemian, a critic of the times, who has outlived his influence and who broods over his old age.

The elegy is combined with the political theme, the old man passing away at virtually the same time as Hal assumes the crown. In the last shot, Falstaff's giant coffin is hauled slowly off by Peto and Bardolph, the camera rising on a crane as the cart bearing the coffin is pulled through the gates of Mistress Quickly's inn. The mistress stands in the gateway, while in the distance, across a

barren field, we see the castle of the new king. Richardson's voice reads from the Holinshed commentary on Henry V: "a majesty was he that both lived and died a pattern in princehood, a lodestar in honor, and famous to the world alway." This judgment of Hal is not entirely untrue to the character we've seen, but in any case it is powerfully ironic, the stark visual juxtaposition of the inn and the castle underlining the conflicts of the film as a whole. Hal has forsaken "sport" for politics, comradeship for an isolated rule; and the result is death.

Everywhere Welles has contrasted the two worlds of the action—the inn and the court. The Boar's Head is a vast, oak-beamed bawdy house, lined with narrow corridors and occasionally filled with revelers. The stench of old beer seems to hang in the air, and Welles has done nothing to give the place the artificial charm of "Merrie England." It is a bare, rough, excremental atmosphere, filled with spontaneous, pansexual displays of affection, where, in the latter parts of the film, imagery of disease and death predominates. Hardly an attractive realm, it is at least preferable to the castle, which resembles nothing so much as the cold vaults of the Thatcher Memorial Library. The film proper opens inside this tomb-like palace, where ceilings are lost in darkness and voices echo down the empty chambers. The king gives audience to the Percys (I, iii of *Henry IV*, part I), and is photographed from a low angle seated at his throne, a "Nuremberg" light burning the edges of his crown. Henry, a victim of age and the sins of his past, is a gaunt,

sepulchral figure whose very breath emits frosty clouds. The light streaming down to where he sits is at once regal and ethereal, but it is also barred like a prison. From the beginning he is depicted as a dying man, a wraith garbed in ornamental clothes; in contrast to his rival Falstaff he is bodiless, and Falstaff's stom-

ach mocks him in the same way that comedy always mocks tragedy. Falstaff, on the other hand, has inflated himself to ridiculous proportions, eating and drinking in defiance of any sense of propriety: one of the film's many paradoxes is that his death will result more from a broken spirit than from bloated flesh.

In Shakespeare's plays, the prince is situated somewhat between the twin excesses of the king and Falstaff, which, as I have suggested, have a relationship rather like the superego and the id; in Welles's film, however, the prince sublimates the body when he moves to the castle and assumes the crown. He becomes not so much a kingly as a priestly presence, his physique melting away and his face assuming the dignity of his father. In the photo above, for example, he is shown giving official forgiveness to Falstaff, who has been guilty of interrupting the coronation. The scene is borrowed freely from *Henry V*, where Falstaff is already dead and the king pardons an anonymous criminal; it is one of Welles's most daring revisions of Shakespeare, but it functions beautifully within this film, Hal's order to "enlarge" the prisoner becoming a crucial pun. The new king looks sadly into the distance, recalling lost youth and friendship, his face already showing a certain strain. Near the beginning of the film he promised to "imitate the sun,/ who doth permit the base contagious clouds/ To smother up his beauty from the world,/ That, when he please again to be himself,/ Being wanted, he may be more wondered at." Now, having become king, he has followed his dying father's advice to "busy giddy minds with foreign wars," and has ordered an imperialist expedition to France. His majestic face, however, is distinctly pale, and the sun behind his head struggles with the "base contagious clouds," diffusing its light ambiguously.

Welles foreshadows this conclusion early in the film, when he turns the prince's most important soliloquy ("I know you all, and will awhile uphold/ The unyok'd humor of your idleness") into a crucial exchange with Falstaff. The two stand in the gateway to the inn, Falstaff in his nightshirt at midday, Hal remarking that "If all the year were playing holidays/ To sport would be as tedious as to work." At the end of the speech, which Hal has delivered partly to himself but within Falstaff's hearing, there is small banter about the jobs Falstaff will be given once the heir apparent becomes king. The old man becomes visibly uneasy as a result of the prince's confession. Hal walks away across the field toward the castle, waving goodbye, while Falstaff stands in the gate, feigning gaiety. The prince's farewell and his physical passage from inn to castle are of course the underlying movements of the story, but his remarkable forthrightness in this scene is also a key to what Welles has called the "beady-eyed" aspects of his character. He is, after all, mainly his father's son, and it is sometimes difficult to tell where his sense of responsibility ends and where his ambition begins. The ending of the film therefore strikes a balance somewhere between tragedy and melancholy satire.

Critics agree that *Chimes at Midnight* is Welles's most satisfying production of Shakespeare, but the reason is not simply the interesting moral and psychological structure I have been trying to describe, nor the fact that the plays are adaptable to his philosophy or temperament. Actually, one reason the film is so good is that the history plays are in some ways more naturally "cinematic" than either *Macbeth* or *Othello*, which have a simpler, more unified design. There is something inherently montage-like in the way Shakespeare juxtaposes the various characters and their worlds, moving from the high seriousness of the court to the comedy of the tavern, or setting off Hotspur's valiant pre-battle promise to "tread on kings" against Falstaff's commentary on "honor." As we have seen, Welles recognized this quality very early in his career, and had tried in *Five Kings* to create the effect of cuts, dissolves, and fades, using elaborate lighting and mobile platforms to give the audience the feeling of movies. With film itself, of course, he had the opportunity to move instantaneously across space, matching and contrasting several plot lines with even greater force.

Throughout the film Welles's free editing of the plays and his fine instinct for abrupt transition serve to heighten the tension between Shakespeare's characters. For example, at the end of the opening scene Hotspur (Norman Rodway) stands glowering in a castle corridor, sneering at "That sword-and-buckler Prince of Wales," wishing to have him "poisoned with a pot of ale." Suddenly we are given a closeup of the prince, who drains a cup of sack and wipes his lips. In the previous shots in the castle, the conspiring

Percy family has been photographed from radically low angles, the camera cutting sharply from one portentous view to another; inside the inn, however, the images are closer to a democratic eye-level and the camera tracks dizzily, moving back from the closeup of the prince as he tosses his cup to a page, then following him as he walks past a row of wine vats and into the arms of four playful whores. Later, the film takes us just as abruptly from the Gadshill robbery to the interior of the castle, reversing the order of Shakespeare's scenes but underlining the conflict between the king and his son: the robbery closes with the prince and Poins skipping down a sunny path, congratulating themselves on the prank they've just played on Falstaff ("Were't not for laughing, I should pity him"); immediately the screen goes dark and a great iron door swings open, the king entering a murky throne room to ask, "Can no man tell me of my unthrifty son?"

During the closing parts of the film, these transitions establish subtle thematic connections between parts of the story, even though the principle of visual contrast remains in force. The king's soliloquy on sleep is shot with Gielgud standing in a dim corridor before a window, and when it ends Welles fades to a closeup of Hal, seated in daylight beside a lake, remarking, "Before God I am exceeding weary"; this speech, in turn, is followed by Falstaff's melancholy exchange with Doll Tearsheet, in which he lies down on a dirty bunk and laments his age and fading strength. Still later, when Hal mistakenly thinks his father has died and takes up the crown only to dicover that the king has risen from a sickbed, Welles is able to break the scene in half, inserting a counterpointed moment with Falstaff, Shallow, and Silence (a much-revised version of a few lines from III, ii of *Henry IV*, part two). Hal takes the crown from his dying father's bed and kneels in a chapel, swearing to guard it against "the world's whole strength," while in the background priests sing a dirge. We then cut briefly to the inn, where the three "comic" characters sit before a fire; the camera never moves, simply watching firelight on faces and allowing a profoundly sad yet funny moment to comment on the inevitability of death. Falstaff sits uncomfortably, drinking sack; the stuttering, nearly deaf and dumb Silence is at the left, holding a pig in his lap; and the shrill-voiced Shallow is at the right, bending across Falstaff's belly to make himself heard:

SHALLOW: And to think how many of my old acquaintances are dead.
SILENCE: We shall all f . . . f . . .

SHALLOW: Certain! Tis Certain! Death, as the psalmist said, is certain to all. All shall die.

(Eight seconds of pure silence, as the three gaze thoughtfully ahead into the fire. Shallow suddenly bursts out with a loud question that startles Falstaff.)

SHALLOW: How a good yoke of Bullocks at Stamford fair?

SILENCE: A good yoke of b . . . b . . .

FALSTAFF: *(Somewhat perturbed)* Death is certain.

Sometimes even bolder ironies are created by presenting two events simultaneously, as in the sequence leading up to the battle of Shrewsbury, where we see heavy armored knights being loaded ridiculously upon horses with the aid of pulleys, while on the soundtrack Hotspur cries out: "Come, let me taste my horse,/ That is to bear me like a thunderbolt/ Against the bosom of the Prince of Wales!"

The battle itself, of course, is a privileged moment, in which the director frees himself almost entirely from a theatrical text so that he may present a sustained wordless action which is nevertheless worthy of Shakespeare's poetry. Staged on a windswept plain that evokes images from both John Ford's cavalry westerns and Eisenstein's late epics, the battle is composed out of hundreds of brief shots and becomes the finest example of rhythmic montage in Welles's career. Interestingly, however, it was photographed as a series of long takes, Welles working on the theory that the combatants wouldn't have time to "warm up" if they performed in brief intervals. "I filmed the battle scenes," Welles said, "with a crane that shifted position very quickly at ground level, as quickly as possible, to follow the action." The mobile crane was important not only because Welles was able to take in broad areas of the field, but

because the rapid editing of what were originally shots in motion creates a different rhythm than the standard battle scene, which uses multiple cameras in relatively static setups. In *Chimes at Midnight* we cut from one dynamic moment to another, the individual images disclosing different levels of action and the camera lending an eerie quality to the blood and gore because of its sudden, almost balletic movements.

Welles also claimed to have edited the battle sequence so that "each shot would show a blow, a counterblow, a blow received, a blow struck, and so on." Critics have generally taken him at his word, but close analysis shows that he did nothing of the kind—and good thing, because the "blow given, blow received" formula would have resulted in monotony. Like most directors he cuts from an army on the left to an army on the right, and frequently shows a mace crashing down on one part of the field only to cut to a man falling in another place. Once in the heat of hand-to-hand combat, however, he simply throws a series of brutal and confused images on the screen; the "center cannot hold," and the men have lost their identity in a struggle for survival.

This is not to say that the battle has no "plot" or artistic logic. The shots reproduced here will give some sense of the overall strategy, as well as the visual qualities of the sequence. It begins with a horse charge over a misty, frost-laden field, but when the lines converge every vestige of separate armies is lost, and images of knights on horseback give way to ranks of ugly footsoldiers, occasionally photographed in fast motion or with confused jerks of the camera, hacking away in the midst of crowds. The battle is initiated with cries of "For Harry and St. George!" only to degenerate into ignoble savagery, with men beating viciously at prone bodies. As the day of carnage wears on, the field becomes a quagmire of mud

and blood, piles of soldiers writhing in slurred motion and falling down atop one another. Occasionally one glimpses a helmeted knight struggling like a dinosaur in quicksand, or a mass of men so caked with mud that, as Pauline Kael has remarked, they seem to have become their own memorial statuary. An extraordinary series of individual images stays in the mind. A dark figure stabbing at a dying man and then, in surrealistically fast motion, moving to another part of the field to thrust his sword into another wounded soldier; groups of men gathered around anonymous shapes on the ground, cutting away like a crowd of jackals surrounding carrion. In one shot (the last of the series), we see the legs of two men writhing in slime, the figure on the bottom jerking spasmodically as if in parody of sexual climax. It is a significant image because it undermines completely Hotspur's eloquent, poetic love of war; early in the film Welles has suggested that a passion for military derring-do is a displacement for sex (the dialogue between Hotspur and Kate is intercut with buglers blowing pompous calls to arms), but here the underlying eroticism of the chivalric code ("Yet once ere night/ I will embrace him with a soldier's arm/ That he shall shrink under my courtesy") is exposed in all its cruel perversity.

The success of the battle scenes, however, has less to do with the manifest content of the images than with the soundtrack and the half-hidden, evocative qualities of the photography. Welles hinted at this fact when he said that he did not "stroll about like a collector choosing images and putting them together." "I am most concerned," he said, "with rendering a musical impression. . . . The visual aspect is that which is dictated to me by poetic and musical forms." Hence the battle is nearly as impressive if one simply listens to the sounds. The grunts of the soldiers and the clang of metal have been weirdly amplified, like radio sound effects, with the noise of combat set in counterpoint to music and choral voices composed by Francesco Lavaginino. The harsh, speeded-up dissonance of battle contrasts with the extreme regularity and slowness of the choral chant, creating a spooky, fatalistic quality, as if all this action were going nowhere but to death. On the screen, the horses and men are obscured by fog and dust, or are photographed in such rapid motion that one barely has time to absorb the details. Welles has commented, "The danger in cinema is that in using a camera you see everything. What one must do is succeed in . . . making things emerge that are not, in fact, visible." In other words, the director's job is to weave a spell, in this case with pure speed and the suggestion of heated violence, none of it fully apparent in the isolated images.

This indirection is a key to Welles's overall approach to the visuals, which represent a special problem in any adaptation of Shakespeare. The richness of the Shakespearian text is of course in its language and its manipulation of theatrical convention; hence too much photographic realism tends to overwhelm the poetry. As

André Bazin once observed of Molière, "The text . . . takes on meaning only in a forest of painted canvas and the same is true of the acting. The footlights are the autumn sun." Because Welles began as a theatrical director he understood this axiom, and was uneasy about the specificity of film in general, preferring instead the "poetic" qualities of an art that suggests more than it shows. The purpose of cinematic images, he said in an interview concerning *Chimes at Midnight*, ought to be to "transform the real, to charge it with a 'character' it does not possess." (A far cry, it will be noted, from the notions about realism that both he and Gregg Toland espoused while working on *Kane*.) In *Othello* he had used Moorish seascapes and Venetian façades as expressively as any studio designer, but the Henry plays presented an even greater difficulty. Although their epic grandeur begs for cinematic adaptation, the "outdoor" spectacle conflicts with period costumes and blank verse. Welles remarked that the only films in which "costumes and nature have learned to live in juxtaposition" are traditional genres like American westerns and Japanese samurai adventures. And while *Chimes at Midnight* is the closest thing to a western Welles ever made, it is a western without a tradition. One of his problems, therefore, was to create a believable natural environment for Shakespeare's men on horseback. He said that he wanted to avoid the feeling he had gotten from Olivier's *Henry V*, where "people leave the castle . . . and suddenly they meet again on a golf course somewhere charging at one another."

Not surprisingly, Welles achieved his ends; he was one of the greatest "period" directors in history, if one considers his success with *Kane, Ambersons,* and *Othello*, where there is never a disharmony between actors and environment. (Or the analogous success of *Touch of Evil*, in which a suburb of Los Angeles becomes a southwestern bordertown.) In *Chimes at Midnight* he once again used the "real" world in an abstract, selective way, disregarding pure historical authenticity (the film was shot on location in Barcelona, Madrid, and other Spanish locations, so that the atmosphere is anything but English) and sometimes ignoring plausibility or coherence. The seasons, for example, change rapidly throughout, and are rarely presented in their proper order; it is fall when Hal and Falstaff go off to war with the Percys, but the battle scenes are fought in a summer landscape.

Clearly the film was shot on a budget that forced these compromises on Welles, but it never suffers as a result. "What I try to do," he said, "is to see with the same eyes the external real world and that which is fabricated." In every shot, therefore, the rocks, trees, and sky are chosen for their expressive possibilities— not the glamorous, haunting expressionism of *Othello* or of Welles's early studio films, but a more homely, gritty style, where occasionally there is a romantic density of air and light. Hence the early parts of the bat-

tle scenes, in which horsemen charge through a wooded landscape, strongly resemble picturesque images from *The Prince of Foxes*; in Henry's camp immediately before the battle, a wind is blowing strongly, sending gusts of smoke and dust across the actors in a manner learned from Ford; meanwhile, the camp of the Percys is shot on a calm and sunny day, from a camera position so low to the ground that it comments derisively on the hubris of the rebellion—the screen is literally filled with sky, and as the Percys stride across the frame they appear to be standing on air.

Many of the landscapes are veiled or dappled, and all are used symbolically. The castle across from Mistress Quickly's inn, for example, is obscured in a cold mist, and in the later parts of the film Falstaff and his companions are photographed in snow, rain, or darkness. The early Gadshill robbery sequence takes place in a Spanish forest rather like the one in *Mr. Arkadin*—scores of straight, narrow trees without underbrush, the sun streaming down on bright autumn leaves. At one point, when Falstaff is being pursued by Hal and Poins, the camera makes a lengthy lateral track across the scene, and the actors become tiny figures running hilariously through rows of fantastic tree trunks. The area begins to resemble a child's playground—the antithesis of the battle of Shrewsbury—where men brandish swords harmlessly and scatter fallen leaves over one another; it is a robbery as carefree as the "paper chase" in a New England woods in *The Stranger*, but, as in that earlier film, the exuberance of "boys" at play has a bittersweet quality, the autumnal background indicating that death must follow from all this ripeness.

In fact nearly the entire film is shot amid a dead or dying nature, the only important exception being parts of the battle, where summer trees make an ironic setting. In the two shots shown on p. 232, for example, Hotspur is shown making his dying

speech, followed by Hal's memorial to him. The leafy trees behind Hotspur are a sign of his premature death, a reinforcement of his comment, "Thou hast robbed me of my youth"; Hal, on the other hand, is photographed against a slightly foggy view, with a solitary horseman passing in the distance. On the soundtrack, a trumpet softly plays a sort of taps, the whole shot being charged with the atmosphere of a military funeral.

Repeatedly Welles indicated that *Chimes at Midnight* is a "human" story done in relatively simple terms—an actor's rather than a director's picture. He disliked being called a formalist, and yet, as the foregoing remarks may indicate, the completed picture is a formalist's delight. It is a triumph of style as meaning; at every moment the "plastics" of cutting, camera movement, and composition translate the story into a nearly universal language, the film as a whole containing as great a range of expressive devices as anything Welles had done previously. For example, as Brian Henderson has noted, the picture is virtually a textbook for the various ways a long take or sequence shot may be constructed: at one extreme is the completely static shot described earlier, where Falstaff, Silence, and Shallow sit before a fire meditating on death; at another is the early scene in the tavern, in which Falstaff, Hal, and Poins discuss plans for the robbery as the camera weaves around them in a little dance. Late in the film, one finds a classic example of what Henderson calls the "theatrical" shot, with the camera positioned at a low angle at one end of the tavern, serving as a kind of proscenium. Shallow and Silence are doing a funny little dance in the middle distance, while Falstaff crosses "upstage" to sit and talk with his page about old times; the dancing couple exits and another page enters to announce Pistol, who comes on excitedly from the right; Falstaff moves forward halfway, learning that Hal is about to be crowned; upon hearing the news, he marches to the extreme foreground, the camera tilting upward to catch his face towering above us like a giant. "Is the old king—*dead?*" he asks rhetorically, his expression showing jubilation and a quick surge of power; he then exits right and the scene closes. In one temporally unified shot Falstaff has moved from dejection to joy, his steady progress forward in the frame marking his lifted emotion, the wide-angle lens making him seem a dot at the beginning and a colossus at the end.

It is a commonplace of writing on the film to say that this formal beauty has been spoiled by a badly synchronized sound-track, which is indeed a serious flaw. But this problem, which often makes *Chimes at Midnight* seem a defaced masterpiece, has tended to obscure the fact that the *idea* of the soundtrack, considered apart from the images, is quite satisfying. It contains some of the most beautiful readings of Shakespeare ever recorded for film— especially in the case of Gielgud's soliloquies—and the musical settings by Lavaginino are uniformly superb. Henry IV's celebrated speech on sleep, for example, begins with the palace musicians playing a soft Renaissance melody, and then slowly becomes a fuller orchestration, expressing a profound yearning as the speech reaches oratorical heights. Gielgud virtually sings the blank verse, and the concluding couplet ("Then happy low, lie down. / Uneasy lies the head that wears the crown") is delivered in perfect harmony with the last chords.

If *Chimes at Midnight* has any true formal problem, as distinct from technical execution, it is not in the director's handling of camera or sound, but in the dramatic curve of the story itself, which presents exactly the same difficulty as the original version of *The Magnificent Ambersons*. It is a film about decline, begin-ning with the last vestiges of celebration for a youth already spent, and then proceeding into a long, slow rendering of dissolution and decay. The delightful Gadshill robbery and the "play extempore" in the tavern have exactly the same function as the Amberson ball and the ensuing sleigh ride—moments of authentic liveliness and charm, laden with ironic foreshadowings of doom, which give way to a somber, almost morbid atmosphere. Thus, except for the battle scene at the center of the film, there is almost nothing to relieve us from extended meditations on disease and death. Joseph McBride describes the problem nicely when he compares Truffaut's *Jules and Jim* with *The Magnificent Ambersons:* "The structure of Truffaut's film, as he admits, weakens in the last sections, as does that of *Ambersons* for reasons not entirely due to the studio's recutting. To create a mood so buoyant as that achieved in the first half-hour of each film and let it down gracefully into destruction proved too taxing for both young directors." But the problem stayed with Welles in his later film, which places him in exactly the same situation. Until the dramatic heights of the coronation scene and the subsequent death of Falstaff, he must render lifelessness or near stupor without allowing the film itself to lag. It seems to me he never quite overcomes this difficulty, and for much of its second half *Chimes at Midnight* demands that the audience give up its desire to be intensely moved or entertained. Like many great works, it contains moments of lethargy which are the price we pay for the power and ambition of the whole.

Luckily, however, the concluding scenes have not suffered the fate of *Ambersons*, and the drama rises to a remarkable pitch, more moving, dignified, and "human" than any previous film by Welles. Falstaff, hearing the news that Hal has become king, rushes precipitously to the coronation, leading Shallow across the snowy landscape we saw at the beginning of the film and promising riches and joy to come. Inside the castle, he realizes that he has forgotten to dress properly, but notes that this will be interpreted as a sign of humility, as if he were a heedless worshipper come to see the Christ child. Welles speaks Shakespeare's lines with virtually no suggestion that Falstaff is cunning or opportune, making him instead a vulnerable innocent, overcome with excitement, proud "to stand stained with travel, and sweating with desire to see him, thinking of nothing else to be done but to see him."

Meanwhile the new king moves past a ceremonial gathering, his crown barely visible beyond clouds of incense and rows of armed men. Without warning, Falstaff bursts through the ranks of celebrants and into Henry's wake, shouting blissfully through stone corridors which until now have heard nothing but solemnity and scheming: "God save thy Grace, King Hal! My Royal Hal! . . . My King! My Jove! I speak to thee, my heart!" There is a hushed, stunned silence, while a guard rebukes the intruder and tries to allow the coronation to go forward. Hal turns, and in closeup makes his famous rejection speech:

I know thee not, old man. Fall to thy prayers.
How ill white hairs become a fool and jester!
I have long dreamed of such a kind of man,

So surfeit-swelled, so old, and so profane,
But being awaked, I do despise my dream . . .
Presume not that I am the thing I was,
For God doth know, so shall the world perceive,
That I have turned away my former self,
So will I those that kept me company.

The prophecy Hal made in the tavern has now come true, and this time his imitation of his father is in unmistakable earnest. When Hal banishes Falstaff, "not to come near our person by ten mile," the old man drops to his knees in pain. The speech is chilling, detached, and ruthless, but the exchange of looks between the two men, shown here, reveals an unspoken communication passing between them. Hal's face, backed by the cold mists of his castle, is nearly a mask, but it has a pale intensity that conveys his anger and his painful recognition of what he is casting aside. Falstaff is on his knees, but he is photographed from a slightly low angle that makes him equal in stature to the king; controlling his grief, he stares back in silent rebuke. The boyish monarch has in fact always been an old man, while his gray-haired subject has been as transparent and naïve as a child. In the irony of their relationship, and in the tension between these two shots, is the essential meaning of what Welles has called a "somber comedy." As in *Citizen Kane*, friendship is revealed as policy, and childhood as a dream.

10

Art about Art

Man ... *the instrument of creation ... will die. ... But what is created by him will never die. And in order to live eternally he has not the slightest need of extraordinary gifts or of accomplishing prodigies. Who was Sancho Panza? Who was Don Abbondio? And yet they live eternally because—living seeds—they had the good fortune to find a fruitful womb—a fantasy which knew how to raise and nourish them, and make them live through all eternity.*

—Luigi Pirandello, *Six Characters in Search of an Author*

Welles's career was littered with abandoned or unfulfilled projects, the residue of a restless, energetic life. After 1955 he worked, in bits and pieces, on a film adaptation of *Don Quixote*, which he wryly predicted would have its title changed to a question he was always asked: *When Will Don Quixote Be Finished?* The picture was started as a half-hour television show, but subsequently grew into a feature film composed of three episodes from Cervantes, framed by scenes of Welles himself explaining the story to child actress Patty McCormack. The episodes are staged in twentieth-century settings; for example, Welles has Quixote assault a movie screen in an attempt to rescue a starlet. Unfortunately Patty McCormack is no longer a child, and the Mexican actor Francisco Reiguera, who plays Quixote, is now dead. Even so, Welles was able to complete most of the film. His former secretary, Audrey Stainton, has written a fascinating memoir in *Sight and Sound* (Autumn 1988), showing how he confronted and overcame many obstacles to the project, incessantly revising it like an impassioned amateur. He had begun shooting with no clear plan in mind, and as the picture slowly expanded, he perpetually added refinements. One of his editors, Mauro Bonanni, became the guardian of an almost finished, hour-and-a-half version—still in need of dubbing and postsynchronization—fragments of which have been shown in Cannes and New York.

In the late sixties in Yugoslavia Welles wrote and directed a thriller called *The Deep*, based on Charles Williams's novel *Dead Calm*, starring himself, Laurence Harvey, and Jeanne Moreau. I have seen an early version of the script, entitled *Dead Reckoning*, which is an almost pure suspense story told in the limited time span of a single day, without flashbacks or even much reference to the past lives of the characters. It all takes place in the middle of the Pacific Ocean, where a honeymoon couple, John and Rae Ingram (played in the completed film by Michael Bryant and Oja Kodar, acting under the name Olga Palinkas), are sailing to an island aboard their ketch, the *Saracen*. One morning on a calm sea they discover a man rowing desperately toward them from a sinking yacht called the *Orpheus*. He is Hughie Warriner (Laurence Harvey), and when he is hauled aboard he tells a gruesome story of how his wife and everyone else on the *Orpheus* have died of food poisoning. He claims he has buried them all at sea and has been adrift ever since, his radio broken and the yacht beginning to sink.

When Hughie collapses of exhaustion John Ingram gets into the lifeboat and rows across to investigate the *Orpheus*. In the half-flooded cabin he discovers Ruth Warriner (Moreau) and Russ Brewer (Welles), both of them alive and hiding in fear of Hughie. Just as he is about to rescue these two, Ingram looks back at his own boat and sees Hughie has regained consciousness and is starting the engines. When Rae struggles with him he strikes her savagely and she collapses on the deck. John makes a frantic attempt to row back to the *Saracen*, but the boat moves off at high speed, leaving him and the two strangers back on board the *Orpheus*. The remainder of the film involves John's desperate attempt to keep the yacht afloat, hampered by the drunken Brewer, a broken engine, and faulty instrumentation. Meanwhile, on board the *Saracen*, Rae Ingram recovers and finds herself confronted with a madman whom she must outwit if there is to be any chance of saving her husband. By the end the Ingrams are in fact reunited, but not before Hughie Warriner and Russ Brewer—each of them revealed as psychotic—have had a fight to the death.

This early draft of the script is exciting to read, and suggests a good many psychological tensions running beneath the suspense plot. It also calls for a number of complex technical effects, including underwater photography, several shots from the top of a ship's mast as it bucks and whirls in the open sea, and a spectacular fire aboard the *Orpheus*. It is, however, a fairly straightforward thriller, in some ways uncharacteristic of Welles. Although shooting on the picture was completed, the soundtrack was incompletely dubbed and Welles had trouble finding a distributor. Other filmmakers had better luck with similar projects: in 1977, Peter Yeats directed a Peter Benchley script called *The Deep*, and in 1989, George Miller directed *Dead Calm*, based on the same Charles Williams novel Welles had used as a source.

In the early seventies, Welles became involved with Films l'Astrophore, a Paris-based company financed by the Iranian government, which proposed to back not only him but Elia Kazan, Sergio Leone, and John Boorman; the company distributed *F for Fake* in Europe and was prepared to support his other work, but then the Iranian revolution changed everything. Meanwhile, to keep his career alive, Welles endorsed Jim Beam whiskey and Eastern Airlines. Throughout the seventies and early eighties, he made frequent TV appearances with Dean Martin, Johnny Carson, and Merv Griffin—and in an infamous series of commercials, he promised that Paul Masson would "sell no wine before its time." Increasingly, he seemed willing to do the kind of jobs that his more puritan admirers thought were a prostitution of talent. He was simple and direct in explaining his motives: "It can be fun," he told an audience in Boston. "I do it for the exposure. If you don't, you get forgotten."

The only theatrical films by Welles to appear in the last decades of his life were two short works, *The Immortal Story* (1968) and *F for Fake* (1976), both minor pieces which are virtually meditations by the director on the nature of his art. Of course, Welles's movies were always self-reflexive, but these two took a distinctly Pirandellian turn, becoming somewhat less public and political. In them he thinks introspectively, immersing himself in notions about artifice and eternity, playing variations on the theme of art and counterfeit. Among his later, still incomplete films is *The Other Side of the Wind*, a movie about Hollywood which he had been shooting since 1970. It would appear to be the ultimate work in this vein—a picture that invites comparison with Fellini's *8½* and Truffaut's *Day for Night*. At the last stage of his life, therefore, he became a cultural legend who, more than ever, exploited the ironies of his own celebrity.

I *The Immortal Story*

The first of these late films is easily the most literary. A sixty-minute work produced originally for French television, *The Immortal Story* is based rather closely on a tale from Isak Dinesen's *Anecdotes of Destiny:* like Welles, Dinesen was an artist in the Gothic tradition who was fond of exemplary fables, and Welles needed to make only minor alterations in the story in order to create meanings relevant to his own career.

The film is in color, but is shot in almost rudimentary fashion, using a spartan decor and few ostentatious camera tricks. It opens in darkness, with an iris into an oriental port city reminiscent of *Broken Blossoms*, and closes with a slow "burn out" to a white screen; periodically we hear a solitary piano playing a haunting melody by Erik Satie. Unfortunately, many individual scenes are marred by technical crudities and breaks in the visual continuity, but on the whole Welles's quiet style is beautifully appropriate. Occasionally one notices his typical mannerisms—a small chorus of townspeople like the ones in *Ambersons*, who provide exposition at the beginning; several deep-focus compositions and radical camera angles; a long, rather bumpy traveling shot down a colonnade; and a couple of scenes on an ornate stairway. But the relative simplicity of the film is in keeping with Dinesen's own style—a prose which is as economical as a biblical parable, and which Welles reads quietly in off-screen narration. The resulting movie is like a charming miniature, a distillation of one of Welles's favorite themes to its most essential level.

Dinesen's tale is set in nineteenth-century Canton, although Welles changes the locale to Macao, the place that in *The Lady from Shanghai* is called the "wickedest city in the world." It tells of a rich merchant, aptly named Clay (Welles plays the character and makes him an American rather than a European), who has lived like a god all his life, controlling the little oriental figures that

move in regular patterns across some of the film's landscapes. As the story begins, Clay has reached a crisis similar to the one that is met by most of Welles's central characters. Like Kurtz in *Heart of Darkness*, like Kane, like Macbeth, his drive to power and autonomy has ended in tragic isolation and a forced recognition of his limits. Dinesen describes him as a "tall, dry, and close old man," who sits in the midst of his rich house, "erect, silent, and alone." Welles combines this comment with a visual allusion to Charles Foster Kane, showing Clay sitting down to eat, his head surrounded by mirrors that multiply his image.

Almost Scrooge-like, Clay is unique among Welles's protagonists in being completely without outward charm or beauty. He believes, as he says later in the film, that his money will be "proof against dissolution," and he contrasts gold with human relations, which always involve some giving over of the self. He has cheated his friend and former business partner, whom we are told was a warmhearted man, and has taken over the partner's house; in his old age his only companion is his accountant, Levinsky (Roger Coggio), a survivor of the 1848 pogrom against Polish Jews, who is equally dry and lonely. Levinsky lives in a solitary flat, viewed discreetly through a window from out in the street as he draws a blind for privacy. "Desire," Welles comments, "had been washed, bleached, and burnt out of him before he had learned to read," and yet "things not to be recounted and hardly to be recalled still moved, like big deep-water fish, in the depths of his dark mind." Both men, in their different ways, have tried to protect themselves against the passage of time and the dangers of life by retreating into their houses, by repressing their feelings, and by giving themselves over to an absolute materialism. Clay devotes himself to his goods, whereas Levinsky marshals columns of figures; between them, as Dinesen says, there is "a kind of relation."

When the drama begins these two are seated in Clay's library, a wide space between them, the warm lights of the room contrasting with blue twilight outside. The old man is lost in a huge chair across from Lévinsky, who sits tiny and hunched over, reading his accounts. At the end of the nightly routine Clays asks, in his perpetually crusty and harsh way, if Levinsky knows of anything else to read. Whereupon the conversation turns to various kinds of books. Besides the accounts, Levinsky has at hand the biblical prophecy of Elisha, which he carefully unrolls from a sheet of aging paper and recites to his master. The prophet speaks of how "God will come with a recompense . . . Then the eyes of the blind shall be opened . . . Then shall the lame man leap as a hart . . . For in the wilderness shall waters break out. And streams in the desert."

Clay, who is all too aware of his own dryness and his gouty foot, recalls another kind of story, about how a lonely sailor was once invited by a rich old man to spend the night with his young wife and make him a child; at the end of the evening the sailor was given five guineas and sent on his way. Levinsky, too, has heard this story, which is told everywhere by sailors, but he reminds Clay that it never happened. "If this story has never happened before," Clay says angrily, "I will make it happen now. I do not like pretense. I do not like prophecies. I like facts."

The rest of the film becomes the tragicomedy of Clay's attempts to turn prophecy into an account book and art into life—to possess the story by becoming both its author (or, more precisely, its *auteur*) and one of its characters. Life, however, resists his efforts. Instead of a randy sailor he hires a virginal and decidedly mystical young castaway (Norman Eshley) who has just been rescued from a desert island and who is trying to find passage to his homeland; instead of a demure young wife he is forced to use a slightly aging local prostitute (Jeanne Moreau), who is the daughter of his former business partner. The lovers—ironically named Paul and Virginie, after the famous couple in Bernardin de St.-Pierre's novel—slowly become willing participants in the drama, meeting in a sweet encounter that is the most explicitly erotic moment in any of Welles's films. But on the morning after, the sailor refuses Clay's money and announces to Levinsky that he will never tell his companions at sea what has happened. Clay dies, having served briefly as puppet-master; his striving for omnipotence and immortality is frustrated because the events he has re-created will have no audience.

Late in the film, in a speech which belongs to Levinsky in the original source, Welles has Clay explain the perpetual appeal of the "immortal story" to sailors: "The sailors who tell this story are poor men who lead a lonely life on the sea. That is why they tell about that rich house and that beautiful lady." Art and fantasy, in other words, grow out of isolation and a longing for impossibilities, and Clay's attempt to bring a Platonic second nature down to the real world is an expression of tragic hubris. A dying man, he tries to become what Pirandello calls a "living character"; meanwhile he tries to dominate Paul and Virginie, asserting his power over their passions, turning them into *objets d'art* like the figures on Keats's Grecian urn: "forever warm and still to be enjoyed, forever panting and forever young." "You," he announces to the lovers from his voyeuristic position on the balcony outside their room, "are young . . . you believe that you are walking and moving according to your own will. But it is not so . . . you are two young, strong, and lusty jumping-jacks within this old hand of mine." Standing outside and listening to the sounds of their lovemaking, he tries to deny his own age, rousing himself vicariously and hence bringing waters into his own wilderness.

As a symbol of humanity, considered apart from his boorishness and cruelty, there is something both vulnerable and sympathetic about Clay. Even though he boasts about money and claims to make other humans move at his will, his control has obvious limits; there is a naïvete and defensiveness in his very seclusion, which is an attempt to wall himself off from those aspects of life he cannot govern. He is also humanized by the fact that he is trying to achieve not just power, but life itself. His age and his sense of being cut off from the living, sexual juices of life are pathetic—indeed Welles seems to heighten the erotic elements of Dinesen's story so as to bring out this theme more forcefully—and toward the end of the film, in the wake of the lovers' passionate night together, one almost wishes him success.

There is a sense, moreover, in which he and all the other characters achieve a kind of victory. Despite the grotesque little charade he produces by hiring an impoverished sailor and a *putain respecteuse* to spend the night in his house, Clay indirectly gives a gift to himself and everyone else. For a time at least, Elisha's prophecy comes true, creating sexual joy and love in the midst of barren lives. Paul and Virginie, after all, are as lonely as Clay and Levinsky, and are linked to them in certain ways. Paul has been lost on an island, where he could only imagine a woman he has never seen. "I sometimes fancied that I had a girl with me, who was mine," he tells Virginie. "I brought her birds' eggs and fish, and some big sweet fruits that grew there. . . . We slept together in a cave." As for

Virginie, who as a little girl lived in the house now owned by Clay, her life has been filled with disappointment. A potentially warm-hearted prostitute (Welles photographs her playing with fortune-tellers' cards, like Tanya in *Touch of Evil*), she wistfully recalls her first love affair, when an earthquake had literally coincided with her pleasure. Ever since she has been in decline, and, as Dinesen remarks, "she would have liked her lovers better had they left her free to love them in her own way, as poor pitiful people in need of sympathy."

Once Clay's little drama begins, however, the story seems to take possession of the actors, their separate longing for renewal and communion being fulfilled in a way that is beyond anyone's control. Reluctantly and contemptuously, the sailor and the woman agree to Clay's plan, Virginie plotting a kind of vengeance upon the man who has been responsible for her father's failure and death, the sailor resisting the corrupt old merchant until the last moment. But when they meet, the lovers are transformed into a Paul and Virginie worthy of St.-Pierre's fiction. The sailor approaches a gauzy, flower-bedecked bedroom where a nude lies waiting for him, and in the romantic dimness he mistakes her for the young girl of his dreams; Welles photographs their lovemaking in a series of almost static images, showing the curve of a back and the flutter of an eyelash, each shot magnified with a telephoto lens in a style uncharacteristic of him. At the height of her passion, Virginie suddenly rises in terror, imagining that the earth has moved as it did in her first affair. Outside on the veranda Clay listens to everything, growing more and more heated, and when the scene is finished the sound of crickets in the garden gives way to the early morning call of birds, the desert having come to life.

At the conclusion all the characters seem fatigued and slightly changed by what has happened. The sailor scoffs when Levinsky asks if he will talk about his adventure. "To whom would I tell it?" he says. "Who in the world would believe it if I told it? I would not tell it for a hundred times five guineas." At the same time he leaves behind a gift for Virginie—a large pink shell "as smooth and silk as a knee" which he found on his island. "When you hold it to your ear," he tells Clay, "there is a sound in it, a song." In another modest alteration of his source Welles has the sailor present the shell to the merchant instead of the accountant. As the youth exits, closing the door to the veranda, Welles cuts suddenly to a closeup of the shell, which is rocking gently on the porch floor; Clay has dropped it in his dying moment, and the rounded pearly shape is an obvious echo of Kane's paperweight. The symbolic meaning of the object is also reminiscent of Welles's first film; it suggests an ideal realm—globed, compacted, and pure—which in this case gives the listener an intimation of immortal beauty. We do not know if Clay has listened to the shell before his death, but Levinsky comments to Virginie that the old man's cup of triumph has been too strong for him. "It is very hard on people who want things so badly," he says. "If they cannot get these things it is hard, and when they do get them, surely it is very hard."

Unlike Kane's death, Clay's suggests a possible triumph, an achieved glory just before extinction. The other characters, too, have been moved by the experience. Virginie comes out of her room and stands on the balcony with Levinsky and the dead Clay, watching her sailor walk away through the garden; he turns as he leaves, and they exchange significant glances, having shared the experience of love. By acting out the "immortal story" they have participated in one of those eternalized "moments" so common to romantic literature, making contact not only with each other but with something transpersonal and hence ideal. In a less direct sense, Clay, too, has been moved by passion and beauty, recapturing the spirit of "jumping-jacks." The world, as Yeats said, is "no country for old men," but the aging merchant has been able to transcend his own body.

The final triumph is reserved for Levinsky, the dark-suited, rather insect-like accountant who has been a silent witness to the action and a go-between for Clay and the lovers. In the last shot, he sits before his dead master's big chair on the veranda, while Virginie stands off in the distance watching the sailor depart. Lifting the shell and placing it to his ear, he listens to the song. "I have heard it before," he says, "long, long ago. But where?" Those passions which we were told have been washed, bleached, and burned out of the man have momentarily returned; he, too, is able to hear the joy of life, and is at least dimly in touch with the "big deep-water fish" of his unconscious. With this recognition, this memory of an elemental life force, the film ends, the screen fading to a white tinged with pink, like the color of a seashell.

The film as a whole has been structured like a nest of boxes, containing a story within a story and reminding us, with constant references to Welles's previous films, that the director himself is like Clay. Thus Welles strives to create fictions that will live, standing outside his actors like a puppet-master, always aware of his mortality; also like Clay, he acts as well as directs, and inevitably there comes a moment when he and all the players are moved more by the fiction itself than by any controlling hand. The director sets a process in motion, only to be consumed by a collective imagination.

It is, to be sure, a highly idealistic notion of art, reducing everything to a fable about eternity, totally unconcerned with the specifics of time and place that made Welles's early work so lively. On its own terms, however, the film succeeds, achieving a serenity and simplicity of visual effect unlike any of Welles's previous movies. The wide-angle views are uncluttered and generally rather static, the backgrounds containing only a few carefully chosen details, such as the tiny figures of Chinese coolies running through a courtyard as Levinsky and Virginie discuss Clay's proposition. The colors are rich and often symbolic—as in the red and gold dining room where Clay reveals his plans to the sailor—whereas the characters themselves are dressed in simple blacks and whites, their bodies making a subtle contrast to the passionate world behind them. There is only one point where it seems to me that Welles fails to create the effect he wants; his own makeup consists of smeared greasepaint and a false pointed nose that looks painfully artificial in closeups. One could argue, of course, that this artificiality is consistent with most of his other films, and that here as in *Mr. Arkadin* he wanted the false face to be noticed. But such quasi-Brechtian theatrics are as much out of keeping with this movie as the painted backdrops which appear at crucial moments in Hitchcock's *Marnie*. The fact is, *The Immortal Story* tries to charm its audience, drawing them into a lovely *mise-en-scène* and sustaining a mood with Satie's music. There is barely any aesthetic justification for Welles to call attention to himself as an actor with a disguise, and he almost destroys several crucial scenes when his painted face appears on the screen. In every other way, he has created a work of modest but real virtue—a film that is ideal for television, if not for the purely theatrical distribution it received in the States.

II *F for Fake*

Welles seems to have arrived at the rather awkward title of this film reluctantly, after trying *Hoax, Nothing but the Truth,* and *!Fake.* In France it is called *Verités et Mensonges,* which, with its suggestion of a pun on "lies" and "dreams," is perfectly appropriate.

At any rate the American title is fitting for a movie which is in some respects bogus, having been composed largely from an old documentary by François Reichenbach. In 1968 Reichenbach took cameras to the Spanish island of Ibiza to profile the art forger Elmyr de Hory, a minor criminal whose adventures and philosophy had been described in Clifford Irving's book, *Fake!* Welles saw the film after the Clifford Irving/Howard Hughes affair had broken into the news, and realized that it had taken on a new significance. As a result he bought up the entire documentary, re-edited huge parts of it, and interspersed Reichenbach's footage with scenes of his own making—some of these composed of scraps of material he had photographed years before under totally different circumstances. What he produced is a nearly unique form of movie; neither documentary nor fiction, it resembles a Chautauqua-speech-cum-magic-show, bound together by Welles's own celebrity presence.

Welles appears throughout in the role of narrator and guide, discussing the relationship between art and forgery, reminiscing about the *War of the Worlds* hoax, interviewing old associates like Joseph Cotten and Richard Wilson, and performing magic tricks. Near the beginning of the film, and periodically thereafter, we catch climpses of Oja Kodar, the beautiful Yugoslavian actress Welles met while working on *The Trial.* In footage which was actually shot some time before *F for Fake* was conceived, we see her strolling through Paris streets in a miniskirt. Ultimately Welles explains her importance. It seems she is the granddaughter of a talented art forger, and she once played an elaborate trick on Picasso. In return for acting as his nude model, she received a series of paintings which she then took to her grandfather; the old man forged copies and destroyed the originals, thus becoming responsible for a whole period of Picasso's career. At the conclusion of this ironic episode, which is impressively edited and dramatized, Welles reminds the audience that near the beginning of the movie he had claimed everything we would see in the next hour would be true; according to his watch, however, we have been watching for ninety minutes, and have ourselves become victims of a sort of confidence game. The Picasso story has been a lie, even though it contains an imaginative truth.

Welles did not in fact shoot a large section of the movie, but it belongs entirely to his personality, and is almost a textbook on how to create new material out of old. *F for Fake* might be described as a collage, like the *Kane* newsreel (which Welles actually parodies at one point, in the form of a biography of Howard

Hughes). It is made up of sharply contrasting types of images, some of them "found," some of them doctored or created, all of them devoted to familiar Wellesian themes. Thus Reichenbach's documentary photography co-exists with several deliberately glamorous, dream-like shots that belong exclusively to the world of the fiction film; notice, for example, the two pictures here, one showing Elmyr de Hory and the other showing Oja Kodar.

The contrast is appropriate, of course, because Welles is exploring the ambiguous relationship between truth and dreams. But even more than that, he is directly confronting the essential "lie" upon which the movies are built—the editing process. In a sense, he finds himself in a position like the Russian filmmakers after the Revolution; short on money and technical facilities, he rearranges a pre-existent film. It was exactly this practice that helped Eisenstein discover that cinema is not reality but a *version* of events—a coded message with ideological biases. For example in his essay "Through Theatre to Cinema" (1934), he speaks with a certain relish about what he terms the "wise and wicked art of reediting the work of others"—an art which all the cutters in the Soviet Union had mastered by the late teens:

I cannot resist the pleasure of citing here one montage *tour de force* of this sort, executed by Boitler. One film bought from Germany was *Danton*, with Emil Jannings. As released on our screens, this scene was shown: Camille Desmoulins is condemned to the guillotine. Greatly agitated, Danton rushes to Robespierre, who turns aside and slowly wipes away a tear. The sub-title said, approximately, "In the name of freedom I had to sacrifice a friend."

But who could have guessed that in the German original, Danton, represented as an idler, a petticoat-chaser, a splendid chap and the only positive figure in the midst of evil characters, that this Danton ran to the evil Robespierre and . . . spat in his face? And that it was this spit that Robespierre wiped from his face with a handkerchief? And that the title indicated Robespierre's hatred of Danton, a hate that in the end of the film motivates the condemnation of Jannings-Danton to the guillotine?

Much of *F for Fake* is built out of a trickery similar to what Eisenstein describes, although the deceit is laid bare and presented to the audience for their contemplation. At one point we see Reichenbach's camera reflected in a mirror, and we repeatedly see Welles at an editing table, rearranging old footage. In the original Reichenbach documentary, Clifford Irving is seen commenting on Elmyr's art and character; but in Welles's re-editing, Elmyr becomes Irving's commentator. As the film proceeds, Reichenbach's documentary is elaborately toyed with before the audience's eyes, revealing what John Russell Taylor has called its ironic "sub-text" of meanings. "In the end," Welles remarks, "Elmyr played a very important role in the life of his biographer . . . Irving, who is a better magician than I, was able to transform himself into a superstar . . . Isn't this revelatory of our age, that a swindler ultimately becomes a celebrity?"

At the same time the film allows Welles to comment on other kinds of deception, particularly on the relationship between art and originality. (No doubt he was obsessed with this topic when he began the project, because Pauline Kael's essay on *Citizen Kane* had unleashed a controversy over the "authorship" of his most distinguished achievement.) One of the chief focuses of his attention is the forger de Hory, who, before Welles's film was released in the United States, committed suicide under the threat of extradition to France. (De Hory's fear of imprisonment is vividly evident in a single frame of documentary footage that Welles isolates for us, showing the dread in the forger's eyes as he talks about the time he once spent in jail.) A charming, dapper rogue, de Hory is seen dashing off a Matisse and then tossing the "masterpiece" into a fire. Later, he forges Orson Welles's signature on a portrait of Michelangelo, which he has painted in Welles's own style; returning the favor, Welles sketches a cartoon of an aging Howard Hughes and signs it "Elmyr."

Rather than condemn de Hory, Welles admires his daring and wit. What is modern art, after all, he asks, except the opinion of "experts" who "speak with the authority of a computer"? He reminds us that experts were called in to validate the handwriting of

Howard Hughes on documents in the possession of Clifford Irving; the authorities testified that the handwriting was genuine, and Welles toys with the amusing idea that it may have been forged by none other than Irving's friend de Hory.

Welles shows that the importance of expertise derives from the commodity status of art; when he talks about the art market, he shows us a montage of McDonald's hamburger stores and parking lots in Los Angeles. Though he does not say so directly, he also suggests that in the industrial age art is significant only when it is original, bearing the style of an admired painter (or *auteur*) who makes it unique and thus marketable. There is, in other words, no connection between labor and value in art, and the romantic notion of the artist, which Welles himself exemplifies, deserves a rigorous questioning. It may be true, as Clifford Irving says at one point, that de Hory failed as a painter because he lacked an "original vision"; his forgeries, however, serve to mock a society that converts originality into capital. He has had the perfect revenge on his critics, and he has proved that the ideal of the supremely gifted artistic genius makes its adherents the prey of swindlers.

To raise such issues is to indicate problems in our culture that run very deep. Some of these have been analyzed brilliantly in recent years by the English critic Raymond Williams, and whether Welles read Williams's *Culture and Society* or not, certain chapters of that book might usefully be considered in relation to *F for Fake.* Williams has noted, for example, that the whole modern notion of the uniquely gifted artist grew out of a reaction against industrialism in the eighteenth century. At about that time, he says, several old words in our language began acquiring new meanings:

> The word *Art*, which had commonly meant "skill," became specialized . . . first to "painting," and then to the imaginative arts generally. *Artist*, similarly, from the general sense of a skilled person . . . had become specialized in the same direction. . . .The emphasis on skill, in the word, was gradually replaced by an emphasis on sensibility; and this replacement was supported by the parallel changes in such words as *creative*, . . . *original*, . . . and *genius* (which, because of its root association with the idea of *inspiration*, had changed from "characteristic disposition" to "exalted special ability," and took its tone in this from the other affective words).

Williams points out that these changes came about because of a need to defend, through art, "certain human values, capacities, energies, which the development of society toward an industrial civilization was felt to be threatening or even destroying." They resulted, as we all know, in the concept of the artist as a bearer of a special, higher truth, a sort of priest whose very existence was a rebuke to materialism. But as Welles and many others came to recognize, the idealistic notion of art had certain pernicious consequences—on the one hand the elevation of the artist into a god (and hence, in Welles's typical view of things, into a Faustian overreacher), and on the other hand the increasing specialization of the artistic product, so that by the middle of the twentieth century the romantic rebellion had become a materialism *par excellence*, a privileged enterprise that was owned or patronized by millionaires.

There is consequently an affinity between Picasso, Howard Hughes, and forgers like de Hory and Irving. For one thing, as Welles suggests, the modern artist is always part idealist and part swindler—a description the young Welles once gave to Charles Foster Kane, and a description that would fit any of the archetypal American tycoons. For another thing, both the artist and the tycoon are celebrities, and celebrity is based on another kind of deception, a public masquerade that forces the real self into greater solitude. "On this overpopulated and mechanized planet," Welles comments, "'it is not so easy to remain oneself." Showing photos of the exterior of Howard Hughes's Las Vegas hotel, he notes that "these mysterious heros, who have done everything to become celebrities . . . end by seeking anonymity." Indeed Howard Hughes's real self, whatever that might have been, has been consumed by a myth more awesome than Kane's, a fiction which other aspirants to fame are able to feed upon. Long before his actual demise, it was rumored that Hughes might be dead anyway, or at least mad and kept prisoner, his image preserved by a group of sinister associates who imitated his telephone voice and forged his signature. Hughes's notoriety had turned him into a sort of Pirandellian "living character," nourished by a fantasy, who could "live through all eternity"; but meanwhile the actual man slowly perished.

If fame is therefore a lie, and if, as Picasso once said, "Art is a lie that makes us realize the truth," then what are de Hory and Irving but the mirror images of the men they have duped? Welles even implies that the manifest forger might be considered a hero, a man who exposes the absurd contradictions in his culture. And this judgment leads him to endorse some paradoxical, almost Wildean epigrams about art. "The important thing," as Clifford Irving says at one point, "is not to know whether a painting is true or false, but whether its falsity is good or bad."

Behind all these observations, of course, is the central paradox of Welles himself, who was a celebrity, an artist, and a self-styled con-man, and whose entire career was marked by a preoccupation with illusionism, magic, and swindles. " I am a charlatan," he comments at the beginning of *F for Fake*, and he repeatedly reminds the audience how much his own success was the result of deliberate fraud—the trick he tried to play upon the Gate Theatre in order to become an actor, the *War of the Worlds* hoax, etc. Indeed the central characters of his films have usually been men who live by false public images (Kane), masquerades (Arkadin), or imposture (Prince Hal). Outside these films, Welles spent most of his time as an actor hiding himself under whiskers, false noses, and a variety of accents; even when he appears as a magician in this movie he is dissembling, and he reminds us of Robert Houdin's theory that "a magician is an actor who plays the role of a magician." At its most personal level, therefore, the movie becomes Welles's confession that he was the prisoner of an illusion, a self-created public image which does not necessarily correspond to the "real" person, and which is potentially destructive.

Such ideas, plus the brilliant collision of montage-pieces in *F for Fake*, create a sort of vertigo of lies, a crazy house which tries to tell the truth about movies, art, and celebrity. It is a minor film which grew out of Welles's anxiety about his culture and his status as a gifted artist, but it was also influenced by a perception Welles once shared with André Bazin: a scoundrel, he remarked—even a scoundrel as dangerous as Harry Lime—becomes charming when he admits his trickery. Thus Welles disarms his audience by confessing to several frauds himself, leaving the question of what constitutes art or genuineness in the realm of mystery. As for truth and reality, they are mundane, he says, like "the toothbrush waiting for you in a glass, a bus ticket, or the grave." The one unalterable truth is that everything passes, and the basic fact of life is "we're going to die."

This emphasis on time passing and the inevitability of death suggests that despite Welles's clever cynicism, *F for Fake* is not so far removed from the romantic tradition after all. Late in the film we see Welles standing before the cathedral at Chartres. "Maybe a man's name doesn't matter that much," he says, observing that the magnificent anonymity of Gothic architecture belongs to an age better than ours. As he speaks, he creates a romantic vision of a prelapsarian world, before the corruptions of industry, and he creates a desire to know those artisans. Ultimately, Chartres becomes as shrouded in mystery and enigma as Howard Hughes's motel penthouse. Thus the film remains partly within the system it criticizes so wittily, leaving us respectful of genius, contemplative, and curious about the mystery of Welles's own personality—a personality which has become a work of art in its own right, a fascinating "lie" designed to make its author remain alive.

And combined with these rather abstract speculations on art and society is the theme of sexuality. For, as in *The Immortal Story*, the worship of flesh becomes a corollary to the tragedy of passing time. When Welles narrates the story of how Oja Kodar bewitched Picasso, we see a lengthy montage of the woman strolling through provincial Spanish streets clad in a bikini, or running in slow motion toward her villa dressed in a transparent gown. These shots are intercut with still photographs of Picasso, who appears to be staring at her, walleyed and ravenous. Welles imagines a little sex comedy in which the old artist is inspired and rejuvenated by the stirrings of desire, a "truth" as inevitable as death. Even Elmyr de Hory, in the earlier parts of the film, has been shown watering his garden and gazing at the sunset with his young homosexual companion, who is a source of comfort and peace in his old age. Art therefore becomes a necessary illusion, a momentary stay against time, but it also reflects beauty and passion, which Welles sees as elemental truths about the human condition.

III   *The Other Side of the Wind*

The Other Side of the Wind is more nearly complete than most of Welles's late films. Like *Don Quixote*, it was in production for over a decade, delayed by Welles's search for money and by what one of his actors, Paul Stewart, has called a "need for perfection." Derived from an earlier script by Welles entitled *The Savage Beasts*, which was about bullfighting, it was transformed into a story about modern-day Hollywood, where an aging director, played by John Huston, attempts to film what turns out to be his last feature. Joseph McBride, who acted in the picture and was present from the first day of shooting, published in *American Film* magazine an account of Welles's complex narrative, and he is worth quoting in detail:

The Other Side of the Wind . . . chronicles the return of Huston's character, Jake Hannaford, from years of retirement to direct a "with-it" low-budget film full of nudity, arcane symbolism, and radical-chic violence. The loose story format allows Welles wide-ranging latitude to satirize both the contemporary Hollywood scene and the grand but antiquated postures of Hannaford and his stooges, whose social views verge on the fascistic. . . .

His framing device in *Wind* is a huge birthday party being given for Hannaford by the character played by Lilli Palmer. The media are there in force, represented by journalists and critics, and by several television and documentary crews with 16mm and Super-8 equipment. The footage shot by these crews is being blown up for incorporation into the film, and Welles has kept a deliberately haphazard look to all of the party footage, giving it the semblance of cinéma vérité. His own crew operates the cameras at the party, and thus appears in the film. . . .

Despite being a movie director with traces of John Ford, Howard Hawks, and Huston himself recognizable in his personality (not to mention Welles, who named the character Jake because Frank Sinatra used to call him that), Hannaford, Welles says, is really based on Ernest Hemingway, with whom he had an edgy acquaintance. . . . In the film, Hannaford is revealed as a "closet" homosexual who develops an intense attachment for his young leading man, John Dale, played by TV actor Bob Random (who comments, "My entire function in the film is to provide silent visual accompaniment for voice-overs"). Hannaford has always been a Don Juan, with a penchant for seducing his leading men's girl friends, but in old age the mask starts to slip away, and he is smitten with the leading man. After Dale spurns Hannaford—who has come to assume a godlike tyranny over the younger man—the old director drunkenly drives off in a sports car he was planning to give Dale, and it crashes. The film follows Welles's favorite narrative structure of starting at the end, with some ironic and portentous narration, and then flashing back to the party. It all occurs on the night of July 2, not coincidentally the date of Hemingway's suicide.

McBride notes that the film resembles Welles's previous work in that it shows "a legendary man being swallowed up in his self-created image and ultimately being destroyed by it." But McBride's own description of the plot suggests that Hannaford is destroyed not so much by his image as by the frustrated, displaced sexuality which lies behind the image. Like Kane, and like most of the other

Welles protagonists, Hannaford is driven to assert mastery and power because he has an unconscious guilt. Hannaford's homosexuality takes its place beside Kane's Oedipal fixation, Arkadin's incestuous love for his daughter, Quinlan's paranoia, and Mr. Clay's impotence; all these shameful truths are barely hidden when the characters try to play god (or, in some cases, when they try to emulate weakling fathers), and when the secrets are revealed, death or suicide results. Thus when Welles told Richard Wilson that *The Other Side of the Wind* would be an "attack on *machoism*" he was only making explicit a theme he had been dealing with all along—the psychoanalysis of male hubris.

Clearly *The Other Side of the Wind* is a more complex, ambitious treatment of this theme than *The Immortal Story*, although McBride reports that it was referred to by Welles's intimates as "the greatest home movie ever made." What gives it an extra dimension and a special fascination for buffs is that in many respects it is a *film à clef*. Despite the fact that Welles himself does not appear, the characters are based almost perversely on his friends and enemies. Peter Bogdanovich, for example, has a major role as a successful young director named Brooks Otterlake, who once idolized Hannaford but has now far surpassed him at the box office. (The Otterlake role, according to McBride, was created after shooting had begun, when Bogdanovich's *The Last Picture Show* became a success.) Howard Grossman, a Bogdanovich assistant, has taken on the role of Charles Higgam (*sic*), a contemptible film historian, and Susan Strasberg plays a bitchy critic who is supposed to remind us of Pauline Kael. Tonio Selwart, a little-known German actor, resembles John Houseman, and a whole gallery of Welles's companions from the Mercury Theatre—including Edmond O'Brien, Norman Foster, Mercedes McCambridge, Benny Rubin, Paul Stewart, and Richard Wilson—are cast in minor roles. Of all the players, however, it is John Huston who is the most interesting, partly because his career had so many parallels with Welles's own. The two men directed their first film within months of each other in 1941, they developed reputations as Hollywood rebels, they became world travelers and *bon vivants* who lived mainly in Europe after the forties, and of course they collaborated many times. In addition, Huston brings to the Hannaford part an authentic macho image, the feeling of a rather courtly tough-guy, so that his appearances can remind us of Welles without actually resembling him.

As a movie about movies, *The Other Side of the Wind* promises to be most impressive at the level of style. From McBride's descriptions and from the excerpts Welles exhibited in public, one can see how much the story acquires meaning from the shifting nature of the imagery. More than *Kane,* which began with an expressionist sequence and then cut to a newsreel, this film is structured around the varieties of cinematic "perception." Super-8 and 16mm footage is intercut with 35mm color, and moving pictures are interrupted with still photographs; the camera, which Welles was fond of calling an "infernal machine," becomes a sort of menacing, omnivorous narrator, always reminding us of its presence, so that we see much of Hannaford's story as if it were a public event being covered by newsmen and paparazzi. Within the fictional world, the characters are often aware that they are being photographed, and have picked up the habit of performing even when they seem oblivious to their surroundings. Thus Hollywood is turned into pure celluloid; "reality" is shown in the process of being altered by film, as opposed to being filtered through it, and Welles appears to be making one of his more pessimistic movies. He envisages a decadent world made from a babel of cinematic "languages" which deny any ultimate truth behind the image; as a humanist, he instinctively recoils from such a prospect and equates it with death.

In February 1975, when Welles decided to show two excerpts from this film before the American Film Institute, he added still another level of significance to the images, turning the televised "Life Award" ceremony into a frame for the sequences he had shot. The Institute's award, of which he was the third recipient, is to some extent a public relations device, enabling the AFI to gather dozens of celebrities in one place and obtain prime-time coverage; Welles, however, was a slightly controversial candidate for the show. A week before the broadcast, syndicated columnist Marilyn Beck publicly chided the Institute for selecting Welles, and wrote that she was not alone in feeling that he had wasted his talents. By contrast, the two previous awards had gone to John Ford and James Cagney—authentically successful American folk heroes whose achievements could be wrapped in the flag; in fact the Ford ceremony was attended by the then president of the United States, and Ford's last public act was to stand before television cameras and shout, in an aging voice, "God bless Richard Nixon!" Thus, even though the Welles program was hosted by such luminaries as Frank Sinatra and Johnny Carson, it seemed much less a major public event.

In this somewhat cloudy, dubious atmosphere, Welles decided to make a pitch for his work in progress. To advertise himself, he exhibited two excerpts from *The Other Side of the Wind* which are critical of Hollywood and the "great man" myth that the AFI had assembled to honor. Reminding the audience of his habit of paying for his own movies out of his acting jobs, and describing himself as a "neighborhood grocery in an age of supermarkets," Welles first showed a highly satiric piece of film depicting a Hollywood celebration in honor of a famous movie director; he followed this episode with a scene in which one of the director's henchmen tries to interest a big studio boss in financing a picture. Taken together, these excerpts gave the awards dinner a breath of fresh air, as well as becoming one of the most interesting examples of Pirandellian theatrics in Welles's career.

Neither of the bits of film can be identified at first glance as being in the style of Orson Welles, although they have a grotesque, somewhat frenzied quality which recalls his earlier work. The first is shot in color, with bumpy, hand-held cameras, using zoom lenses to capture occasional closeups, jump cuts to shatter the action, and overlapping speeches to give the illusion of unmanipulated reality. The setting is Jake Hannaford's birthday party. The director, followed by his entourage and a bewildering crowd of photographers who might well be shooting this very footage, moves slowly through the night air toward a California-style house; meanwhile we hear a cocktail-party piano playing "It's Delovely," and a smattering of applause for the guest of honor. Drink in hand, Hannaford turns and gives a weary smile to the people waiting to receive him, his face caught in the painful glare of movie lights. He walks forward carefully, with a graceful, loping stride, while various figures gather around; suddenly a man in an orange shirt runs frantically from behind the crowd of photographers, shouting "Mr. Hannaford! Mr. Hannaford!" As one of Jake's cronies (Benny Rubin) raises an arm and yells, "Happy Birthday, Jake," the running man circles in front of Hannaford and offers to shake his hand. "Mr. Hannaford," he says with great earnestness, "I'm Marvin P. Fassbender." "Of course you are," Hannaford says, like a doctor trying to reassure a mental patient, and then continues moving toward the house.

Everyone on the lawn seems to start and pause along with Hannaford, sucked along in the wake of celebrity. After a moment Hannaford stops at a doorway and turns to look behind, the camera zooming in for a closeup of his pained, slightly open-mouthed expression. A reverse angle shows a line of photographers, lights, and sound equipment scurrying forward *en masse.* Glancing to his left and then his right, Hannaford sees that he is flanked by more photographers moving their equipment toward him, knocking one another down in an attempt to gain a position in the front row. Defensively, he breaks out in a huge smile, providing a "photo opportunity" and forcing the crowd to halt for a good shot. In closeup, we see the intently serious face of a young girl in rimless glasses holding lights aloft.

We now cut to the interior of the house, with the party in progress. The action appears to have been shot casually, using multiple, hand-held cameras, but behind the apparent randomness there is a careful plan, so that figures move in and out of range at the proper dramatic moments. The scene opens with Brooks Otterlake casually waving aside a reporter with a gesture of *noblesse oblige:* "This is Mr. Hannaford's night," he says. "Let's save the questions for him, okay?" As the scene develops, however, it becomes clear that Hannaford is a relative bystander, with Otterlake claiming the center of attention in the room; thus when the young director moves out of view, one of the reporters walks into the frame and asks, "You two are very close, aren't you?" "Yes, I'd like to ask you about that," a woman's voice says, and the camera pans to find the Susan Strasberg character seated on a desk top, brandishing a cigarette. "Come on, Otterlake," she says, hopping off her perch and crossing the room. "Why do you think you have to be as rude as *he* is?" "As rude as *you* are," Otterlake answers. "In print, anyway."

The director and the critic begin circling one another like prizefighters, moving cautiously in deference to each other's power; meanwhile Hannaford stands on the sidelines with the rest of the crowd, reacting occasionally. "She wasn't that kind to me in her review," Otterlake says, raising his voice so he can be heard by everyone. "Not that you did me much harm." Suddenly he breaks into a Cagney imitation to disguise a boast: "I mean, how can you do much harm to the *third biggest grosser in movie history?*" Hannaford now interrupts with mock awe: "Do you *really* make that much? How marvelous!" "Yes!" Strasberg chimes in, ostensibly speaking to Hannaford but really aiming the remark at Otterlake. "Did you know that when his own production company goes public that your friend there stands to walk away with forty million dollars?" The camera quickly pans with Otterlake as he crosses to

Hannaford and attempts to soothe him with flattery. "Yes, and she's going to keep on writing that I stole everything from you, Skipper. I'm never gonna walk away from that." Hannaford looks around in apparent innocence. "It's all right to borrow from each other," he says. "What we must never do is borrow from ourselves."

The first excerpt ends here, punctuated with a cynical joke in the manner of *Citizen Kane*. The second, even more calculatedly bewildering and technically complex than the first, takes place in a major studio screening room, where an influential young producer—modeled quite obviously on Robert Evans of Paramount—is waiting to be shown rushes from Hannaford's latest film. The action inside the room is photographed in black and white, with a hand-held camera; but when the actors are introduced, the movie footage is intercut with still photographs taken from slightly different angles, sometimes in color. As a result everything comes to a stop, the faces and gestures of the two players momentarily frozen on screen, each photograph accompanied by the click-whizz of a camera shutter. Later, as Hannaford's film is projected, we see 35mm color footage, done in a sort of parody of Antonioni, played off against a conversation between the producer and Hannaford's representative. Welles cuts directly back and forth between the film and the conversation, so that Hannaford's images occupy the full screen and are never framed by the "real" studio. The episode as a whole is therefore composed of several different grades of film stock in different media, moving rapidly and without transition from a documentary look, to still photographs, to wide-screen color.

At the beginning the producer (Jeffrey Land) is shown in two stills which create a stop-motion effect. A handsome young man dressed in a stylish leather jacket and aviator glasses, he glances impatiently at his watch. Soon Hannaford's stooge arrives (played by Norman Foster, Welles's collaborator on *Journey into Fear* and *It's All True*), and nervously introduces himself as "Billy Budd." Trying to ingratiate himself, he calls the producer "Max" and reminds him that they are both former actors; almost instantly he recognizes that he has made a social error, and his voice trails off lamely. Opening a bag of gum drops, he takes a seat in the row directly behind the producer, signaling the projectionist to begin. We hear the bleep of a synchronized soundtrack, a production leader flashes past, and in big screen color we see a woman in a lavender dress (Oja Kodar) walking across a horizon and entering a phone booth. Subsequent footage, all of it wordless and Antonioni-like, shows the woman being followed by a young man on a motorcycle. The action is drawn out and is interrupted at one point by a title reading "scene missing." Billy explains that everything we are seeing is in rough form, with only the slates cut out. When the male lead appears in a huge, glamorous closeup, Billy remarks, "According to Jake the box likes him." "The box?" says the producer. "Yeah, the old magic box." The producer pauses and then asks rhetorically, "Suppose the actor doesn't like the old magic director?"

As the Hannaford footage runs by, the producer begins asking questions in a flat, hostile tone. Occasionally Welles cuts to a tight closeup of him, with Billy leaning over his shoulder.

PRODUCER: What happens here?

BILLY: I'm not really sure , Max.

PRODUCER *(reacting to shots of Oja Kodar walking down the steps of a building with a bag slung over her shoulder)*: What's in the package?

BILLY: You mean what's she got in her purse?

PRODUCER: It's either a bomb or her lunch. . . . What's the bomb for?

BILLY: I don't know, maybe he's changed his mind and there won't be any.

PRODUCER *(reacting to shots of Bob Random looking at a series of wind-up toys)*: What are the toys about? . . . When does the bomb go off?

BILLY: Well . . . we don't actually know.

PRODUCER *(turning back over his shoulder to give Billy a hostile look)*: He's just making it up as he goes along, isn't he?

BILLY: *(The camera zooms in for a slightly larger closeup of his strained expression. He shrugs his shoulders.)* He's done it before.

Indeed Welles *was* making it up as he went along—changing certain characters, building relationships into the story, adding sequences, just as he had before. Like Porter, Griffith, Chaplin, and most of the directors who worked prior to the studio or package-unit systems of production, he often composed films in his head, incorporating new ideas during the shooting. And in a decade when nearly all movie directors were growing intensely self-conscious—a decade when Orson Welles became one of the cinema's central myths—he had found a nearly inexhaustible subject, capable of endless elaboration. He simply turned the cameras on the working world around him, portraying the director as part hustler, part frustrated artist, and part aging Don Juan. This man is a flawed figure, but the disparity between his legend and his actual circumstances makes him seem at once tragic and fraudulent. We must assume that Welles had an intimate understanding of such phenomena, having made himself at a very early age into a kind of show business superman, and having developed at the same time an almost morbid fascination with the dangers of fame. He knew that as much as he wanted and needed power, its effects were corrosive.

"I'm just a poor slob trying to make movies," Welles once complained when a critic charged him with an inability to complete his films. In fact, he had always been able to make dramatic material out of the tension between a "poor slob" and his public image. He was one of our last romantics, but his romanticism was tempered by irony and intelligent detachment, the prerequisites for turning oneself into the basis of fiction. However unfinished and unruly his last projects might have been, whatever doubts may continue to be expressed about his "genius," he was one of the few American filmmakers whose work will remain eccentric, significant, and new.

11

Between Works and Texts

*H*ow can we define a work amid the thousands of traces left by
a man after his death?
—Michel Foucault, "What Is An Author?"

I

Foucault's rhetorical question seems especially relevant to Welles,
who left a collection of "traces" comparable to the vast inventory of
Xanadu. Consider the holdings in the Welles archive at the Lilly
Library in Bloomington, Indiana. At the center of the archive are
the files of the Mercury Theatre, purchased from Welles and
Richard Wilson in 1978, documenting Welles's career during the
thirties and forties. There are 19,875 items in the Mercury files,
ranging from personal correspondence, publicity clippings, and
family photographs, to the scripts and working records of some of
America's most celebrated movies, plays, and radio programs. At
one extreme, the collection includes such fascinating trivia as Rita
Hayworth's application for a driver's license and Eleanor Roosevelt's autograph; at another, it is a mine of information about U.S.
foreign policy, the nations and culture of Latin America, and a
variety of social issues with which Welles was concerned. Among
the manuscripts are several unproduced items by writers other
than Welles—for example a play entitled *Emily Brady* by Donald

Ogden Stewart, and *Snowball*, a radio drama of 1943 by Howard Koch. (Koch's script—a story about lynch mobs—is accompanied by a letter from CBS executive Lymon Brysom informing Welles that "the present attitudes of stations in very large sections of the country" were such that they would not carry the program. "They would accuse us," Brysom writes, "of insisting on the importance of the race question with disproportionate emphasis.") A preponderance of the material, however, consists of things signed by Welles himself, often containing holograph revisions and production sketches—such as *Marching Song*, the unproduced play he co-authored with Roger Hill during the early thirties. In this category alone there are over a dozen film scenarios, scores of essays, some charcoal drawings and set designs, and a smattering of unremarkable poetry—even a set of "classroom notes" for teaching *The Merchant of Venice*, together with a fascinating series of study questions and a lengthy fill-in-the-blanks examination.

In looking through the archive, one is repeatedly confronted with the epistemological problem raised by Foucault: which of these things shall we define as the "works" of Orson Welles? The problem is especially vexing because most of the material is either incomplete or dependent upon something absent. For instance, we could make a good-sized volume from the manuscripts of Welles's public speeches, but even though the volume would contain some incisive political commentary it would have no particular literary value and would do very little to explain why Welles was one of this country's most effective platform speakers. What is missing is his voice, which, with its slightly drawling transatlantic accent and its rich timbre, could make the *City Directory* sound Shakespearian. As an actor, Welles often played men who mesmerized audiences on formal public occasions: he was Charles Foster Kane delivering an election speech, Father Mapple giving a sermon, Clarence Darrow summing up a case; and he was almost Kurtz, the anit-hero of *Heart of Darkness*—a man whose voice, as Conrad tells us, "rang deep to the very last." His script for the unfilmed *Heart of Darkness* project is in fact one of the most interesting documents in the Mercury archive, and it ought to be transformed into that unique twentieth-century genre, the published screenplay. Nevertheless, readers would be haunted by a desire to see the images it describes, and they would surely want to hear Welles speaking those famous last words, "The horror! The horror!"

A similar feeling of absence hovers over the playscripts and set designs of Welles's theatrical productions, such as his adaptations of *Julius Caesar* and *Native Son*. Theatrical literature, as Brecht once noted, is always "provisional," taking its specific form not only from movement, voice, and lighting, but also from the interaction of performers and audience on a specific occasion. Once the occasion passes, the performance survives only in memory or in fragmentary records. Hence Welles's work for the stage, like that of all great theatrical personalities, has passed into the realm of mere legend. His actual productions, such as *Around the World*, are hardly less present to us than the shows he *nearly* directed. For example, *Moby Dick Rehearsed*, the play he staged in London in 1955, has roughly the same evidentiary status as the "oratorio" based on the same novel, which he attempted without success to produce in New York in 1947. The London play was quasi-Brechtian, but the proposed New York production, based on a script by Brainerd Duffield and a score by Bernard Herrmann, would have been Wagnerian and explicitly Freudian; according to the notes preceding its text, it was intended to pay tribute to an American author who, "driven by neurosis to create works of libidinal intensity," had "enunciated Freudian truths in an era which made prudery a fetish." Welles's stage presentation would "lay bare the basic poetic stuffs of the novel itself. . . . Melody, symphonic and choral, movement, dance-gesture, light and color—all would blend in patterns to kindle the spectator's latent responses."

We can only speculate about what such an event might have been like, armed with the more permanent record of Welles's films. But the evidence of the films is also partial. As this book indicates, anyone who tries to analyze Welles's career in movies must inevitably confront questions of textual authenticity. How can we arrive at an accurate account of his intentions for *The Magnificent Ambersons*? How should the newly discovered footage of *It's All True* be assembled? Which is the "purer" form of *Touch of Evil*— the short version released in 1958 or the longer version, possibly containing a few shots by another director? Which *Macbeth* should we exhibit—the release print or the recently issued film containing Scottish accents? Of the two versions of *Mr. Arkadin*, one of them titled *Confidential Report*, which comes closest to the design Welles had in mind?

Some of these questions have answers, but I doubt that anyone will ever respond confidently to all of them, or to the many others that are raised by Welles's unreleased and mostly incomplete pictures, such as *Don Quixote, The Deep, The Other Side of the Wind,* and *The Merchant of Venice.* Perhaps significantly, one of the obsessive images of his cinema is a room crammed with objects and figures, its crowded space distorted by a wide-angle photography that recedes into some vague horizon. In similar fashion, his career was cluttered and just beyond our grasp. Certainly he left behind a substantial body of material that ought to be restored, preserved, and exhibited. Nevertheless, his reputation will always depend to some degree on fragments and traces. Like Coleridge's unfinished poem "Kubla Khan," his life's work denies us scholarly closure; a romantic artifact, its oneiric quality is heightened by a sense of unfulfilled possibility.

Coleridge tells us that while writing "Kubla Khan" he was interrupted by an unnamed "person from Porlock," who knocked on the door at an inopportune moment and broke the mood of composition. Welles was beset by a variety of less quaintly literary frustrations, most of which I have discussed in the preceding chapters. For the sake of clarity, however, I should probably emphasize that none of these frustrations had anything to do with what Charles Higham has called a "fear of completion"—an idea born of vulgar auteurism and pop psychology. The absence to which I refer is more pervasive and overdetermined, resulting partly from the evanescence of theatre itself and partly from the material and ideological conflicts of Welles's career. Let me also emphasize that I do not intend to close this book with a chapter on the death of authorship—even though literary theory over the past two decades has taught us to think of both authors and works as reifications of bourgeois ideology. According to the theory, it does not matter who is speaking, since everyone is spoken *by* a language contract, which in turn is mediated by a social contract. Clearly, however, we do not need to adopt a textual utopianism or a romantic notion of creativity in order to insist upon what Edward Said calls the "worldliness" of discourse. Indeed we should recognize that films—like books and critical commentary—are forms of language through which real historical subjects carry on struggles for power. This idea was never lost upon Welles, who attained worldwide celebrity as a result of the Mars panic, and who, as we have seen, devoted many of his subsequent projects to the theme of demagoguery. From Kane, who declares that people will think "what I tell them to think," to Henry V, who intends to "busy giddy minds with foreign wars," the leading characters in Welles's films often use language as a hoax, attempting to become colonizers of consciousness. Given the possibility of such ambition, it matters very much for us to know who is speaking and toward what ends.

Welles the *auteur* was himself driven by a kind of will to power, signified not only in the dynamic excess of his style but also in his embattled relation with the movies and the stage. He had taken his theatrical identity from a turn-of-the-century tradition of flamboyant directors, and throughout his career he struggled to maintain that identity in the face of a changing, increasingly corporate, culture. In an important early essay entitled "The Director in the Theatre Today," published by the Theatre Education League in 1939, he wryly commented on his art, pointing out that the profession of director was relatively new to theatrical history. Even as late as the nineteenth century, he noted, drama had been virtually directorless, centered on the emotional expressiveness of a lead player:

For thousands of years the director was a stage manager. . . . When Mr. Sullivan, for instance, arrived in a town like Galway to play "Macbeth," . . . he would arrive at the theatre at seven o'clock for a consultation with this stage manager.

"I always come in at the center for 'They have tied me to the stake,'" Mr. Sullivan would declare. . . . "Please have Lady Macbeth when she takes the daggers away take them by the blades."

"All right. Is there anything else?"

"No. Just have everyone else stand six feet away and do their damnedest."

Welles recognized that the "six feet away" school, laughable as it might sound to contemporary audiences, had produced the most impressively emotional actors in Western theatre. But he also recognized that in the period between the 1880s and the 1920s a new fashion had evolved, devoted to carefully designed spectacles such as the ones managed by David Belasco or Hardin Craig, or to director-centered ensembles like the ones founded by Stanislavski or Meyerhold. Welles remarked, "We are so proud of the fact that we don't allow these old-time stars on the stage today, we forget that their influence from the fifth row center can be much more insidious."

For Welles, the special business of the new director was "to make his playhouse a kind of magic trick in which something quite impossible comes to be." This credo was obviously intended to point up his interest in magicians, but it also reminds us that stage magic had evolved in the same way as theatre as a whole. Turn-of-the-century performers like Howard Thurston and Georges Méliès were in fact actor-directors, their presence in the spotlight signifying their power over the entire physics of the playhouse. The Mercury Theatre was clearly indebted to this type of spectacle, becoming a mixture of magical effect, Shakespearian acting, and thirties-style political drama—everywhere designed to manifest Welles's skill as orchestrator. It mattered little whether he actually wrote the words or built the sets. "The great field of the director," according to Welles, was "conception," or the ability to control meaning. "The script of a play in most cases," he claimed, "is a wandering and loosely knit affair embracing many plays. If a director is good enough he can use all these plays. . . . If he has a special point to make, he will select only one or two." The stage setting would in turn be governed by the director's central conception. "One director, for instance, presenting a Molière comedy may decide that the whole play shows the fundamental hardness of the world . . . and so his conception of the visual element in his production leads him to erect on stage a setting of stainless steel, which he decorates with rose leaves to show a kind of hopeless beauty. . . . Such a director has a feeling about texture." As an illustration of his own practice, Welles commented on the Mercury production of *Julius Caesar:* "I wanted to present 'Julius Caesar' against a texture of brick, not of stone, and I wanted a color that had certain vibrations of blue. In front of this red brick wall I wanted levels and places to act; that was my conception of the production."

For a time Welles was able to maintain the working conditions he described in his essay on direction. According to Robert Lewis, one of the founders of the Group Theatre and the Actor's Studio, Welles's importance to American theatre lay precisely in the fact that he was one of the first exponents of what we now know as "conceptual drama." He built an image of himself as a sort of youthful Prospero, becoming the star of an acting company that somehow partook of the collectivist politics of the era while at the same presenting his own ideas of spectacle. Like Stanislavski or Meyerhold, but in his own terms, he imposed a style upon an ensemble and appropriated a body of literature to his ends. Remarkably, he even transported his company to the movies, where for three or four years it was relatively free of the studio system. In 1939, speaking before a symposium on Hollywood composed chiefly of

New York academics and intellectuals, he announced his opposition to the film industry as it was then organized: "What I don't like about Hollywood films," he said, "is the 'gang' movie and I don't mean the Dead End Kids. I mean the assembly line method of manufacturing entertainment developed in the last fifteen years or so, and I share this prejudice with practically everybody whose craft is the actual making of a movie and not just . . . the business of selling it. When too many cooks get together they find, usually, the least common denominator of dramatic interest."

This was the typical complaint of directors against studios, but in Welles's case it was an especially insistent demand. The entire apparatus of representation in the Mercury Theatre was keyed to his idiolect, allowing his manner to become so recognizable and impressive that later in his career it could occasionally assert itself in movies where he was ostensibly nothing more than an actor. Even as late as the 1970s, when the Mercury was long since dissolved and Welles was reduced to doing magic tricks on the Johnny Carson show, the signs of his theatre could still be seen in the way he presented the illusion. The movement of an assistant from point A to point B, the disposition of magical paraphernalia on the stage, the pace and tempo of the act—all these things bore the traces of his earlier work, as if they were motivated by the same structural logic.

To borrow a witticism from Sandra Gilbert and Susan Gubar's *No Man's Land*, we might say that Welles's art was less about *jouissance* than about *puissance*. In retrospect, however, his surviving films are interesting because of the way they dramatize the futility or fakery behind most assertions of authority. In this sense his art is deeply paradoxical, born of a belated romanticism that tends toward modern and postmodern irony. One of the signatures of his visual style is an extreme low-level shot, looking up through a wide-angle lens at a male figure who towers over us as if to assert phallic power; but at the same time the narrative context makes the character seem pathetic, ludicrous, or fascistic. Similar effects can be seen at other levels of his pictures. *Citizen Kane*, for example, perpetuates the notion of the "great man" even while it deconstructs the biographical enterprise; and *F for Fake*, which is based on material from documentaries signed by François Reichenbach, functions both as an expression of Welles's personality and as a subtle comment on the "theft" or appropriation of one person's language by another.

These ironies are homologous with the contradictions in

Welles's whole approach to his art. On the one hand, he resembled what Antonio Gramsci has termed the "traditional intellectual": an anti-bourgeois with European tastes, he was cynical about industrialization and progress, interested in preserving a canonical dramatic literature, and nostalgic for certain values of the nineteenth century. On the other hand, he also resembled Gramsci's opposite type, the "organic intellectual": a progressive and a populist from the American Midwest, he was a lifelong opponent of racism and fascism, a dazzling impresario of the age of mechanical reproduction, and a show-business personality. For a while he managed to hold these tensions in splendid equilibrium, generating a kind of egocentric leftism in theatre, radio, and film. From the beginning, however, his plans were thwarted by the very institutions he sought to energize. Federal censors closed his and John Houseman's one attempt at truly radical drama, *The Cradle Will Rock*, forcing it into a stunning improvised performance that was also the most "directorless" show of Welles's career. Afterward, in the commercial realm, the Mercury Theatre became increasingly dependent on box office receipts, sponsors, and movie studios, until finally the irreconcilable tendencies in Welles's career split apart, giving him two public images. ("What you don't realize," Kane says to Thatcher, "is that you are talking to two different people.") To his admirers, he seemed a Byronic loner, forced into European exile and beleaguered independence (in his own words, a "neighborhood grocery in an age of supermarkets"). To his detractors, he seemed bombastic and anachronistic, an ex–boy genius who was the butt of Joan Rivers's jokes and the narrator of *Bugs Bunny Superstar*. Meanwhile the sense of Welles as adversary political artist was repressed or forgotten altogether.

Partly because of the contradictions in his public roles, and partly because of the very nature of his art, Welles produced relatively few things that could be called his "works." His stage success is a matter of record, but the shows themselves have vanished. His reputation as a film director has grown steadily, but most of his movies after *Citizen Kane* were incompletely realized; they did not reach the screen, or they were inadequately financed, or they were recut by his producers. This does not mean, however, that he left no marks. Using terminology from one of Roland Barthes's most influential essays, we could say that Welles's artistic activity usually manifested itself somewhere between "works" and "texts." That is, it never became a series of neatly finished commodities that signify his full intentions or conceptions; nor did it become a radicalized, collective, or corporate discourse that bears no signs of an enunciating author. It operated instead in the "provisional" zone of theatre, cinematic fragments, and archival material—a zone where, with varying degrees of success, he established an unorthodox way of speaking. In this zone his dramatic "conceptions" and political attitudes were constantly at play, but they never assumed a definitive shape.

II

By way of illustrating the situation I have just outlined, let me now turn to some specific cases from the Mercury archive. I shall concentrate on a single phase of Welles's career: the period 1943–47, just after his contract with RKO ended, when his fortunes seemed in precipitous decline. During that five-year period, which I have already discussed in chapter 5, he can hardly be said to have been inactive. He wrote a syndicated newspaper column; he directed *Around the World* on the New York stage; he made dozens of public speeches about theatre or politics; he appeared regularly on the radio; he placed almost weekly orders for magical equipment; he wrote or supervised several film scripts that never found backers (among them *Salomé, Fully Dressed and in His Right Mind*, and *Carmen*); he co-starred in three pictures; and he adapted, directed, and acted in two memorable Hollywood thrillers, one of which is generally regarded as a masterpiece of *film noir*. Purely for the sake of convenience, my remarks center on the last two films, both of which are problematic "works," released in a form different from what Welles planned and shot. I do not have space to treat them in detail, but I can at least indicate certain features of their prerelease construction that were not known to me when this book was originally published and that no other writers have described.

The Stranger, produced by Sam Spiegel's International Pictures and first shown in May 1946, was reduced in length by almost thirty minutes. I have said that it is Welles's most conventional movie; but if we were able to see it in its long version that judgment might need qualification. Both the shooting script (presumably written by Anthony Veiller, John Huston, and Welles) and the studio's production log reveal that the film was originally structured as a flashback narrative. It began with a mysterious sequence in which Mary Rankin rises from her bed at midnight, makes her way through a graveyard, and emerges into a New England town square, where she enters the door of a church and begins to climb an enormous clock belfry. A crowd gathers in the square, armed with scythes, pitchforks, shotguns, and any weapon at hand. From their viewpoint, we see two figures emerge onto the ledge of the clock tower—a male and a female, locked in a struggle. Both figures topple from the ledge and fall to their death. The crowd is as shocked and baffled as we are, and people begin to ask questions: "Know who they were?" "What happened?" "Who was he?" Fade out. Against a dark screen the main title of the picture appears. Behind it, the grotesque figure of an iron demon moves forward out of the darkness and toward the camera. As the credits appear, the camera tracks backward, revealing that the demon is part of a huge clockwork. Moving out of a portal, it turns and begins to circle the pedestal of the clock, followed by another figure that enters behind it—an iron angel in feminine robes, brandishing a sword. Just as Welles's name appears as the final credit, the clock strikes twelve.

This witty, "magical" introduction was followed by a surreal opening passage in which Konrad Meinike—an escaped Nazi war criminal who is clearly schizophrenic—tries to locate a man named Franz Kindler in Argentina, so that he can deliver a message from God. Meinike is picked up by fellow Nazis and taken to the offices of a dog-training farm somewhere in the countryside, where he is given truth serum and questioned. Throughout the sequence, we hear the vicious barking of German shepherds in the background:

FARBRIGHT: Why do you want to see [Franz Kindler]? What is so
    important about it?
MEINIKE: I have a message from him.
FARBRIGHT: From whom?
MEINIKE: From the All Highest.
(The three inquisitors instinctively stiffen. FARBRIGHT's heels
    actually click.)
FARBRIGHT: Why did you not tell us this before?

Muttering incoherently and still feeling the effects of the drug, Meinike is then sent to a white-walled city morgue, where a bored night attendant sits at a desk trimming his toenails. The attendant explains the procedure for making fake passports. Taking papers from a corpse, he tells Meinike to visit a photographer—indeed we glimpse that visit in the released version of The Stranger, and it is among the most striking, characteristically Wellesian moments of the entire picture.

Welles frequently commented on the loss of the Latin American sequences of *The Stranger*, which were far more eerie and complex than my summary indicates. He even told Barbara Leaming that he received a scar on his leg while shooting them—almost the only mark left to remind him they once existed. "You don't know what it was like on the screen!" he said, and attributed the loss to Ernest Nims, an editor "who believed that nothing should be left in a movie that did not advance the story." To my knowledge, however, Welles never mentioned that Nims also removed material from a later point in the film, when Mary Rankin discovers that the man she has married is in reality Franz Kindler, one of the architects of the Nazi death camps. Mary collapses; at this point we were supposed to see an expressionistic, forties-style dream sequence, showing Mary's brother Noah suspended from an infinitely high ladder, a barking dog below him. Suddenly Noah transforms into Kindler. Meanwhile, on the soundtrack, accompanied by what the shooting script describes as "queer music," we were supposed to hear dialogue representing "quite realistically" what goes on in the room after Mary faints: Noah arrives, accompanied by the investigator Wilson and Judge Longstreet, and calls the police. The last line of dialogue is spoken by a doctor: "We'll get her to bed and she'll be fine. . . . You need have no fear." As the line is spoken, Mary's delirium takes over completely. The figure of Kindler, holding the rungs of a "cosmic ladder," turns and addresses the camera, repeating the doctor's words: "You need have no fear." The camera moves in on his face until one of his eyes fills the screen. "Failing to speak," he says, "you become part of the crime."

This sequence is pregnant with Wellesian possibilities, including an interesting montage of conflicts between sound and image. We cannot know exactly how it was realized, but at least we have Welles's next, more ambitious, film, *The Lady from Shanghai*, to show us what he could accomplish with similar material. As I have already explained, however, *The Lady from Shanghai* is also incomplete, reduced by almost one hour from its prerelease form. Welles had begun shooting the film at Columbia Pictures on October 2, 1946, and had completed the principal photography on January 22, 1947; from that point until mid-March 1947, the film was substantially revised, with Harry Cohn ordering various cuts and retakes. Production then resumed for about eleven days to reshoot certain material and add closeups. (The last shot photographed was a close-up of Welles in front of a process screen, making his famous speech about hungry sharks off the coast of Brazil; in the earlier version the speech was played on location in a tightly framed composition involving four people.) By the time the next stage of postproduction was completed, *The Lady from Shanghai* had gone about four hundred thousand dollars over budget and was a much shorter picture. Many of its most celebrated passages—including the "Morning Beach" scenes in Acapulco, the drunken seaside "Barbecue," the San Francisco aquarium sequence, the chase through the Chinese theatre, and the apocalyptic "Crazy House" finale—were abridged in order to bring the film down to ordinary length. Welles's evocative offscreen narration was added at the last minute, to smooth over the ragged condensation. Finally, after a somewhat disappointing preview, the film was given a new music score and was cut once again by Viola Lawrence—who, according to Welles, made drastic changes.

In later years Welles said little about what had been done to the film, although he often complained about the score Columbia used. It is clear from the correspondence in the Mercury archive that he had specific ideas about music; he wrote detailed instructions about how certain actions on the screen ought to be scored, and he and Richard Wilson negotiated long and unsuccessfully for the rights to a song entitled "Caminante del Mayab," which they hoped would be performed by the Mexican singer Pedro Vargas. The archival material also makes clear, however, that Viola Lawrence's editing of the film involved major alterations, leaving whole sequences on the cutting room floor.

In its penultimate form, *The Lady from Shanghai* was a complex but slightly more comprehensible narrative, articulating the motives of the characters and the convolutions of the murder plot in greater detail. Like all of Welles's Hollywood films, it had an impressively atmospheric, somewhat enigmatic opening development. But here again, as in the case of *The Stranger*, the opening was largely eliminated, apparently because Welles did not follow the straightforward logic of classic studio cinema. One of the scripts in the archive—a cutting continuity labeled "Scenes as Shot," dated early January 1947—enables us partly to reconstruct his design. He had intended to begin with a sinister network of actions, structured by crosscutting and a series of intersecting movements of camera and players. First we would have seen a brief montage of New York spires and tenements suffering under the heat of an August night. Cut to a tracking shot of a man following a woman down the streets until she enters Central Park. Cut to El Morocco, where George Grisby, described in the script as a "sweaty, aging playboy," is scribbling doodles on a tablecloth as "hot rumba music" fills the room. A waiter enters the frame, leans down to Grisby's apprehensive ear, and whispers, "She hasn't called." Dissolve to a radio, with the El Morocco music coming tinnily through its speaker. A telephone beside the radio rings, and Arthur Bannister picks it up. "Yes?" he says, and reaches for a bottle of pills. (These pills were supposed to function as a motif; later, in another scene that was cut, Elsa Bannister tells Michael O'Hara that she would like to take enough of her husband's pain pills to end her own life—a remark that becomes ironic in light of the courtroom sequence toward the end, when O'Hara himself takes them.) "What do you mean—*you lost her?*" Bannister shouts angrily into the telephone. Cut to Sidney Broom, speaking from a phone booth in a garage; he tells Bannister that he has followed Elsa into Central Park, where she hired a horse and buggy. Cut to Central Park, where Michael O'Hara is strolling along and singing a tune as Elsa's carriage trots past him.

Welles had initiated the chance encounter between Michael and Elsa with a lengthy tracking shot—quite similar to the one he would use later in *Touch of Evil*—showing Elsa in the carriage, Michael on foot, and a police car cruising past as the couple ultimately meet at a stoplight and exchange words. Shortly afterward Michael comes across Elsa at another place in the park and rescues her from a mugging. As he drives her hackney cab back to the city, we were supposed to see a longer conversation between the two, in which their characters were developed. At one point in these missing scenes, Michael compares the horse to Rosinante and himself to Don Quixote. "I remember," Elsa says, "Rosinante was the old nag Don Quixote rode when he went out after those windmills. . . . You'd better be careful. Things have changed." This remark was intended to function as another of the film's motifs; for example, in a later scene Elsa would accuse Michael of trying to "act like books," and he would disagree, insisting that people could actually be "better than books." But in a memo to the studio cutters, Harry Cohn ordered virtually all such references cut from the release print.

I could go on at length, noting various deletions and changes, but two further examples should be sufficient to show how the studio's revisions affected some of the film's most ingeniously planned episodes. First, consider the scenes at "Morning Beach" in Acapulco, where Grisby tempts O'Hara, taking him up to a mountaintop and offering him money to participate in a fake murder. In the final shooting script this sequence is much more explicitly satiric. As Grisby and O'Hara stroll up the hillside from the beach, Grisby's remarks are systematically played off against American tourists in the background, whose conversations about money become obsessive and nightmarish. We see a little girl attempting to get her mother to buy her a fancy drink: "But mommy," she says, "it ain't even one dollar!" Then a honeymoon couple walks past. "Sure it's our honeymoon," the young man says, "but that's a two million dollar account." An older lady and her husband cross in front of the camera, arguing about taxi fare. "I practically had to pay him by the mile," the lady complains. A gigolo speaks to a girl seated on a rock. "Fulco made it for her," he announces. "Diamonds and emeralds— must've cost a couple of oil wells. And she only wears it on her bathing suit." Another young couple walks up the steps from the beach, the man rubbing his nose with zinc oxide as he mutters, "But listen, Edna, you've got to realize pesos is real money." Two girls enter the scene, one of them saying, "Heneral—that means General—in the army like. Only this one's rich." Meanwhile, through all this, Grisby babbles about the atomic bomb and the end of the world, ultimately turning and asking O'Hara, "How would you like to make five thousand dollars, fella?"

As I indicate in chapter 5, some of this material remains in the released film; but the sound mix and the retakes—most of them involving reaction shots of Welles against a process screen— deprive the sequence of its rhythm, its counterpointed dialogue, and its hallucinatory intensity. In similar fashion, the spectacular concluding sequences, when Elsa, Bannister, and O'Hara confront one another in an amusement park Crazy House, have been condensed significantly. For example, we have lost a scene where O'Hara talks with Bessie, Elsa's black maid, just outside the hall of mirrors. (Nearly every sequence involving Bessie, played by Evelyn Ellis and described in the script as "no Aunt Jemima," was cut or reduced by the film's editors.) Also lost are various practical jokes that O'Hara encounters as he makes his way through what Welles called the "Caligari" room of the funhouse—including a moment when a skeletal figure looms out at him, garbed in a blonde wig and clothing similar to Elsa's.

According to the script, the initial version of the film contained a slightly longer exchange between the three principal characters in the mirror maze. This condensation must have been especially troubling for Welles, not only because the sequence as it now stands is among the most admired set pieces in his career, but also because it is the culmination of an idea he had nursed from the time he first came to Hollywood. Near the end of *Citizen Kane* he had shown the protagonist walking along a mirrored corridor that cast his reflection into infinity. In August 1941, not long after the release of *Kane*, he had hoped to elaborate the mirror effect in *Love Story*—a script written by John Fante about the relationship between a working-class Italian couple living in the North Beach area of San Francisco in 1909. (This short film would have been an episode in a longer project called *It's All True*—a North American precursor to the movie Welles later tried to make in Brazil.) The opening of *Love Story* would have shown the couple meeting and carrying on a courtship against the background of a series of "attractions" in a North Beach amusement park. They would have looked into a penny-picture machine showing a movie called *Sins of Paris*; boarded a "Scenic Railway" that traveled to exotic places; entered a "Foolish House" that frightened people with spooky practical jokes; and walked through the "Crystal Maze," carrying on a conversation while "faced by a thousand reflections."

Welles never made *Love Story*, but in 1944, soon after leaving RKO, he tried to use the mirror idea once again in a project called *Don't Catch Me*, based on a book by Richard Powell, written with Bud Pearson and Les White. Trade papers of that year announced he would direct the picture, which never obtained backing. A genial comic thriller described as a "farce melodrama," *Don't Catch Me* told the story of a sophisticated honeymoon couple named Arab and Andy who, rather like Nick and Nora Charles, uncover a ring of Nazi spies working on Long Island. In terms of sexual politics the script was considerably more advanced than the MGM *Thin Man* series, and it might have made Welles seem a slightly less misogynistic director. Equally important to my argument, it would have given him an opportunity to stage the amusement park scene he had long imagined. He wanted to end the story with a chase through a deserted funhouse; Arab, Andy, and the Nazi spies would find themselves lost in a Gothic "Tunnel of Love" and end up in a mirror maze, where their reflections would be multiplied endlessly.

It is doubtful that either of these films would have shown us a hall of mirrors to equal the one in *The Lady from Shanghai*. I mention them chiefly because they illustrate how one of Welles's ideas went through a process of rewriting and revision, ultimately finding a context in which it was executed brilliantly. When it finally reached the screen, however, the mirror sequence was a fragment, with no clear point of origin and no definitive conclusion. (Welles continued to experiment with the same idea as late as *The Other Side of the Wind*, where, in a bewildering movie-within-the-movie, he shows the reflections of Oja Kodar and Bob Random reflected in a maze of window glass on a building in Los Angeles.) By the same token, many of the films Welles directed after *Kane* never became "works." Even if we could recover every frame of film he shot we would not be able to restore his career to an imagined fullness; nor could we transform his various projects into a neatly catalogued set of objects, like volumes on a shelf. At best we could only point to a web of performing situations or texts through which he tried to assert what, in his AFI acceptance speech, he called his "contriety."

The scholarly attempt to define or restore Welles's works is therefore rather like Thompson's search for Rosebud: it leaves us confronted with an inventory, feeling that a missing piece might complete a puzzle, yet knowing that even when the piece is found it cannot sum up the story. As Thompson recognizes, however, the meaning of an inquiry lies not in a goal we arrive at but in a process we go through. In this sense there are no endings anywhere, and no completed works. During the mid-forties, when he was plagued by debts and Hollywood producers, Orson Welles must have adopted a roughly similar attitude, viewing his art with a good deal of irony. If I had to choose one piece of evidence as proof, it would be a line that was cut from *The Lady from Shanghai*. Variations of the line were supposed to occur at several junctures, becoming another of the film's motifs. Michael O'Hara speaks it first during his conversation with Elsa Bannister in Central Park, and I appropriate his words here, for the sake of my own qualified summing up: "Sure, you can't decide about anything till it's all over and done, and even then you can't be certain, because who knows when anything's done with—for good and all."

Bibliographic Notes

In place of footnotes or a formal bibliography, I am providing an account of my chief sources for each chapter. Certain items have been used often enough to warrant a separate listing. These are:

Bazin, André. *Orson Welles*, Preface by Jean Cocteau (Paris: Editions Chavane, 1950).

Bessy, Maurice. *Orson Welles. Cinéma d'Aujourd'hui* series No. 6 (Paris: Editions Seghers, 1970).

Cowie, Peter. *A Ribbon of Dreams: The Cinema of Orson Welles* (New York: A. S. Barnes, 1973).

Gottesman, Ronald, editor. *Focus on "Citizen Kane"* (Englewood Cliffs, N.J.: Prentice-Hall, 1971).

—— *Focus on Orson Welles* (Englewood Cliffs, N.J.: Prentice-Hall, 1976).

Higham, Charles. *The Films of Orson Welles* (Berkeley: University of California Press, 1970).

Kael, Pauline. *The Citizen Kane Book* (Boston: Little, Brown, 1971).

McBride, Joseph. *Orson Welles* (New York: Viking Press, 1972).

I have also made extensive use of *The New York Times, Newsweek, Time, Variety, The Hollywood Reporter,* and *Motion Picture Herald.*

I The Prodigy

Biographical information is drawn chiefly from Russell Maloney, "Orson Welles," *The New Yorker* (Oct. 5, 1938); Alva Johnson and Fred Smith, "How To Raise a Child," *The Saturday Evening Post* (Jan. 20–27, Feb. 3, 1940); Roy Alexander Fowler, *Orson Welles, A First Biography* (London: Pendulum Publications, 1946); Peter Noble, *The Fabulous Orson Welles* (London: Hutchinson, 1956); John Houseman, *Run-Through: A Memoir* (New York: Simon and Schuster, 1972); Mícheál MacLiammóir, *All for Hecuba* (London: Methuen, 1950). Quotations from *Bright Lucifer* are courtesy the Center for Theater Research, Wisconsin State Historical Society, Madison, Wisconsin. Useful background information on theatre and radio in the thirties is contained in Gerald Rabkin's *Drama and Commitment* (Bloomington: Indiana University Press, 1964), and in *Radio Drama in Action*, ed. Eric Barnouw (New York: Farrar and Rinehart, 1945). See also Hadley Cantril's *Invasion from Mars* (New York: Harper and Row, 1966). A brief history of RKO may be found in "RKO Radio: An Overview" by Tim Onosko in *The Velvet Light Trap*, No. 10 (Fall 1973). See also John Davis's "Studio Chronology" in the same issue. Jonathan Rosenbaum's discussion of *Heart of Darkness*, together with excerpts from Welles's script, appeared in *Film Comment* (Nov.–Dec. 1972). Information on *Smiler with a Knife* and *The Way to Santiago* was obtained courtesy of Richard Wilson and the Wisconsin State Historical Society.

II The Magician

My arguments on deep-focus photography and motion picture soundtracks were influenced by Noel Burch's *Theory of Film Practice* (New York: Praeger, 1973). Burch is also important to my understanding of "self-reflexive" cinema. Gregg Toland's essay on his photography for *Kane* appeared first in *American Cinematographer*, but is conveniently reprinted in *Focus on "Citizen Kane."* See also André Bazin's "The Evolution of Film Language" in *What Is Cinema?* Vol. I (Berkeley: University of California Press, 1967); and Brian Henderson's "The Long Take" in *Film Comment* (Summer 1971). A useful reference on optical printing and other techniques of motion picture photography is *Practical Motion Picture Photography*, ed. Russell Campbell (Cranbury, N.J.: A. S. Barnes, 1970). For an "orthodox" view of how lenses should be used in the classic

Hollywood movie, see Jay Donohue, "Focal Length and Creative Perspective," *American Cinematographer* (July 1966). David Bordwell's essay *"Citizen Kane"* appeared first in *Film Comment* (Summer 1971), and is reprinted in *Focus on Orson Welles*. Hiram Sherman is quoted from Richard France's *"The Shoemaker's Holiday* at the Mercury Theatre," in *Theatre Survey* (Nov. 1975). George Coulouris's remarks appear in an interview with Ted Gilling in *Sight and Sound* (Summer 1973). François Truffaut's comments on Welles's acting are taken from the official program of the AFI "life award" ceremony honoring Welles.

III   *Citizen Kane*

See David Bordwell's essay on *Kane*, mentioned in the notes to chapter 2. See also Robert Carringer's "Rosebud, Dead or Alive," *PMLA* (March 1976), and *"Citizen Kane, The Great Gatsby*, and Some Conventions of American Narrative," *Critical Inquiry* (Winter 1975). Carringer's research into the scripts of *Kane* was not yet published as this book went to print, but I am grateful to him for allowing me to see his conclusions. For a useful discussion of self-reflexive narrative in *Kane*, I recommend Kenneth Hope's unpublished thesis, "Film and Meta-Narrative" (Bloomington, Indiana University, 1975). The various biographies of W. R. Hearst include Mrs. Freemont Older, *William Randolph Hearst, American* (New York: Appleton-Century, 1936); Ferdinand Lundberg, *Imperial Hearst* (New York: Modern Library, 1937); W. A. Swanberg, *Citizen Hearst* (New York: Scribner, 1961). For comments on the politics of *Kane*, see Charles Eckert, "Anatomy of a Proletarian Film," *Film Quarterly* (Spring 1975), pp. 65–76. See also Harry Wasserman, "Ideological Gunfight at the OK Corral," *The Velvet Light Trap*, No. 11, pp. 22–31.

IV   *The Magnificent Ambersons*

I am grateful to Richard Wilson, who allowed me to glance at the Mercury files on the production of *Ambersons*, including the last pages of the cutting continuity. I also consulted two scripts of the film at the Museum of Modern Art, and the RKO pressbook at the Lilly Library in Bloomington, Indiana. For a discussion of the theme of pastoral in English literature, see Raymond Williams, *The Country and the City* (New York: Oxford University Press,

1973). See also Michael Wood, "Parade's End," *American Film* (March 1976). Bernard Herrmann's remarks on the original conclusion of the film are quoted from an interview at England's National Film Theatre, published in the *Miklos Roja Society Newsletter* (Summer 1974). For information about "The Two Black Crows" I am indebted to the Archive of Contemporary Music at Indiana University.

V   The Radicalization of Style

John Houseman's comments, here as elsewhere, are quoted from *Run-Through: A Memoir.* Welles's newspaper column is quoted from *The New York Post,* where it appeared on weekdays between Jan. 22 and June 15, 1945. See also "The Big Show-Off," by Jerome Beatty, *American* (Feb. 1947). I obtained background information on *Around the World, The Lady from Shanghai,* and *Macbeth* from interviews with Richard Wilson.

VI   *Touch of Evil*

Albert Zugsmith's recollections of *Touch of Evil* appear in an interview with Todd McCarthy and Charles Flynn in *Kings of the Bs* (New York: Dutton, 1975). Henry Mancini is interviewed in the AFI *Dialogue on Film* (Jan. 1974). Dennis Weaver is quoted from the AFI "life award" program. See also Stephen Heath, "Film and System," *Screen* (Spring and Summer 1976).

VII   The Gypsy

Welles's interviews with André Bazin appeared in *Cahiers du Cinéma* in June and Sept. 1958. See also Micheál MacLiammóir, *Put Money in Thy Purse* (London: Methuen, 1952). Jack Jorgens's essay on *Othello* is found in *Focus on Orson Welles.* Welles's essay in *The Fortnightly* is entitled "Thoughts on Germany," and was published in March 1951. Welles's novel, *Mr. Arkadin,* appeared originally in French, and was published by Gallimard, Paris, in 1954. An unauthorized translation was issued by W. H. Allen, London, 1956.

VIII *The Trial*

On Kafka, see Georg Lukács, *Realism in Our Time* (New York: Harper and Row, 1962); see also Ernst Fischer, *The Necessity of Art* (London: Penguin Books, 1963), and Walter Benjamin, *Illuminations* (New York: Harcourt Brace, 1968). A script of *The Trial*, together with Welles's interview on the film with *Cahiers du Cinéma*, has been published by the Modern Film Script series, Simon and Schuster, New York, 1970.

IX *Chimes at Midnight*

For commentary on the Henry plays, see William Empson's "Double Plots" in *Some Versions of Pastoral* (New York: New Directions, 1950). See also C. L. Barber, *Shakespeare's Festive Comedy* (Princeton: Princeton University Press, 1959). Welles's comments on the film appeared in *Cahiers du Cinéma in English* (Winter 1965). Pauline Kael's essay is collected in *Kiss Kiss, Bang Bang* (Boston: Little, Brown, 1968).

X Art about Art

Welles is quoted from a brief interview reported by David Ansen in *The Real Paper*, Boston, Jan. 22, 1977. See also the special issue on Welles published by *Positif*, No. 167 (March 1975). Background on the production of *F for Fake* appears in *Ecran* (Feb. 1975). Raymond Williams is quoted from *Culture and Society* (New York: Harper and Row, 1958). Joseph McBride's report, "The Other Side of Orson Welles," is in *American Film* (July–Aug. 1976).

XI Between Works and Texts

Unless otherwise indicated, the quotations in this chapter are taken from documents in the Welles archive of the Lilly Library in Bloomington, Indiana. Edward W. Said is quoted from *The World, the Text, and the Critic* (Cambridge: Harvard University Press, 1983), pp. 31–53. Robert Lewis's comments on Welles were made at a New York University symposium in May 1988. Roland Barthes's essay, "From Work to Text," was translated by Josue V. Harari, and appeared in *Textual Strategies*, edited by Harari (Ithaca: Cornell University Press, 1979), pp. 73–81.

Additional Bibliography

Since 1978, several important new books and articles on Welles have been published. Here is a partial list:

Bates, Robin. "Fiery Speech in a World of Shadows: Rosebud's Impact on Early Audiences." *Cinema Journal* (Winter 1987): 3–26.

Bazin, André. *Orson Welles: A Critical View*, trans. Jonathan Rosenbaum (New York: Harper and Row, 1978).

Bordwell, David, and Kristin Thompson. "Style in *Citizen Kane*," in *Film Art* (New York: Knopf, 1986).

Brady, Frank. *Citizen Welles* (New York: Charles Scribners Sons, 1989).

Carringer, Robert. *The Making of Citizen Kane* (Berkeley: University of California Press, 1985).

Comito, Terry, editor. *Touch of Evil*, screenplay by Orson Welles (New Brunswick, N.J.: Rutgers University Press, 1984).

France, Richard. *The Theater of Orson Welles* (Lewisburg, Penn.: Bucknell University Press, 1977).

Higham, Charles. *Orson Welles: The Rise and Fall of an American Genius* (New York: St. Martin's Press, 1985).

Leaming, Barbara. *Orson Welles: A Biography* (New York: Viking Press, 1985).

Lyons, Bridget Gellert, editor. *Chimes at Midnight*, screenplay by Orson Welles, adapted from Shakespeare. (New Brunswick, N.J.: Rutgers University Press, 1988).

McBride, Joseph. *Orson Welles, Actor and Director* (New York: Harvest Books, 1977).

Naremore, James. "Orson Welles and the FBI," forthcoming in *Film Notes and Queries*, vol. 1, no. 1, 1990.

Pells, Richard H. "The Radical Stage and the Hollywood Film in the 1930s," in *Radical Visions and American Dreams* (Middletown, Conn.: Wesleyan University Press, 1984).

Rosenbaum, Jonathan. "The Invisible Orson Welles: A First Inventory," *Sight and Sound* (Summer 1986): 164–71.

Sartre, Jean-Paul. "*Citizen Kane*," trans. Dana Polan, *Post Script* (Fall 1987): 60–65.

Simon, William G., editor. *Persistence of Vision* (no. 7), special issue on Welles, 1989.

Stainton, Audrey. "*Don Quixote*: Orson Welles's Secret," *Sight and Sound* (Autumn 1988): 253–56.

Thomson, David. "Orson Welles and *Citizen Kane*," in *America in the Dark* (New York: William Morrow, 1977).

Welles, Orson. *The Big Brass Ring,* screenplay with Oja Kodar, preface by James Pepper, afterword by Jonathan Rosenbaum (Santa Barbara: Santa Teresa Press, 1987).

Wollen, Peter. *"Citizen Kane,"* in *Readings and Writings* (London: Verso, 1982).

Filmography

I have not attempted to catalogue Welles's extensive work in theatre, radio, and television; for a partial account of these appearances, the reader may consult the special issue of *Persistence of Vision* listed in the additional bibliography. The following list was compiled from a number of sources, including McBride, Peter Noble's *The Fabulous Orson Welles*, Charles Higham's *The Films of Orson Welles*, and the filmography by Henry Moret printed in *Ecran*, Feb. 1976. A few items do not appear in other publications.

DIRECTED BY WELLES

The Hearts of Age (1934)
   Directors: Orson Welles and William Vance
   Cast: Welles, Virginia Nicholson, William Vance
   A four-minute, 16mm film made in Woodstock, Illinois.
   A copy may be seen in the Library of Congress film archives.

Citizen Kane (1941)
   Director: Orson Welles
   Script: Herman J. Mankiewicz, Welles, and (uncredited) John
      Houseman
   Photography: Gregg Toland

Camera Operator: Bert Shipman
Art Direction: Van Nest Polglase, Perry Ferguson
Special Effects: Vernon L. Walker
Set Decoration: Darrel Silvera
Music: Bernard Herrmann
Costumes: Edward Stevenson
Sound: Bailey Fesler, James G. Stewart
Editors: Robert Wise, Mark Robson
Producer: Orson Welles
Associate Producer: Richard Barr
Assistant Director: Richard Wilson
Cast: Welles *(Kane),* Joseph Cotten *(Jed Leland),* Everett Sloane *(Bernstein),* Dorothy Comingore *(Susan Alexander),* Ray Collins *(Jim Gettys),* William Alland *(Jerry Thompson and newsreel narrator),* Agnes Moorehead *(Mary Kane),* Ruth Warrick *(Emily Norton),* George Coulouris *(W. P. Thatcher),* Erskine Sandford *(Herbert Carter),* Harry Shannon *(Jim Kane),* Philip Van Zandt *(Rawlston),* Paul Stewart *(Raymond),* Fortunio Bonanova *(Matisti),* Georgia Backus *(Curator of Thatcher Library),* Buddy Swan *(Kane, age 8),* Sunny Bupp *(Kane, Jr.),* Gus Schilling *(Waiter),* Richard Barr *(Hillman),* Joan Blair *(Georgia),* Al Eben *(Mike),* Charles Bennett *(Entertainer),* Milt Kibbee *(Reporter),* Tom Curran *(Teddy Roosevelt),* Irving Mitchell *(Dr. Corey),* Edith Evanson *(Nurse),* Arthur Kay *(Orchestra conductor),* Tudor Williams *(Chorus master),* Herbert Corthell *(City Editor),* Benny Rubin *(Smather),* Edmund Cobb *(Reporter),* Francis Neal *(Ethel),* Robert Dudly *(Photographer),* Ellen Lowe *(Miss Townsend),* Gino Corrado *(Gino the waiter),* Alan Ladd, Louise Currie, Eddie Coke, Walter Sande, Arthur O'Connell, Katherine Trosper, and Richard Wilson *(Reporters).*
Production Company: A Mercury Production at RKO, 29 June–23 Oct. 1940. U.S. premiere in New York, May 1941. 119 mins.

The Magnificent Ambersons (1942)
Director: Orson Welles (added scenes by Freddie Fleck and Robert Wise)
Script: Welles, based on Booth Tarkington's novel.
Photography: Stanley Cortez (added scenes by Russell Metty and Harry Wild)
Art Direction: Mark-Lee Kirk
Set Decoration: Al Fields

Special Effects: Vernon L. Walker
Music: Bernard Herrmann (added music by Roy Webb)
Costumes: Edward Stevenson
Sound: Bailey Fesler, James G. Stewart
Editors: Robert Wise, Jack Moss, Mark Robson
Producer: Orson Welles
Associate Producer: Richard Wilson
Assistant Director: Freddie Fleck
Cast: Orson Welles *(Narrator)*, Tim Holt *(George Amberson Minafer)*, Joseph Cotten *(Eugene Morgan)*, Dolores Costello *(Isabel Amberson Minafer)*, Agnes Moorehead *(Fanny Minafer)*, Anne Baxter *(Lucy Morgan)*, Ray Collins *(Jack Amberson)*, Richard Bennett *(Major Amberson)*, Don Dillaway *(Wilbur Minafer)*, Erskine Sandford *(Roger Bronson)*, J. Louis Johnson *(Sam)*, Gus Schilling *(Drugstore clerk)*, Charles Phillips *(Uncle John)*, Dorothy Vaughan and Elmer Jerome *(Spectators at funeral)*, Olive Ball *(Mary)*, Nina Guilbert and John Elliot *(Guests)*, Anne O'Neil *(Mrs. Foster)*, Kathryn Sheldon and Georgia Backus *(Matrons)*, Henry Roquemore *(Hardware man)*, Hilda Plowright *(Nurse)*, Mel Ford *(Fred Kinney)*, Bob Pittard *(Charlie Johnson)*, Lillian Nicholson *(Landlady)*, Billy Elmer *(House servant)*, Maynard Holmes and Lew Kelley *(Citizens)*, Bobby Cooper *(George as boy)*, Drew Roddy *(Elijah)*, Jack Baxley *(Rev. Smith)*, Heenan Elliott *(Labourer)*, Nancy Gates *(Girl)*, John Maguire *(Young Man)*, Ed Howard *(Chauffeur/Citizen)*, William Blees *(Youth at accident)*, James Westerfield *(Cop)*, Philip Morris *(Cop)*, Jack Santoro *(Barber)*, Louis Hayward *(Ballroom extra)*.
Production Company: A Mercury Production at RKO, 28 Oct. 1941–22 Jan. 1942. U.S. premiere Aug. 1942. 88 mins. (originally 131 mins.)

Journey into Fear (1943)
Director: Norman Foster (and, uncredited, Orson Welles)
Script: Joseph Cotten, Orson Welles, based on Eric Ambler's novel.
Photography: Karl Strauss
Art Direction: Albert S. D' Agostino, Mark-Lee Kirk
Set Decoration: Darrell Silvera, Ross Dowd
Special Effects: Vernon L. Walker
Music: Roy Webb

Costumes: Edward Stevenson
Editor: Mark Robson
Executive Producer: George J. Schaefer
Producer: Orson Welles
Cast: Joseph Cotten *(Howard Graham)*, Dolores Del Rio *(Josette Martel)*, Orson Welles *(Colonel Haki)*, Ruth Warrick *(Stephanie Graham)*, Agnes Moorehead *(Mrs. Mathews)*, Everett Sloane *(Kopeikin)*, Jack Moss *(Banat)*, Jack Durant *(Gogo)*, Eustace Wyatt *(Dr. Haller)*, Frank Readick *(Mathews)*, Edgar Barrier *(Kuvelti)*, Stephen Schnabel *(Purser)*, Hans Conried *(Oo Lang Sang, the Magician)*, Robert Meltzer *(Steward)*, Richard Bennett *(Ship's Captain)*, Shifra Haran *(Mrs. Haklet)*, Herbert Drake, Bill Roberts.
Production Company: A Mercury Production at RKO, 1942–43. U.S. premiere, Feb. 1943. 71 mins.

The Stranger (1946)
Director: Orson Welles
Script: Anthony Veiller assisted by John Huston
Story: Victor Trivas, Decla Dunning
Photography: Russell Metty
Art Direction: Perry Ferguson
Music: Bronislaw Kaper
Orchestration: Harold Byrns, Sydney Cutner
Costumes: Michael Woulfe
Sound: Carson F. Jowett, Arthur Johns
Editor: Ernest Nims
Producer: S. P. Eagle (pseudonym of Sam Spiegel)
Assistant Director: Jack Voglin
Cast: Orson Welles *(Franz Kindler alias Professor Charles Rankin)*, Loretta Young *(Mary Longstreet)*, Edward G. Robinson *(Inspector Wilson)*, Philip Merivale *(Judge Longstreet)*, Richard Long *(Noah Longstreet)*, Byron Keith *(Dr. Lawrence)*, Billy House *(Mr. Potter)*, Martha Wentworth *(Sarah)*, Konstantin Shayne *(Konrad Meinike)*, Theodore Gottlieb *(Farbright)*, Pietro Sosso *(Mr. Peabody)*, Isabel O'Madigan.
Production Company: International Pictures (RKO Studios), 1945. U.S. premiere, May 1946. 85 mins. (originally 115 mins.).

The Lady from Shanghai (1946)
Director: Orson Welles
Script: Welles, from Sherwood King's novel, *If I Die Before I Wake.*
Photography: Charles Lawton, Jr.
Camera Operator: Irving Klein
Art Direction: Stephen Gooson, Sturges Carne
Set Decoration: Wilber Menefee, Herman Schoenbrun
Special Effects: Lawrence Butler
Music: Heinz Roemheld
Musical Director: M. W. Stoloff
Orchestration: Herschel Burke Gilbert
Song "Please Don't Kiss Me": Allan Roberts, Doris Fisher
Costumes (gowns): Jean Louis
Sound: Lodge Cunningham
Editor: Viola Lawrence
Assistant Director: Sam Nelson
Executive Producer: Harry Cohn
Associate Producers: Richard Wilson, William Castle
Cast: Welles *(Michael O'Hara)*, Rita Hayworth *(Elsa Bannister)*, Everett Sloane *(Arthur Bannister)*, Glenn Anders *(George Grisby)*, Ted de Corsia *(Sidney Broom)*, Gus Schilling *(Goldie)*, Louis Merrill *(Jake)*, Erskine Sandford *(Judge)*, Carl Frank *(District Attorney Galloway)*, Evelyn Ellis *(Bessie)*, Wong Show Chong *(Li)*, Harry Shannon *(Horse cab driver)*, Sam Nelson *(Captain)*, Richard Wilson *(D. A.'s Assistant)*, players of the Mandarin Theatre.
Production Company: Columbia Pictures, filmed in Hollywood, Mexico, and San Francisco, 1946. U.S. premiere: May 1948. 86 mins. (cut from 155 mins.).

Macbeth (1948)
Director: Orson Welles
Script: Welles, adapted from Shakespeare
Photography: John L. Russell
Second unit photography: William Bradford
Art Direction: Fred Ritter
Set Decoration: John McCarthy, Jr., James Redd
Special Effects: Howard and Theodore Lydecker
Music: Jacques Ibert
Musical Director: Efrem Kurtz

Costumes: Orson Welles, Fred Ritter, Adele Palmer
Makeup: Bob Mark
Sound: John Stransky, Jr., Gary Harris
Editor: Louis Lindsay
Dialogue Director: William Alland
Assistant Director: Jack Lacey
Executive Producer: Charles K. Feldman
Producer: Orson Welles
Associate Producer: Richard Wilson
Cast: Welles *(Macbeth)*, Jeanette Nolan *(Lady Macbeth)*, Dan O'Herlihy *(Macduff)*, Edgar Barrier *(Banquo)*, Roddy McDowall *(Malcolm)*, Erskine Sandford *(Duncan)*, Alan Napier *(Holy Father)*, John Dierkes *(Ross)*, Keene Curtis *(Lennox)*, Peggy Webber *(Lady Macduff)*, Lionel Braham *(Siward)*, Archie Heugly *(Young Siward)*, Christopher Welles *(Macduff child)*, Brainerd Duffield *(1st Murderer)*, William Alland *(2nd Murderer)*, George Chirello *(Seyton)*, Gus Schilling *(Porter)*, Jerry Farber *(Fleance)*, Lurene Tuttle *(Gentlewoman)*, Robert Alan *(3rd Murderer)*, Morgan Farley *(Doctor)*; the witches have been listed variously as Peggy Webber, Lurene Tuttle, Brainerd Duffield, and Charles Lederer.
Production Company: A Mercury Production at Republic Studios, Summer 1947. U.S. premiere, Oct. 1948. 107 mins. (cut to 86 mins.).

Othello (1952)
Director: Orson Welles
Script: Welles, adapted from Shakespeare
Photography: Anchise Brizzi, G. R. Aldo, George Fanto, Obadan Troiani, Alberto Fusi
Art Direction: Alexandre Trauner
Costumes: Maria de Matteis
Sound: Piscitrelli
Editors: Jean Sacha, John Shepridge, Renzo Lucidi, William Morton
Assistant Director: Michael Washinsky
Producer: Orson Welles
Associate Producers: Giorgio Patti, Julien Derode, Walter Bedone, Patrice Dali, Rocco Facchini
Cast: Welles *(Othello)*, Micheál MacLiammóir *(Iago)*, Suzanne Cloutier *(Desdemona)*, Robert Coote *(Roderigo)*, Michael

Lawrence *(Cassio)*, Hilton Edwards *(Brabantio)*, Fay Compton *(Emilia)*, Nicholas Bruce *(Lodovico)*, Jean Davis *(Montano)*, Doris Dowling *(Bianca)*, Joseph Cotten *(Senator)*, Joan Fontaine *(Page)*.

Production Company: A Mercury Production, filmed at Scalera studios in Rome and on location in Morocco and Italy, from 1949 to 1952. U.S. premiere, June 1955. 91 mins.

Mr. Arkadin [British title: *Confidential Report*] (1955)
Director: Orson Welles
Script: Welles, based on his novel
Photography: Jean Bourgoin
Art Direction: Orson Welles
Music: Paul Misraki
Costumes: Orson Welles
Sound: Jacques Lebreton, Jacques Carrère
Editor: Renzo Lucidi
Executive Producer: Louis Dolivet
Production Manager: Michael J. Boisrond
Assistant Directors: José María Ochoa, José Luis de la Serna, Isidoro Martínez Ferri
Cast: Welles *(Narrator/Gregory Arkadin)*, Paola Mori *(Raina Arkadin)*, Robert Arden *(Guy Van Stratten)*, Akim Tamiroff *(Jacob Zouk)*, Michael Redgrave *(Burgomil Trebitsch)*, Patricia Medina *(Mily)*, Mischa Auer *(The Professor)*, Katina Paxinou *(Sophie)*, Jack Watling *(Marquis of Rutleigh)*, Grégoire Aslan *(Bracco)*, Peter Van Eyck *(Thaddeus)*, Suzanne Flon *(Baroness Nagel)*, Tamara Shane *(Woman in apartment)*, Frédéric O'Brady *(Oskar)*.

Production Company: A Mercury Production at Sevilla studios (Spain)/Film Organization (France). (A Spanish version with a different cutter, and different players as Sophie and the baroness, was apparently shot at the same time. See Moret's filmography in *Ecran*.) Filmed in France, Spain, Germany, and Italy, 1954. U.S. premiere, Oct. 1962. 100 mins.

Touch of Evil (1958)
Director: Orson Welles (added scene by Harry Keller)
Script: Welles, adapted from an earlier script by Paul Monash, which in turn was based on Whit Masterson's novel *Badge of Evil*

Photography: Russell Metty
Camera Operator: John Russell
Art Direction: Alexander Golitzen, Robert Clatworthy
Set Direction: Russell Gausman, John P. Austin
Music: Henry Mancini
Musical Supervisor: Joseph Gershenson
Costumes: Bill Thomas
Sound: Leslie I. Carey, Frank Wilkinson
Editors: Virgil Vogel, Aaron Stell, Edward Curtiss
Producer: Albert Zugsmith
Production Manager: F. D. Thompson
Assistant Directors: Phil Bowles, Terry Nelson
Cast: Welles *(Hank Quinlan)*, Charlton Heston *(Mike Vargas)*, Janet
Leigh *(Susan Vargas)*, Joseph Calleia *(Pete Menzies)*, Akim
Tamiroff *("Uncle Joe" Grande)*, Valentin De Vargas *("Pancho")*,
Ray Collins *(District Attorney Adair)*, Dennis Weaver *(Motel
"Night man")*, Joanna Moore *(Marcia Linnaker)*, Mort Mills
(Schwartz), Marlene Dietrich *(Tanya)*, Victor Milan *(Manolo
Sanchez)*, Lalo Rios *(Risto)*, Michael Sargent *(Pretty Boy)*,
Mercedes McCambridge *(Gang Leader)*, Joseph Cotten *(Police
surgeon)*, Zsa Zsa Gabor *(Owner of strip joint)*, Phil Harvey
(Blaine), Joi Lansing *(Zita)*, Harry Shannon *(Police Chief
Gould)*, Rusty Wescoatt *(Casey)*, Wayne Taylor, Ken Millar,
and Raymond Rodriguez *(Gang members)*, Arlene McQuade
(Ginnie), Dominick Delgarde *(Lackey)*, Joe Basulto *(Delin-
quent)*, Jennie Dias *(Jackie)*, Yolanda Bojorquez *(Bobbie)*,
Eleanor Dorado *(Lia)*, John Dierkes *(Plainclothes cop)*.
Production Company: Universal Studios, location scenes in
Venice, California, 1957–58. U.S. premiere, Feb. 1958. Two ver-
sions exist (93 mins. and 108 mins.), neither of them definitive.

The Trial (1962)
Director: Orson Welles
Script: Welles, based on Kafka's novel
Photography: Edmond Richard
Camera Operator: Adolphe Charlet
Art Direction: Jean Mandaroux
Music: Jean Ledrut, and the *Adagio* of Tomaso Albinoni
Costumes: Hélène Thibault
Sound: Jacques Lebreton

Sound Recording: Julien Coutellier, Guy Villette
Pin-screen Prologue: Alexandre Alexeieff and Claire Parker
Editors: Yvonne Martin, Denise Baby, Fritz Mueller
Producers: Alexander and Michael Salkind
Production Manager: Robert Florat
Assistant Directors: Marc Maurette, Paul Seban, Sophie Becker
Cast: Welles *(Narrator/Advocat Hastler)*, Anthony Perkins
(Joseph K.), Jeanne Moreau *(Miss Burstner)*, Romy Schneider
(Leni), Elsa Martinelli *(Hilda)*, Suzanne Flon *(Miss Pittl)*,
Madeline Robinson *(Mrs. Grubach)*, Akim Tamiroff *(Block)*,
Arnoldo Foà *(Inspector)*, Fernand Ledoux *(Clerk of the Court)*,
Maurice Teynac *(Director of K.'s office)*, Billy Kearns *(1st
Police officer)*, Jess Hahn *(2nd Police officer)*, William Chappell
(Titorelli), Raoul Delfosse, Karl Studer, and Jean-Claude
Remoleux *(Executioners)*, Wolfgang Reichmann *(Usher)*,
Thomas Holtzmann *(Student)*, Maydra Shore *(Irmie)*, Max
Haufler *(Uncle Max)*, Michael Lonsdale *(Priest)*, Max Buchs-
baum *(Judge)*, Van Doude *(Archivist in cut scenes)*, Katina
Paxinou *(Scientist in cut scenes)*.
Production Company: Paris Europa Films, FI-C-IT, Hisa-Films.
Filmed at Studio de Boulogne, Paris, at the Gare d'Orsay, and in
Zagreb, March–June 1962. U.S. premiere, Feb. 1963. 118 mins.

Chimes at Midnight (1966) [later U.S. title, *Falstaff*]
Director: Orson Welles
Script: Welles, adapted from Shakespeare's *Richard II, Henry IV
parts I and II, Henry V,* and *The Merry Wives of Windsor.*
Commentary from Raphael Holinshed's *The Chronicles of
England.*
Photography: Edmond Richard
Camera Operator: Adolphe Charlet
Second Unit Photography: Alejandro Ulloa
Art Direction: José Antonio de la Guerra, Mariano Erdoza
Music: Angelo Francesco Lavagnino
Musical Director: Carlo Franci
Costumes: Orson Welles
Sound Recording: Peter Parasheles
Editor: Fritz Mueller
Executive Producer: Alessandro Tasca
Producers: Emiliano Piedra, Angel Escolano
Production Manager: Gustavo Quintana

Assistant Directors: Tony Fuentes, Juan Cobos

Cast: Ralph Richardson *(Narrator)*, Orson Welles *(Sir John Falstaff)*, Keith Baxter *(Prince Hal, later Henry V)*, John Gielgud *(King Henry IV)*, Jeanne Moreau *(Doll Tearsheet)*, Margaret Rutherford *(Mistress Quickly)*, Norman Rodway *(Henry Percy, called Hotspur)*, Marina Vlady *(Kate Percy)*, Alan Webb *(Justice Shallow)*, Walter Chiari *(Silence)*, Michael Aldridge *(Pistol)*, Tony Beckley *(Poins)*, Fernando Rey *(Worcester)*, Andrew Faulds *(Westmoreland)*, José Nieto *(Northumberland)*, Jeremy Rowe *(Prince John)*, Beatrice Welles *(Falstaff's page)*, Paddy Bedford *(Bardolph)*, Julio Peña, Fernando Hilbert, Andrés Mejuto, Keith Pyoft, Charles Farrell.

Production Company: Internacional Films Española (Madrid)/ Alpine (Basle). Filmed in Barcelona, Madrid, and various Spanish locations, 1964–65. U.S. premiere, March 1967. 119 mins.

The Immortal Story (1968)

Director: Orson Welles

Script: Welles, based on the story by Isak Dinesen [Karen Blixen]

Photography: Willy Kurant

Color: Eastman Color

Assistant Cameramen: Jean Orjollet, Jacques Assuerds

Art Direction: André Piltant

Music: piano pieces by Erik Satie, played by Aldo Ciccolini and Jean-Joel Barbier

Costumes for Jeanne Moreau: Pierre Cardin

Sound: Jean Neny

Editors: Yolande Maurette, Marcelle Pluet, Françoise Garnault, Claude Farny

Producer: Micheline Rozan

Production Manager: Marc Maurette

Assistant Directors: Olivier Gérard, Tony Fuentes, Patrice Torok

Cast: Orson Welles *(Narrator/Mr. Clay)*, Jeanne Moreau *(Virginie Ducrot)*, Roger Coggio *(Elishama Levinsky)*, Norman Eshley *(Paul)*, Fernando Rey *(Merchant)*.

Production Company: ORTF/Albina Films. Filmed in Paris and Madrid, Sept.–Nov. 1966. U.S. premiere, Sept. 1968. 58 mins.

F for Fake (1973)

Director: Orson Welles, using material from an earlier film by François Reichenbach.

Script: Orson Welles
Photography: (U.S. and Toussaint) Gary Graver, (France and Ibiza) Christian Odasso. In 16mm color.
Music: Michel Legrand
Editors: Welles, Marie Sophie Dubus, Dominique Engerer
Titles: Lax
Sound Recording: Paul Bertault
Producers: Dominique Antoine, François Reichenbach
Associate Producer: Richard Drewett
Cast: Orson Welles, Oja Kodar, Elmyr de Hory, Clifford Irving, Edith Irving, François Reichenbach, Joseph Cotten, Laurence Harvey, Richard Wilson, Paul Stewart, Howard Hughes, Saša Devčić, Gary Graver, Andrés Vincent Gomez, Julio Palinkas, Christian Odasso, François Widoff *(as themselves)*, Peter Bogdanovich, William Alland *(off-screen)*.
Production Company: les Films de l'Astrophore (Paris)/Saci (Tehran)/Janus Film (Munich). Filmed in France and the U.S., 1973. U.S. premiere, Oct. 1974. 85 mins.

The Deep (Unreleased)
Director: Orson Welles
Script: Welles, based on Charles Williams's novel, *Dead Calm*.
Photography: Willy Kurant
Color: Eastman Color
Cast: Orson Welles *(Russ Brewer)*, Jeanne Moreau *(Ruth Warriner)*, Laurence Harvey *(Hughie Warriner)*, Olga Palinkas *(Rae Ingram)*, Michael Bryant *(John Ingram)*.
Filmed at Hvar, Yugoslavia, 1967–69.

The Other Side of the Wind (Incomplete)
Director: Orson Welles
Script: Orson Welles and Oja Kodar
Photography: Gary Graver
Color: Eastman Color
Production Design: Polly Pratt
Cast: John Huston *(Jake Hannaford)*, Peter Bogdanovich *(Brooks Otterlake)*, Lilli Palmer *(Zarah Valeska)*, Susan Strasberg *(Juliette Rich)*, Oja Kodar *(the actress)*, Bob Random *(John Dale)*, Howard Grossman *(Charles Higgam)*, Joseph McBride *(Mr. Pister)*, Tonio Selwart *(The Baron)*, Cathy Lucas *(Mavis Hensher)*, Norman Foster *(Billy)*, Edmund O'Brien *(Pat)*,

Cameron Mitchell *(Matt)*, Mercedes McCambridge *(Maggie)*, Benny Rubin, Richard Wilson, John Carrol, Paul Mazursky, Curtis Harrington, Dennis Hopper, Henry Jaglom, Claude Chabrol, Stephane Audran, Gary Graver.

Filming began Aug. 1970. Filmed in Los Angeles and Flagstaff, Arizona.

WELLES AS ACTOR

1943   *Jane Eyre* (d. Robert Stevenson)
1944   *Follow the Boys* (d. Edward Sutherland)
1945   *Tomorrow Is Forever* (d. Irving Pichel)
1947   *Black Magic* (d. Gregory Ratoff)
1948   *Prince of Foxes* (d. Henry King)
1949   *The Third Man* (d. Carol Reed)
1950   *The Black Rose* (d. Henry Hathaway)
1953   *Trent's Last Case* (d. Herbert Wilcox)
       Versailles (d. Sacha Guitry)
       L'Uomo, la Bestia e la Virtù (d. Stefano Vanzina)
1954   *Napolean* (d. Sacha Guitry)
       Three Cases of Murder (episode directed by George More O'Ferral)
1955   *Trouble in the Glen* (d. Herbert Wilcox)
1956   *Moby Dick* (d. John Huston)
1957   *Man in the Shadow* (d. Jack Arnold)
       The Long Hot Summer (d. Martin Ritt)
1958   *The Roots of Heaven* (d. John Huston)
1959   *Compulsion* (d. Richard Fleischer)
       David and Goliath (d. Richard Pottier, Fernando Baldi)
       Ferry to Hong Kong (d. Lewis Gilbert)
1960   *Austerlitz* (d. Abel Gance)
       Crack in the Mirror (d. Richard Fleischer)
       The Tartars (d. Richard Thorpe)
1961   *Layfayette* (d. Jean Dréville)
1962   *RoGoPaG* (episode by Pier Paolo Pasolini)
1964   *Marco the Magnificent* (d. Denys de la Patellière, Noël Howard)
1965   *Is Paris Burning?* (d. René Clément)
1966   *The Sailor from Gibraltar* (d. Tony Richardson)
       A Man for All Seasons (d. Fred Zinnemann)
1967   *Casino Royale* (episode by Joseph McGrath)

I'll Never Forget What's'isname (d. Michael Winner)
Oedipus the King (d. Phillip Saville)

1968   *House of Cards* (d. John Guillermin)
        The Southern Star (d. Sidney Hayers)

1969   *The Battle of the River Veretva* (d. Veljko Bulajic)
        Michael the Brave (d. Sergui Nicolaescu)
        Teppea (d. Giulio Petroni)
        Twelve Plus One (d. Nicholas Gessner)
        The Kremlin Letter (d. John Huston)
        Start the Revolution without Me (d. Bud Yorkin)
        Mihai Viteazu (d. Sergui Nicolaescu)

1970   *Catch-22* (d. Mike Nichols)
        Waterloo (d. Sergei Bondarchuk)
        Upon This Rock (d. Harry Rasky)

1971   *A Safe Place* (d. Henry Jaglom)
        The Toy Factory (d. Bert Gordon)
        Get To Know Your Rabbit (d. Brian de Palma)
        La Décade Prodigieuse (d. Claude Chabrol)
        The Canterbury Tales (d. Pier Paolo Pasolini)
        To Kill a Stranger (d. Peter Collinson)

1972   *Sutjeska* (d. Stipe Delic)
        Malpertuis (d. Harry Kümel)
        Necromancy (d. Bert Gordon)
        Treasure Island (d. John Hough, Andrea Bianchi)

1977   *Voyage of the Damned* (d. Stuart Rosenberg)

1979   *Never Trust an Honest Thief* (d. George McCowan)
        The Secret of Nicolai Tesla (d. Krsto Papic)
        The Muppet Movie (d. James Frawley)

1981   *Butterfly* (d. Matt Cimber)

1982   *The Muppets Take Manhattan* (d. Frank Oz)

1983   *Where Is Parsifal?* (d. Henri Helman)

1987   Someone to Love (d. Henry Jaglom)

WELLES AS NARRATOR (EXCLUSIVE OF TV FILMS)

1940   *The Swiss Family Robinson* (d. Edward Ludwig)

1946   *Duel in the Sun* (d. King Vidor)

1956   *Lords of the Forest* (d. Henry Brandt and Heinz Sielman)

1958   *The Vikings* (d. Richard Fleischer)

1959   *High Journey* (d. Peter Baylis)
        South Seas Adventure (d. Carl Dudley)

1961 *King of Kings* (d. Nicholas Ray)
1962 *River of the Ocean* (d. Peter Baylis)
1963 *The Finest Hours* (d. Peter Baylis)
1970 *To Build a Fire* (d. David Cobham)
1971 *Sentinels of Silence* (d. Robert Amrom)
      Directed by John Ford (d. Peter Bogdanovich)
1972 *The Crucifixion* (d. Robert Guenette)
1973 *Future Shock* (d. Alex Grasshoff)
1975 *Bugs Bunny Superstar*
1976 *The Challenge of Greatness* (d. Herbert Kline)
1979 *The Late, Great Planet Earth* (d. Robert Amram)
1981 *Genocide* (d. Arnold Schwartzman)
      History of the World, Part I (d. Mel Brooks)

INCOMPLETE OR UNREALIZED PROJECTS

I offer here a partial list. Welles announced dozens of films that were never started. At one extreme is a project like *It's All True*, which was virtually completed before RKO withdrew its support; at the other are films that never got beyond a script or an outline.

1939–40 *Heart of Darkness*
         Smiler with a Knife
1941 *The Way to Santiago* (Mexican Melodrama)
      The Pickwick Papers
      It's All True (A North American version of the anthology film Welles later shot in Brazil, composed of three episodes: *Love Story*, *The Captain's Chair*, and an untitled story about New Orleans jazz. Writers included John Fante and Robert Flaherty.)
1942 *It's All True*
1944 *The Landru Story* (became Chaplin's *Monsieur Verdoux*)
      War and Peace
      Don't Catch Me (script by Welles, Bud Pearson, and Les White)
1945 *Henry V* (based on Pirandello)
      Crime and Punishment
      Enrico Caruso
1947 *Moby Dick*

Fully Dressed and in His Right Mind
Cyrano de Bergerac
Bolivar's Idea (adapted from a radio show of 1942)
Carmen (script by Brainerd Duffield)
Portrait of an Assassin (This title is listed in Charles
  Higham's biography of Welles. It may refer to a
  script Welles worked on with Charles MacArthur,
  about the assassination of Archduke Ferdinand at
  Sarajevo.)

1948?   *Salomé* (script by Welles and Fletcher Markle)
         Ulysses (script by Ernst Bornemann)
         Around the World in 80 Days
1950   *Paris by Night*
1953   *Julius Caesar*
1957   *Don Quixote*
?   *Operation Cendrillon* (a film about a Hollywood movie
           company working in an Italian town)
         Carmilla
         The Naked Lady and the Musketeers
         Alexandre Dumas
         Lovelife (described by Welles as "a film about sexual
           obsession")
         Salomé, Two by Two, and Abraham (three stories from
           the Bible)
1960   *Catch-22*
1969   *The Merchant of Venice*
1970–80 *The Other Side of the Wind*
         The Big Brass Ring
         King Lear
1978   *The Dreamers* (based on fiction by Isak Dinesen)
1984   *The Cradle Will Rock* (a "docudrama" about the WPA
           production of Marc Blitzstein's musical play)

Index